NOOKS AND CRANNIES

Books written, illustrated, and designed by David Yeadon

NOOKS AND CRANNIES

WHEN THE EARTH WAS YOUNG

HIDDEN CORNERS
1. New England
2. Mid-Atlantic States

NEW YORK BOOK OF BARS, PUBS
AND TAVERNS

SUMPTUOUS INDULGENCE ON A
SHOESTRING (a cookbook)

SMALL TOWNS IN AMERICA
1. Southern California
2. Northern California

HIDDEN RESTAURANTS OF CALIFORNIA
1. Southern California
2. Northern California

WINE TASTING IN CALIFORNIA

COOKING WITH SPIRITS
LET ME HELP YOU

TOWARD INDEPENDENCE

NOOKS AND CRANNIES

AN UNUSUAL WALKING TOUR GUIDE TO NEW YORK CITY

written and illustrated by
DAVID YEADON

CHARLES SCRIBNER'S SONS
NEW YORK

Copyright © 1979 David Yeadon

Library of Congress Cataloging in Publication Data
Yeadon, David.
  Nooks and crannies

  Includes index.
  1. New York (City)—Description—1951–   —Tours.
I. Title.
F128.18.Y42   917.47'1'044   79-11057
ISBN 0-684-16084-6

1 3 5 7 9 11 13 15 17 19 V/P 20 18 16 14 12 10 8 6 4 2

Printed in the United States of America

For NORAH
and her smile

CONTENTS

LIST OF ILLUSTRATIONS

NOOKS AND CRANNIES

INTRODUCTION

There was a time, about two years ago, when I thought I knew New York City. I'd visited all the main attractions and dozens of other lesser-known museums, parks, and historic niches described in the better guidebooks. I'd written about the city, sketched it, photographed it, and used up at least a dozen pairs of shoes on its sidewalks. Yet, as I was soon to learn, I hardly knew the city at all.

One summer morning on the Upper West Side a friend happened to show me Pomander Walk, a charming little alley of Tudor-style cottages graced with privet hedges and tiny lamp posts. I was suddenly in England. The din and bustle of Broadway was left outside the iron gates; inside it was as cozy as a Somerset village. Someone was sitting on a doorstep reading a newspaper and drinking tea, sparrows chirped among the window boxes brimming with geraniums, and a lady with a feather duster (I hadn't seen a feather duster since my last visit to Yorkshire) peered at me through an upstairs window framed by bright blue shutters. I smiled and, wonder of wonders, she smiled back.

So began my rediscovery of the city. Soon, thanks to advice from friends and their friends, I accumulated a tantalizing list of riverside walks, architectural oddities, markets, strange museums, forgotten parks (even precise directions to an unspoiled river gorge), a farmhouse in the heart of the city, a rooftop jungle, a bank where concert pianists gave lunchtime renditions of Chopin, the most authentic (and least-known) Italian neighborhood in the five boroughs, and a Maine-flavored fishing village easily reached by subway.

1

Nook-and-cranny exploration began to absorb most of my weekends, then a good portion of my weeks. Projects stalled and faltered as I scampered off, sketchbook in hand, to visit Dead Horse Bay, a 1694 Quaker meeting house in Flushing, exotic gingerbread mansions in Bay Ridge, the most ornate cemetery entrance and gatehouse in the country (just a short stroll from Prospect Park), an unspoiled ravine complete with waterfalls and deep pools, a silent hemlock forest in the midst of turbulent urbanity, Aunt Len's Doll and Toy collection in northern Manhattan, a famous "mystics" museum, and a row of Greek "temples" along the waterfront on Staten Island.

I found a place to rent a horse in the heart of Manhattan, I went deep-sea fishing with an ex-naval captain, listened to Reverend Ike's "gospel of green power" at the most sumptuous theater in the city, visited an ocean liner in dock, ate a vast buffet dinner for free in a midtown pub, strolled the conservatory gardens in Central Park (one of its lesser-known attractions), watched the auctions at Parke-Bernet, and relaxed on the green of a "typical" English village in the heart of Queens.

And that was merely the beginning.

It's taken a long time—far longer than I expected—to put this book together. The problem was knowing where and when to stop. Even now my files are packed with unused clippings, photographs, hand-scribbled notes, and messages from friends beginning "I've just found this wonderful . . ." But publishers get a little nervous about thousand-page books and authors occasionally need a rest. So, readers should regard the book's 500-plus "unusual-things-to-see-and-places-to-go" as not necessarily all-encompassing, but a significant introduction to a lesser-known New York. The book should be used as a starting point for fresh discoveries and even more varied walking tours. The "Mini-Tours" section particularly is designed to encourage users to plan their own itineraries and routes. Newcomers will find opportunities to leave the tourist crowds and the trinket stands behind; long-time residents will rediscover their city and sense again the thrill of exploring one of the most exciting and kaleidoscopic urban environments in the world.

New York, New York—you're still the greatest!

WALKING
TOURS

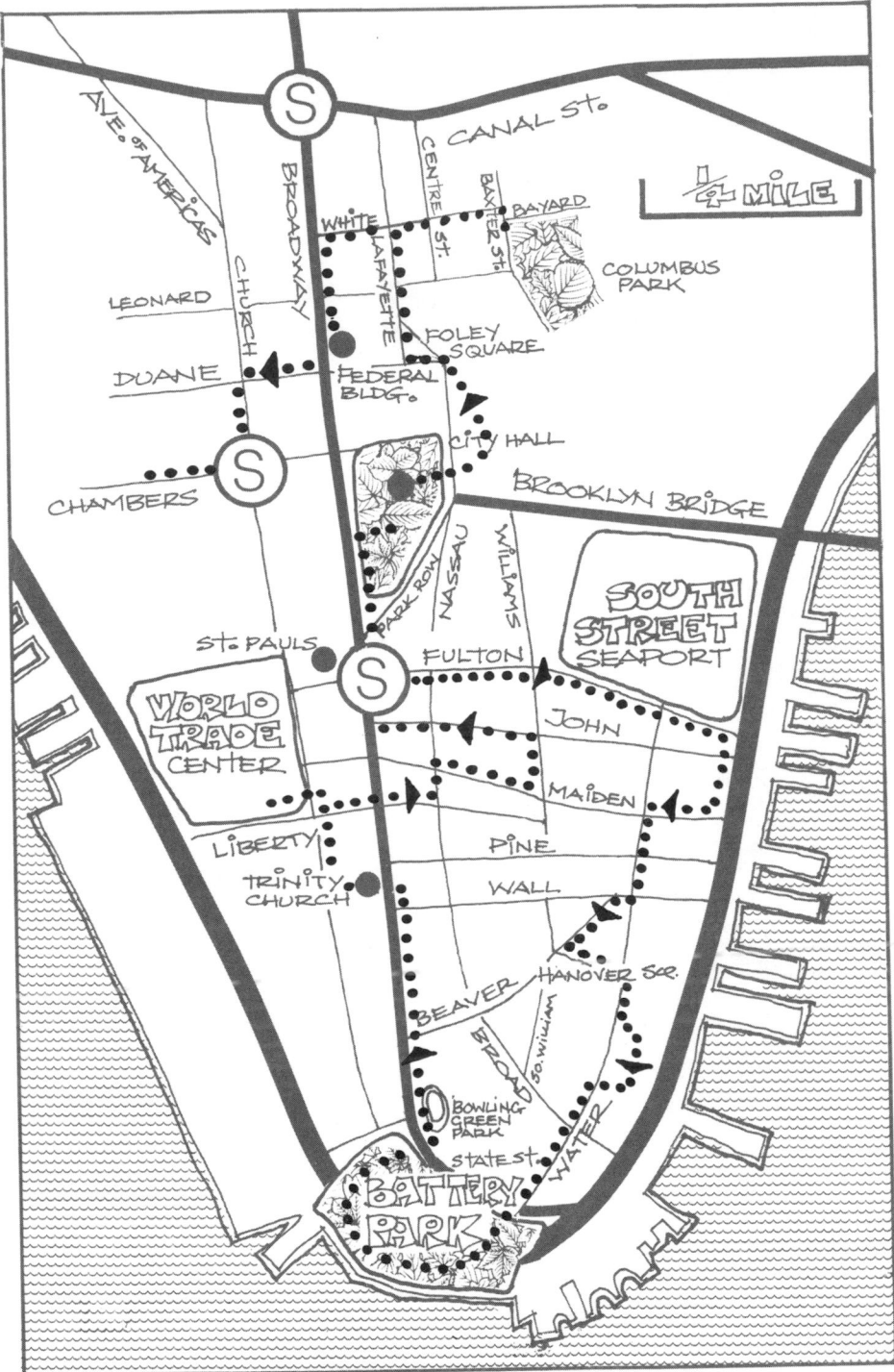

1
DOWNTOWN

Peering into the canyons of downtown, one feels on the edge of a mythical city—a Dürer-like creation of towers, turrets, pinnacles, battlements, Gothic traceries, Romanesque arches, flying buttresses, and cloud-whipped eyries. Dark passages pierce the lower gloom of the crevasses while high up, scores of stories above the insectlike scurryings of the sidewalk crowds, the sun burnishes brilliant gold spires and highlights the grotesque gargoyles, the godlike statues of toga-clad damsels and bearded, sword-wielding men of herculean proportions. (That some of the most exotic towers and spires are mere water tanks in disguise in no way detracts from their romantic appearance.)

But downtown possesses other moods, other images. Four A.M. on a cool spring morning, for example, is the best time to visit the South Street Seaport area at the east end of Fulton Street. The fish market is a hullaballoo of roaring trucks, bawling merchants, hook-wielding hands tugging hundred-pound tuna across the slippery cobbles, and workers taking a break at the Paris Bar, downing their early-morning beers and boiler-makers (see chapter 7, "Manhattan Markets").

———————— **DIRECTIONS** ————————

Subway: *Start:* IRT 4, 5 to Fulton Street/Broadway or IND A or CC to Fulton Street/Nassau Street
Bus: *Start:* M1, M6
  Return: IRT 1, 2, 3 from Chambers Street/West Broadway
  Return: M1, M6

5

Then there are the quiet places—little-known parks, narrow alleys with an almost Amsterdam flavor, secluded museums, and silent churches smelling of incense and redolent with history. Downtown is all this and much more, as we'll discover on this leisurely stroll.

We begin at South Street. Come just after breakfast on a weekday morning, say around 9:30 A.M., and beat the crowds of tourists to the Seaport restoration. If you've never spent time here before pick up some of the abundant descriptive literature and enjoy this worn remnant of New York's maritime era. Visit the tiny museums in the area (the display of old printing equipment in the Bowne and Company building at 211 Water Street is a must), the stores selling old prints of the harbor and contemporary artworks of sailing ships, the display of restoration models in the Seaport Museum, the Fulton Market with its antiques, trinkets, and some of the finest clams on the half-shell in Manhattan. Across South Street at Pier 16 are the ships themselves—the full-rigged *Wavertree*, the paddle-wheeler *Alexander Hamilton*, the *Clearwater* sloop, the schooner *Black Pearl*, and other seafaring creations from tugs to ferryboats. By the time the crowds arrive you'll have completed your explorations and be ready for the rest of our saunter around downtown.

Beyond the Fulton Market at 127 John Street is Emery Roth's "fun tower," a relatively standard glass-face office block transformed into a riot of color and activity by the addition of "neon tunnels," brightly painted seats and benches, fountains, swaths of canvas awnings, odd bits and pieces of sculpture, and the largest digital clock in the world. Even the utilities level (about halfway up the building) is a carnivallike mélange of blue, red, and yellow pipes, valves, and boilers—altogether a wonderfully refreshing creation.

Inside, at the New York Cocoa Exchange, the environment is a little more traditional although there's always plenty of activity between 9 A.M. and 2:30 P.M. Monday to Friday (recent bomb scares have resulted in the temporary closing of the visitors gallery but you're still welcome to pick up the literature and watch the bawling and the bustle through the trading floor doors). By New York Stock Exchange standards it's a diminutive gathering (membership is limited to 183 individuals). Everybody knows everybody and there's a spirit of joviality around the circular table in the center of the floor. The odd barrage of sounds makes the place seem more like a farmyard than a futures market.

At South William Street (Beaver and William streets) we enter a tiny enclave of delicately detailed stores and restaurants with a distinctly mid-nineteenth-century flavor. Before the emergence of the great skyscrapers much of downtown looked like this. Dutch-style trimmings were popular and the meandering streets still followed the line of New Amsterdam cow paths. The mood continues as we wander into Hanover Square itself, a pleasant breathing space with a small park and the finely proportioned India House. Originally founded as the Hanover Bank it later became the headquarters of the New York Cotton Exchange and today contains one of the best-known businessmen's clubs in lower Manhattan.

Here in the square one can sense the richness of the "new" downtown. All around are the cloud-clutching towers of the nation's largest banks, their curtain-walls soaring high above the imaginative promenades and plazas, the sculptures and gardens. Take time to explore the niches. Follow signs up and down the escalators to underground shopping malls, raised decks overlooking the East River, "picnic" areas where office workers lunch in a cacophony of bass-heavy radios, and Jeanette Park, a "hard" plaza of outstanding design which during the summer is a hub of activities in the area. The little-known branch of the Whitney Museum of American Art (a welcome if rather small annex of the main museum at Madison Avenue and 75th Street) is located at the top of the escalator at 55 Water Street and features regularly changing exhibitions of American artists (call 483-0011 for details).

Across from Jeanette Park is the ever-popular Fraunces Tavern, which somehow manages to contain behind its refined neo-Georgian façade (a "conjectural restoration") a popular restaurant, an invariably crowded bar, and an extensive museum dedicated primarily to the commemoration of George Washington's famous farewell to his officers on December 4, 1783 (Monday–Friday 10 A.M.–4 P.M. Free). Other displays include the Flag Room, collections of eighteenth-century dinnerware and crystal, clocks, prints, portraits, and Revolutionary War memorabilia. Although the museum is a highlight of most downtown walking tours and can become a little overcrowded, it's still worth a visit.

Where Water Street ends at Battery Park is the lesser-known Shrine of Saint Elizabeth Seton located in the last of a once-refined row of Federal-style townhouses. Part of the building, the eastern wing below the raised dormers, is a 1793 structure and the remainder with its odd combination of bowed façade, oval side windows, and delicate columns (which are sections of masts from old sailing ships topped with Ionic capitals) is an 1806 addition attributed to City Hall architect, John McComb, Jr. Inside, masses are celebrated regularly in the oval chapel. It's a pleasant place to rest; the silence and the pastel shades of the walls and pews offer welcome respite from the racket outside.

Next door at the Seamen's Church Institute (on the site of Herman Melville's birthplace) is a second chapel bathed in a soft mellow light from the stained-glass windows facing the street. Back in the early 1800s the chapel was a floating structure tied to an East River pier at the end of Pike Street. Photographs in the entranceway show a simple Gothic-style clapboard structure perched on a float and surrounded by a burly contingent of seamen parishioners ("our parish is the world"). Today the institute contains scores of lodging rooms for sailors (some of the older residents love to recount tales of their maritime exploits), a library, a school, and a cafeteria that in recent years has gained a reputation as one of downtown's best bargain eateries. Take time to stroll the halls and corridors on the first three floors. Almost every inch of wall space and every spare niche is taken up with ship models, etchings, prints, displays of ship knots and decorative rope-working, bells (a fine collection just outside the cafeteria), and the inevitable canvases of turbulent seascapes. "I did most of that," an elderly sailor told me as I gazed at a framed display of intricate ropework. "Couldn't do it too good now, though." He held up his gnarled fingers, swollen at the joints. "That's what twenty years at sea does to you. Can't move them now hardly worth a damn." He invited me to join him in the residents' lounge and after a few self-conscious coughs began to tell me of his merchant-ship exploits and how he'd traveled around the world fifteen and a half times ("We got beached on one trip somewheres off Nigeria, so I count

Bowling Green Park

that as half"), skippered his own small steamship at the age of thirty ("I tell you there ain't too many who's been captainin' at that age"), and played banjo at a celebration for the Chiefs of Staff at the end of the Second World War. "Hell, I was good on the five-string. Could have had my own band. The 'Lightnin' Licker' they called me. My fingers moved so fast all you saw was a big blur. Leastways that's what they told me," he added modestly and looked down sadly at his hands. "You wouldn't think it, would you?"

Battery Park, across from the institute, is always full of life during the summer. Tourists throng its pathways waiting for the boats to take them on the Statue of Liberty/Ellis Island trips. Bongo drummers and promising jazz musicians blast-boom the afternoon away while lithe-limbed girls in halter tops and frayed shorts ogle and giggle, and bronzed boys jog along the Admiral Dewey promenade past the Good Humor carts and the "I love New York" stickers. Around Castle Clinton (the smoothed remnants of a yet-to-be-used fortress, built 1807–11) are a plethora of monuments to Wireless Operators, the Walloon Settlers, John Ericsson (builder of the *Monitor,* America's first iron warship), the Salvation Army, Giovanni da Verrazano, and Emma Lazarus, who helped raise funds for the erection of the Statue of Liberty across the bay with her immortal words, "Give me your tired, your poor/Your huddled masses yearning to breathe free . . ."

If the park's a little too hectic (and it can hardly be described as either a nook or a cranny) stroll north up State Street past Cass Gilbert's United States Custom House (one of the most splendid examples of Beaux-Arts architecture in the country and regrettably closed at the time of writing) to the recently restored Bowling Green Park. Surrounded by its original 1771 fence is Manhattan's first official park and, if the lunchtime crowds are any gauge, the city's best-used space. It was here on July 9, 1776, a few hours after the Declaration of Independence arrived in the city from Philadelphia, that a rioting crowd of citizens and militia destroyed the statue of George III, which for years had gazed in somber dignity over the comings and goings of the colonial populace.

A short distance farther north look for the entrance to a post office on the west side of Broadway. The restrained gray façade of the old Cunard building, which now houses the post office, conceals one of the most ornate entrances to any commercial structure in the world. The richly decorated vestibule with its profusion of terra-cotta and tiled arches, its bas-reliefs of sea nymphs, dolphins, and chubby children of Neptune is merely a modest preparation for the overwhelming opulence of the Great Hall itself. Step inside and look up at the main dome and the richly decorated half-domes. Magnificent frescoes by Ezra Winter roaring with the fury of the ocean depict the Viking vessel of Leif Ericson, Columbus's galleon, and the sturdy ships of John Cabot and Sir Francis Drake, all surging through turbulent seas to the New World. Subterranean gods and goddesses cavort across the ceiling and walls with mermaids and sea creatures in a riot of line and form that is almost audible. Barry Faulkner's finely executed world maps on the side walls provide rare segments of visual relief. And somehow, in the middle of all this, doe-eyed postal workers and their customers make their transactions oblivious to their surroundings. Even in the vestibule more people seem to be attracted by the tiny Philatelic Exhibition Center with its displays of special U.S. commemorative stamps than by the bewitchingly naked nymphs floating above their heads. (Someday I would like to make my own addition to New York's burgeoning displays of graffiti with the simple phrase "LOOK UP" tastefully stenciled on sidewalks and curbs at salient points around the city. There's a whole realm of riches above the six-foot level, as every nook-and-cranny explorer knows.)

Continuing north on Broadway past an odd row of single-story stores reminiscent of 14th-Street-type outlets—cheap clothing, cut-price hi-fi equipment, discount record stores, and so on—stroll into the Art Deco–flavored Irving Trust Company Building at the junction of Broadway and Wall Street and enjoy its rich gold-and-crimson mosaic interior. Then next door, at the Bank of Tokyo, look high up (once again) at the building's Broadway façade and notice the huge flowing statues decorating the upper floors. The strict rhythm of the façade makes them almost come alive, seeming to float effortlessly in front of the building.

If you've never taken one of the more traditional tours of the downtown area you may, at this point, wish to stroll east on Wall Street to the New York Stock Exchange and the adjacent Federal Hall National Memorial where George Washington took the oath of office as first President of the United States on April 30, 1789. Both contain extensive exhibits and abundant descriptive literature. The only problem is that during the summer in particular they tend to be inundated with tourists and it's difficult to appreciate all that's offered.

So much has been written about Trinity Church that it is unnecessary to repeat its long and fascinating history here. (If you'd like more information, pick up one of the pamphlets inside the church or a copy of the "Heritage Trail Walking Tour of Downtown".) Suffice it to mention that this 1846 Richard Upjohn creation is the third church to occupy the site and that the burial ground contains such notables as Alexander Hamilton and Robert Fulton. It also provides a wonderful setting for lunchtime relaxation and occasional concerts, and a convenient link between Broadway and Church Street (Trinity Place). Stroll through the church and down the steps at the back to the American Stock Exchange across the street (Monday–Friday 9:45 A.M.–3 P.M.). What originated as a curbside marketplace (there's an amusing life-size portrayal of some early stockbrokers in action at the top of the escalator) is now an immense 20,650-square-foot trading hall with room for over 1000 people. Some sit quietly in tiered booths around the edge of the room, while others run rampant across the trading floor bawling and gesticulating with all the fervor of distraught Yankee fans. Even behind the thick glass of the visitors' viewing platform the hullaballoo can be deafening. The crisp, clearly designed display boards explaining every nuance of stock transactions are in marked contrast to the turmoil below, and compared with the New York Stock Exchange the exhibits are usually less crowded and visitors can absorb the abundant information at a more leisurely pace. (If you're unclear as to the exact function of the exchange pick up the pamphlet *Market for Millions* from the information desk.) Also not to be missed is the unusual restaurant downstairs—Harry's at the American Stock Exchange. Here, along a replica of a narrow eighteenth-century street, is a series of distinct dining rooms with such appropriate names as the Patent Office, the Exchange Club, the Harbor Grill, and the Back Office Bar. Harry Poulakakos (who also owns the Harry's at Hanover Square restaurant and bar in India House) and his wife Edrienne cater to a remarkably varied clientele (at least for a downtown restaurant) and it's worth taking a peep before moving on with the walking tour.

Exchange watching can be a fascinating pastime and if you'd like a little more action continue north on Church Street to 4 World Trade Center and the relatively little-known Commodities Exchange Center (floors 8 and 9, Monday–Friday 10 A.M.– 3 P.M.). Here one emerges from the elevator into an environment of stainless-steel trim, gray and maroon carpets, recessed lighting, and futuristic booths from which sophisticated ladies provide information as readily and accurately as computers. But in the distance you can hear it again—the bawling and bellowing, the same racket we experienced at the American Stock Exchange. On the eighth floor you look directly into the exchange—the plush carpets are covered in the traditional confetti of order slips and around the walls figures flash on large boards marked as silver, gold, palladium, platinum, zinc, cotton, sugar, coffee, potatoes, and beef—but you'll learn more about the commodities and the action from the visitors' gallery on the ninth floor.

Of course, if you'd really like to understand not only how the stocks-and-commodities game works but how the whole money system ebbs and flows, then cross Church Street from the World Trade Center and visit Merrill Lynch's "Money Tree" display in the United States Steel Building at 1 Liberty Plaza (Monday–Friday 9 A.M.–5 P.M.). Unfortunately, there's no take-away literature, but it's a relatively small and well-documented exhibit, so give it a try. For those unfamiliar with the complexities of money supply and demand it's a useful—and novel—overview.

And as long as we're dabbling in pecuniary matters, where better to go next than the massive palacelike Federal Reserve Bank of New York at Nassau and Liberty streets, where at the end of a one-hour tour you'll see more actual money in gold form than in any other place in the world. After all the paper pushing in the exchanges, where "real" money never changes hands, it's a pleasure and a relief to know that here at least is a tangible foundation for the nation's currency. Unfortunately though, one can't just walk in off the street and take a tour. You must write or call (791-6130) at least a week in advance and indicate your preference for day and hour of visit (tours are Monday–Friday 10 A.M., 11 A.M., 1 P.M., and 2 P.M.). But if you have the slightest interest in the subject, it's worth taking the trouble to make advance arrangements.

And now let's forget about money and go in search of a few more of downtown's hidden nooks and niches. Behind the Federal Reserve Bank is the Home Insurance Company at Maiden Lane and William Street. On the fifteenth floor visitors are invited to browse through a fascinating fire-fighting museum (Monday–Friday 9 A.M.–4:30 P.M.) filled with ancient "piano" engines, fire marks, hand pumpers, helmets, badges, trumpets, and the desk where Home adjuster H. H. Walker paid out $3,151,106 in claims after the great Chicago fire of 1871 (a remarkable sum in those days). Notable features of the collection, which according to the company's brochure is the largest of its kind in the world, include a complete restoration of the Eagle Engine Company 13 firehouse once located on Maiden Lane, a two-hundred-year-old underwriters' "box" from Lloyds of London, and at the other end of the hall a re-creation of a late-nineteenth-century agent's office complete with pot-belly stove, a "summator" machine for calculating premiums, and authentic policies of that era in the principal's roll-top desk. Even if you never took much interest in fire-fighting equipment, you're likely to be impressed by the excellent displays here and the effective presentation of a complex subject.

Across from the Home Insurance Company stroll through the imaginative galleria at 100 William Street, lined with shops, to John Street (one wishes downtown had more such arcaded streets) and then head west toward Broadway, passing the diminutive John Street United Methodist Church. This is the site of the first Methodist church in America, erected in 1768, and the current 1841 structure is the third house of worship to be built here. Usually the doors are open, so walk inside and enjoy its simple intimacy. Note the sturdy hand-carved pulpit and the candelabra, all features of the church since its founding.

For an unusual sequence of contrasts after this modest structure, enter the columned halls of the American Telephone and Telegraph Building at John Street and Broadway, an impressive reminder of the immense wealth and power of America's corporate lynchpins. Then pause in the almost-feminine interior of St. Paul's Chapel immediately to the north (there are occasional noonday concerts here). In a sumptuous setting of a gilded pulpit, Water-ford crystal chandeliers, and a pink, blue, and cream decor one can see George Washington's pew in the north aisle and the pew of the first governor of New York, George Clinton, in the opposite aisle. If the sweet richness of the interior begins to pall, stroll in the simple churchyard before moving north to the Woolworth Building, fourth in this unusual sequence of interior spaces. Take a deep breath and enter a monument to one of the nation's most renowned capitalist entrepreneurs, a "cathedral of commerce," and one of the most exotic Gothic-Revival structures ever built. On the outside, Cass Gilbert, the architect, used almost every element and nuance of the Gothic era—spires, turrets, flying buttresses, gargoyles, and endless variations on the pointed arch.

Inside under a vaulted ceiling of floral motifs in glass mosaics and gold-leaf-covered wrought-iron cornices one can stroll through bronzed hallways faced in marble from the Isle of Skyros, admire the ornate elevator doors, and even chuckle (quietly of course) at the caricature sculptures of Cass Gilbert holding a model of his creation, Louis Horowitz the builder, and F. W. Woolworth himself nickel-and-diming it in the niches. Miller's Restaurant hides away in the arched catacombs while secretaries peer through palatial windows into the inner courtyard surrounding the main staircase and visitors stand wide-eyed on the polished terrazzo floors. Those who would like more information on the building itself and its founder (Woolworth paid fifteen million dollars in cash for the structure and for seventeen years—from 1913 to 1930—could claim the headquarters of his vast empire as the world's tallest building) should ask one of the guards for a pamphlet.

It's time for a rest, so stroll across to City Hall Park and select a bench for a few minutes. Look at the buildings surrounding this welcome swathe of grass and shade. Park Row, once appropriately known as "Newspaper Row," contained from the mid-nineteenth century to the early years of the twentieth century most of the city's newspaper offices. Their names bring tears to the eyes of older journalists—the *New York World*, the *Sun*, the *Tribune*, the *Mail and Express*, the *Recorder*, the *Evening Post*, the *New York American*, and at least a dozen more. In the park itself, statues of Horace Greeley and Benjamin Franklin are the last tangible remnants of what used to be one of the most hectic corners in town.

The offices overlooked City Hall and all the comings and goings of the "Boss" Tweed era, where graft was often openly flaunted as the big wheelers and dealers jostled for position and power. The famous Tweed courthouse, immediately behind City Hall, took almost ten years to build and cost the city more than ten million dollars, most of which ended up in the pockets of Tweed and his Tammany clique. City Hall itself, though, reflects a rather more decorous period of civic growth. It was completed in a combined Georgian/French-Renaissance style ("petit palais" is an oft-used phrase to describe its regal character) in 1812 and is generally regarded as one of New York's finest architectural treasures (open to the public Monday–Friday 10 A.M.–4 P.M. Free). Stroll through the lobby housing Jean Antoine Houdon's life-size statue of George Washington, and ascend the curved stairway of the rotunda. This light and delicate space was an essential element of the original design and is said to be based upon a similar feature at Wardour House in Wiltshire, England. The dome, like much of the exterior of the building, is a reconstruction. In fact it's rather amazing that anything is left of the original structure. Fires, neglect, and the annoying tendency of Massachusetts marble (originally used for the south façade) to erode rapidly have necessitated extensive and repeated restorations since the late 1800s.

The Governor's Room is the primary area open to the public and contains mainly city-commissioned portraits by John Trumbull of such notables as George Washington, George Clinton, Alexander Hamilton, and Governor Peter Stuyvesant. Across the rotunda is the Council Chamber, which is usually also open to the public.

Outside again, across Centre Street we pass under the ornate tower of the Municipal Building, topped by Adolph Weinman's golden statue of "Civic Duty," into Police Plaza, one of the few and certainly one of the most attractive pedestrian spaces in the city. The contemporary salmon-color building directly ahead (past Rosenthal's sculpture of interlocking steel circles) is the Police Headquarters Building, where tours are available (call 374-5320 for details), and slightly to the south is the last remnant, a window, of the Rhinelander Sugar House, which contained as many as a thousand American prisoners during the Revolutionary War.

As the paved walk curves around toward Foley Square note St. Andrew's Church (without doubt one of the darkest churches in

the city), where special services used to be held for printers working along Newspaper Row at 2:30 in the morning.

The irregular-shaped Foley Square is certainly one of the city's
more unusual civic spaces and a favorite haunt of court-watchers
who flock in daily (and nightly—see "Mini-Tours") to watch the
legal machinations in the Family Court, the County Court House,
and the U.S. Court House. My favorite distraction here is an incredibly ornate architectural gem at the north end of this cluster of
courts. Napoleon Le Brun's "chateau-style" fire station for Engine
Company 31, although no longer in use, is one of downtown's
most exquisite buildings (Lafayette and White streets) and one of
the subjects I most enjoy sketching (see "Mini-Tours"). For
another diversion in this area, stroll east on White Street to Columbus Park at Bayard and Baxter streets for a glimpse of a more
relaxed corner of Chinatown. It's a part of the neighborhood most
visitors miss.

Then it's west on Leonard Street to Broadway and the Institute
for Art and Urban Resources' "Clocktower" gallery. Take the elevator to the twelfth floor and then walk the remaining flight to a
rather bedraggled but certainly active complex of studio space
and galleries where the works of lesser-known "pioneer" artists
are shown in a series of exhibitions from September through May.
Brendan Gill has been an active supporter of the Institute since its
creation and claims that the Clocktower and PSI (Project Studios
One) in Long Island City, Queens, provide two of the most valuable centers in the city for artist interaction in a noncommercial atmosphere (Wednesday–Saturday 1 P.M.–6 P.M., September–May;
233-1096. Free).

South on Broadway to Duane Street we pass the Federal Building which, surprisingly, often has interesting displays open to the
public as well as a marvelous bookstore (Monday–Friday 9 A.M.–5
P.M.) full of obscure (but authoritative) government pamphlets
and books on such varied topics as pickle and relish making, the
rings of Saturn, how to breed your own Angus cattle, Mariner explorations of Mars, how to start your own car wash, advice on infant care, barbecue-cooking techniques, and bee-raising (25,000
titles in all!). If you've never browsed through one of these places,
allow yourself quite a bit of time.

At Duane Street, just west of Broadway, we discover the Fire

Fire Department Museum

Department Museum, one of the city's lesser-known official attractions. (Monday–Friday 9 A.M.–4 P.M., Saturday 9 A.M.–1 P.M. Free.) Occupying three floors of an old firehouse is a large collection of old engines (incredibly ornate affairs complete with finely painted trim), pumpers, trophies, photographs, helmets, trumpets, and all the paraphernalia of firehouse tradition during the nineteenth and early twentieth centuries. The Model-T Ford Chief's car (circa 1920) is still in good working order and is often seen in city parades, but the most popular attractions are the early red engines with their endless arrays of brass trimmings and crenellated boiler chimneys—virtual caricatures of themselves.

Well, that just about completes the tour of downtown although there are two final diversions for those still curious about this area's hidden delights. Take Chambers Street west from Broadway and enjoy "Mr. Auction's" magnificent monologue as he sells everything from so-called crystal goblets and "genuine" Ming vases to TV sets and coffee machines (90 Chambers Street). Then continue west on Chambers to Cheese of All Nations and sample the wares in one of the most redolent stores in the city or enjoy inexpensive and unusual cheese dishes in the upstairs restaurant—a splendid way to end a day's exploration of one of Manhattan's most delightful neighborhoods.

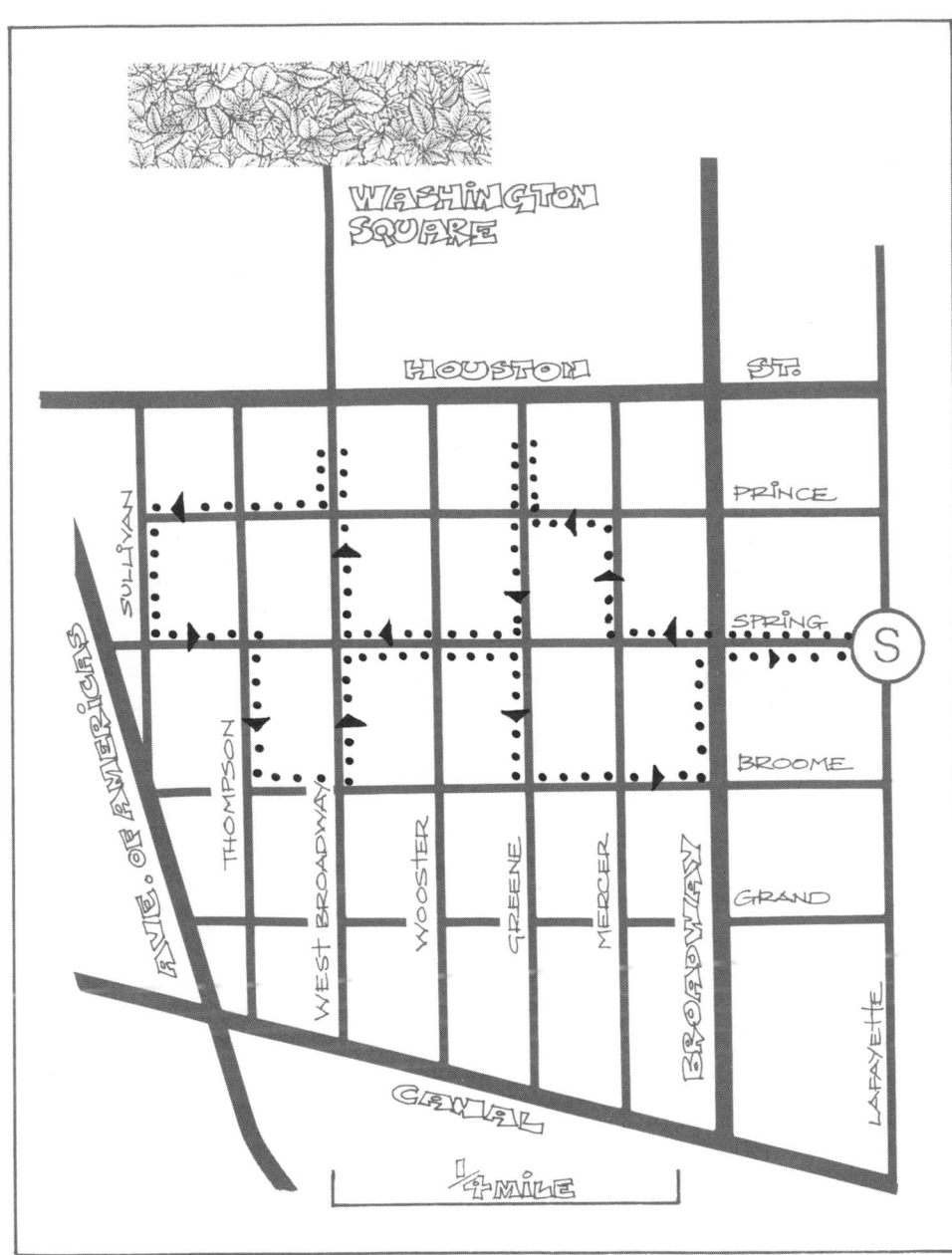

2
SOHO

In the early morning the streets are silent. The paint-flaked pillars of the cast-iron façades glow in a fresh light. Bits of cardboard boxes and shards of brightly colored cloth litter the sidewalks and the cobbled streets. There's a faint rumble of traffic along Canal Street to the south but here, deep in Soho, nothing moves. It's cat-quiet in the canyons.

By midafternoon the neighborhood is transformed. Machines pound and churn in a thousand print shops, cloth-cutting outlets, rag converters, window-shade manufacturers, corrugated-box makers, and twine jobbers. Open doors give glimpses of cavern-ous sweatshops where workers hunch over long tables in the half light or wrestle with pallets piled high with paper and boxes. Everybody shouts. The streets become thrombosisized veins, clot-ted with Mack trucks and delivery vans. Horn-honking is a popu-lar pastime; that and bawling out the guy in front, and the world in general. "Hey you, buster, get that thing outta here. Look at that guy, willya. Jus' look at that."

A door smothered in cheap-print flyers bursts open and smashes against a pile of boxes brimming with leather remnants. A short man, beer-bellied and sweating, emerges and sits on the

―――――――――― **DIRECTIONS** ――――――――――

Subway: IRT 6 to Spring Street and Lafayette Street
Bus: M1, M2, M3, M5, M6 (north/south), M12, M21 (east/west)

broken iron steps lighting a cigar. He watches the street with vacant eyes and then slowly raises his head to look at the blue sky high above the crenelated cornices of the ten-story warehouses and workshops. A young girl in a long peasant-print skirt and with a baby in a papoose on her back walks slowly past carrying a plastic bag full of bits of cut cloth and hessian. Two artists follow, one at either end of a ten-foot-wide canvas. They look identical —long black hair, long black beards, rimless spectacles, faded jeans—and have the same dedicated, serious expression on their faces as they slowly maneuver the painting down the street. It's a classically simple creation, a single strand of wormlike white paint squeezed directly from a tube onto a light blue background. The fat man on the steps watches them for a moment and then turns his head toward the gloomy workshop beyond the door.

"Hey, Al." Al dutifully appears, a little man, very thin, rubbing his hands on an oily rag. The fat man gestures with his head toward the artists now negotiating a rather difficult section of cobbled street around the rear end of a Mack truck that effectively blocks the sidewalk. A confrontation seems inevitable. The two men are moving alongside the truck, the driver is just about to open the door. He hasn't seen them, they are oblivious to him. Any moment the canvas will be sent flying. The fat man saves the day, bawling across the street to the two artists, "Hold it—hey, you two, hold it!" They stop immediately. The truck door swings open, missing the canvas by less than a foot. The driver climbs down and stares in bewilderment as the startled artists scurry around the trucks to regain the comparative safety of the sidewalk. The masterpiece is saved. The driver, the fat man, and Al stare after them as they disappear through a tall gallery doorway.

"Jesus!" mutters the fat man and saunters back into the dark workshop. Al follows, slamming the poster-smothered door behind him.

Soho is a crazy kind of place.

A few years back the twenty or so blocks in the area *so*uth of *Ho*uston Street (hence So-Ho) were ripe for the wrecker's ball. A 1962 study by the City Club of New York called the area "the wastelands of New York city" and concluded there were "no buildings worth saving." The central part of the district around Spring, Broome, and Greene streets was labeled "commercial slum no. 1." The Fire Department was even more adamant and pointed out that "Hell's Hundred Acres" was one of the most dangerous working environments in the city. A loft fire at 633 Broadway in March 1958 killed twenty-four people and the newspapers exposed the woefully inadequate enforcement of codes in the area. One beleaguered city official claimed, "The only way to enforce the codes is to pull all the bloody blocks down!" No one really paid much attention to these remarks until the proposal was made to plow the Lower Manhattan Expressway straight through the heart of the district. Actually, the concept had been on the map for more than twenty years but had gone unnoticed. New York, after all, is known for its pipe dreams and Robert Moses-inspired idiosyncrasies that never leave the bottom drawer of the planner's office.

But suddenly the project came alive along with ambitious ideas for swaths of sunken pavement, overpasses, intersections, and lots and lots of lovely traffic—an engineer's dream. The outcry was instantaneous and unified. Led by architectural professors, media notables, and the city's cultural clique, citizens of Manhattan "discovered" Soho. They were told of its outstanding nucleus of cast-iron structures—the finest in the country—huddled along the dark streets north of Chinatown. Nikolaus Pevsner described it as "a veritable museum of cast iron architecture." TV documentaries discussed its fascinating history, first as an elite residential area developed by John Jacob Astor and other perceptive entrepreneurs in the early 1800s, then as the city's elaborately exotic red-light district around 1850, followed by the cast-iron era of the later 1800s when the tight blocks became the base for the world's largest silk manufacturers, lace makers, garment cutters, and dry-goods distributors, and Broadway flourished with its ornate hotels and department stores. Architectural scholars had a field day analyzing the range of styles and influences in the ornate cast-iron façades of the warehouses and cramped factories—Italianate, neo-Grec, Victorian Gothic, Second French Empire, Renaissance, and a score of other hybrid combinations.

Students with measuring tapes, cameras, and drawing boards rushed out to record the intricate details of this "magnificent repository of American ingenuity and craftsmanship." Descriptive texts eloquently gushed about architraves, caryatids, spandrels, quoins, pilasters, modillions, capitals, and cornices. Experts discussed the comparative merits of "the cast-iron architects"—Henry Fernbach, Isaac Duckworth, Griffith Thomas, Jonathan Snook, Robert Mook, Jarvis Morgan Slade, and even debated the individual characteristics and quirks of the casting companies.

Soho was "in" and the expressway was "out," as was a later proposal for a vast sports complex and other city-inspired projects considered detrimental to the preservation of the area. Soho rose from abysmal anonymity to historic district status in less than four years.

Prior to the uproar, painters, sculptors, writers, and others seeking inexpensive spacious living areas had slowly filtered down from the more affluent neighborhoods to the north and settled quietly in empty lofts above the warehouses and workshops. Though they lived illegally in this nonresidential area, the city usually turned a blind eye to this minor transgression. After the spotlight became focused on Soho, however, the surge of "loft dwellers" increased dramatically and the inevitable confrontation with building inspectors and fire marshals was avoided only by formal legalization of loft living in 1970. At that time there were less than a thousand studios in Soho. Today the number has increased to three thousand and continues to grow rapidly. Loft living has become popular not only with the macro-canvas artists but with hip lawyers, doctors, and Dry Dock Country people attracted by big spaces in a bohemian atmosphere and the increasingly chic image of the neighborhood. The original pioneers of Soho are concerned. "Keep it Dirty" says a spray-paint sign across a splintered doorway. "This happens every time," Alex Matheson, a Soho artist, told me as we sat on a rusty loading bay on Greene Street. "We find a low-rent area, go in quietly and fix it up a bit—just enough to make it livable. Then someone opens up a gallery or a restaurant—whatever. Then the fur-coaters come and a few decide to stay and there's a piece in *New York* magazine, and then the whole cycle begins—more galleries and restaurants, rents up, old tenants forced out, new tenants in. A few make it big—y'know you get a little clique of artists and buyers and critics and gallery owners all together and some win out—but most have to move somewhere else. There's other Sohos all over town—under the Brooklyn Bridge near the Watch Tower, up by the 59th Street

Bridge, even over in Hoboken. Maybe there's nothing you can do about it. You get pissed off though, always having to move."

Alex's complaint can be heard over and over again in Soho. Marginal businesses are being forced out to increase loft space; fancy bars, restaurants and art galleries are being opened up to cater to wealthier residents and the "Saturday crowd." Another artist, Glenn Paulsen, admitted that if it weren't for the abundance of raw materials for his art he'd have left long ago. "I can't really afford it. I've had to sublet part of my loft. But I need those remnants (scores of boxes are left out on the streets filled with cloth, leather, and metal remnants—throwouts from the sweatshops). I build these creatures"—he pointed to a gallery full of life-size carnival creatures that moved and played cymbals, drums, and gongs at the pull of a string—"they're ninety percent street junk and this is the best street-junk area in town."

Let's begin our exploration of this rapidly evolving neighborhood by strolling westward along Spring Street from the subway at Lafayette. Pause briefly at Broadway and admire the remarkable range of architectural styles and materials. Cast-iron, brick, stone, and a few scattered contemporary structures adorn both sides of this imposing thoroughfare. In 1854 *Putnam's Monthly* magazine gushed that Broadway was "altogether the most showy, the most crowded, and the richest thoroughfare in America . . . the most famous street in the United States." The imposing private homes had rapidly given way to the great emporiums of wealth—Arnold Constable, Wanamaker's, Lord and Taylor, and Tiffany. Hotels, music halls, theaters, and beer gardens abounded. At 521-23 are the last remnants of the famous St. Nicholas Hotel, center of the city's social whirl. The statistics were staggering. Built at a cost of two million dollars in 1853, the hotel boasted a 275-foot frontage on Broadway, 600 rooms for more than 1000 guests, a staff of 400, 2 miles of halls, 30 miles of piping, and the most expensive—some said the most vulgar—furniture manufactured in America.

Nearby, the great six-story Niblo's Hotel, built on the site of Niblo's Garden (a landscaped series of promenades for theatergoers in the area), was joined by other equally magnificent monoliths—the Collamore, Metropolitan, American, and Prescott. The cobbled side streets leading off into Soho contained the "ladies' boarding houses" catering to every whim and taste of a discerning clientele, with Miss Lizzie Wright's "French Belles," Mrs. Hathaway's prim and proper "fair Quakeressess," and Madame Kanth's house of "Germanic Order." Alas, such interesting diversions have long since disappeared.

The Down East store at 93 Spring Street is a refreshing oasis of a different kind. The windows brim with hiking equipment, books on walking and climbing, and maps of America's little-known wilderness regions. I once watched a girl inside sewing a custom-designed parka filled with duck down. Pristine photographs of the Sierra and Cascade ranges contrasted all too vividly with the shadowed streets outside. Devotees of the outdoor life quietly compared hiking routes and equipment while traffic snarled by a few feet away.

Mercer Street, otherwise known as "Scavenger's Row," is one of the best remnant-hunting streets in Soho. Every weekday brings a constant flow of scrap connoisseurs sifting and sorting through the boxes and piles of cloth cutouts, metal strips, cardboard tubes, leather clippings, and the occasional odd bits and pieces of wood. It's a dignified procedure. At one point I watched three residents, all very artist-looking, standing patiently in line with their plastic bags waiting for a fourth member of the group to complete his selection of leather remnants from a huge cardboard box on the sidewalk. When he'd finished he smiled at the next one in line, who promptly moved into position and half disappeared into the box in search of his desired quota—and so on. "There's always plenty for everyone," the last artist in the line told me. "I use this stuff in collage work primarily. If I don't find what I need tonight, there'll be more at lunchtime tomorrow. I'll just get here earlier."

To many residents Fanelli's Café at Prince and Mercer is true Soho. Here the warehousemen, sweatshop workers, local businessmen, artists, and writers gather against the ornate bar and in the tiny dining room to enjoy the cold ale and generous "working-men's specials" of roast beef, ravioli, corned beef, and spare ribs on tables covered with crisp white tablecloths. The decor is bar-basic. Browned photographs of old boxing champions are reminders of the days when the place was a popular center for the city's fight crowd. Mike Fanelli has seen every kind of patron in his corner tavern with the erratic neon sign. I asked him how Soho had changed in the last decade. "I still get my regulars. Some guys' been coming here since repeal, some before that. But there's more of your fur-coaters nowadays, 'specially Saturdays. That used to be a real dead day. Now you should see it."

He's right. Saturday is promenade day. The streets, particularly West Broadway, are filled with visitors from other parts of the city and out-of-towners who come for a little gallery-hopping and pub-crawling. Personally, I don't care for Saturdays in Soho, but the gallery owners and restaurauteurs love it. "Oh, most of them come just to browse and giggle," a gallery girl told me, "but the darlings talk—they go home and they talk and the next week they'll bring their friends down. Eventually they buy something. You can get hooked on this place." It's true. West of Fanelli's the galleries start to proliferate. In a five-block area I counted twenty-three, and more are opening all the time. And the shows are often brilliantly produced. The wide, white spaces with an occasional Corinthian-top cast-iron pillar provide abundant space for the huge canvases, sculptures, and "constructions." Visitors are often invited to participate directly in the art forms by walk-throughs, climb-ups, pushbuttons, rope-pulling, and in one unusual exhibition of "stuffed shapes," punching and kicking. The tight snobbishness of some of the Madison Avenue galleries is replaced here by a brilliant airiness, a sense of experiment for experiment's sake, and, best of all, a sense of humor both in the displays and the artworks themselves.

A brief diversion north on Greene Street will encompass, at last count, seven galleries and the Aesthetic Realism Foundation, which boldly propounds the teachings of Eli Siegel ("art is the oneness of opposites") and exhibits prints of masterworks that supposedly confirm his principles.

Soho is alive with ideas. Sit in the coffeehouses, the bars, or stroll the galleries; listen to the artists, the people who live here; read the billboards and the signs pinned on noticeboards. Ideas are created as rapidly as the silk hats and feathered frills that streamed from the somber sweatshops at the turn of the century. Exhibitions, seminars, workshops, video experiments, theater, mime, music, jazz, film, photography, neon sculpture, you name it, somewhere in Soho someone will be working on it—conceiving it, twisting it, shaping it, testing it, turning it inside out, tying it in knots, defending it, rejecting it. It's a great stewpot of creativity.

Watch out for Richard Haas's wall painting at 112–114 Prince Street just west of Greene. Look carefully. At first it appears to be the side elevation of the neo-Grec frontage complete with ornate cast-iron detailing, window blinds, plants, and a cat—then suddenly you realize (actually the peeling surface helps a little) that it's a "trompe l'oeil" creation, a magnificent three-dimensional illusion on a flat surface.

Further west on Prince Street, the Dean & Deluca store is all too real, a wonderful potpourri of gourmet foods and cookware with such obscure creations as portable solar cookers and a Raclette oven for creating those redolent browned-cheese concoctions supposedly so popular with European mountaineers. Sausages and hams dangle on ropes or nestle together comfortably in their display cases. Cheeses, over 180 different varieties, beam up at the goggle-eyed customers. Pickles, salads, pâtés, pasta-makers, and a thousand more pots, pans, and paraphernalia await the jaded cook, tired of using Joy and Teflon II. Appropriate adjuncts to this fairly recent arrival in Soho are the adjoining Cheese Store, the Whole Food Emporium, and the nearby Food Restaurant (one of Soho's most traditional eating places).

A short diversion north on West Broadway includes four more galleries along with the very popular Let There Be Neon. On the opposite side of the street Mama Siltka's and the Ballroom (note Marion Pinto's large painting here depicting some of Soho's leading personalities) usually provide live entertainment along with dinner, and the Axis, a little lower down, is one of Soho's best-known jazz cafés.

Continuing west on Prince Street, past Alex Streeter's tiny jewelry store at 152, the Damron Hall stoneware and glass store, and the enticing "Untitled" shop brimming with art postcards, we enter a more restrained section of Soho. The Vesuvio Bakery, and, farther down, Raoul's Bar, mark the eastern fringe of an old Italian neighborhood that once dominated the southern part of Greenwich Village. The street clubs are still here—Fanelli's Republicans, and the Sullivan Knights. North on Sullivan Street itself there's Mario Amarino's Italian butcher shop, the Zampieri Bakery with a windowful of glazed Panettone di Milano cakes (some over ten pounds), and the Canevari Sausage shop. Cardine Canevari insisted that her homemade creations—cotegino, lugigana, and capicolla—were northern-style sausages. "I use lots of salt and ground pepper, sometimes a bit of parsley or cheese, not too much else. Northern food is not so spicy as the southern. Most of the people around here, they're northerners. I come from the north too. I know these recipes. I learned them from my mother." Cardine took over the store almost ten years ago, when her husband died. She has seen the neighborhood change rapidly. "Oh, we're all right here in this street—things are still pretty much the same. But over there, what a difference, so many things—and so quickly!"

Aldo Boya, on the bocci court near Sullivan and Spring, agrees. "You see that place on the corner there?" He pointed to the Soho Charcuterie and Restaurant, a resplendent niche of homemade gourmet fare and elaborate prices, on the corner of Spring. "You should see the cars, 'specially 'round lunchtime. Great black limousines lining the street halfway to Vinnie's Bar—Rolls, Caddies, Lincolns, the lot. You could keep an army warm in the fur coats at that place." He paused to aim and throw. "What the hell they wanna put that there for? There's no ritzy people living 'round here."

At the corner of Thompson and Spring, just by the play area, a Portuguese crowd gathers daily for its street forum—a huddle of dark faces in dark clothes and even darker hats. Joe's Grocery just north on Thompson Street next to Dominick Barbato's Pork Store sells many hard-to-find Italian and Portuguese delicacies to a devoted clientele. Across the street in the O G Dining Rooms equally enthusiastic devotees devour the establishment's fluffy, crusty creations from its bake shop, at tiny tables in a Depression-flavored setting. South on Thompson Street past the fish market is Pinto and Guedes, another Portuguese store.

Around the corner, heading east on Broome Street, close your ears to the terrified screeches of hens about to meet untimely demises at the Live Poultry Market. A large man in a blood-stained apron sits outside, nearly overwhelming an upright cane chair that creaks pitifully as he moves. An elderly Italian woman emerges with a white bird wrapped in newspaper, its head lolling hideously.

The large man leers up at me. "Chicken?" he asks with what can only be called "a menacing grin." Across the road a group of rusty street sculptures huddle creaturelike in the middle of the road.

I pause—with relief—at Kenn and Bobb's Broome Street Bar, a delightful Soho pub at the corner of Broome and West Broadway. Outside, a gilded lion's head dangles over the doorway of this diminutive structure dwarfed by the colonnaded façades of nearby loft buildings. Inside, Kenn Reisdorff mingles with a very Soho clientele and occasionally takes over the bar to administer restorative draughts of Pryor's Dark, McSorley's Ale, and Stegmaier Porter to a thirsty clientele. Talking is thirsty work, and the babble here never ceases. If voices wear out there are blackboards and multicolored chalks available for budding graffiti artists. Kenn boasts that his pub was once a renowned German restaurant, when the partially developed neighborhood was known as Klein-deutschland (Little Germany). Later it was owned by the seven burly Wagner brothers, Italian, not German, and all boxers. Today along with his wife's smaller establishment, Berry's at Spring and Thompson, the Broome Street Bar is one of Soho's most popular watering holes.

The blocks north and east of Broome Street are the cultural heart of the neighborhood. North on West Broadway are most of the primary galleries. At 484 Broome Street, in the middle of another synergism of galleries, is the Kitchen, an intriguing experimental center for music and video recording offering a broad range of public presentations. Similarly, the Museum of Colored Glass and Light, the Open Space Theater, and the Performing Garage, all on Wooster around Broome, attract a steady stream of supporters. There's also the Museum of Holography at 13 Mercer Street (just north of Canal), with one of the most unusual exhibits in town (see "Mini-Tours").

Then there are the bars and restaurants. Stroll north on West Broadway from the Broome Street Bar past the galleries and poster stores and peep into the splendidly ornate interior of Oh-Ho-So, the bibliotecque-style spaces of Skrambles, the orange-and-brown niches of 162, the dark, rich recesses of WPA, and the light and airy Spring Street Natural Restaurant and Bar. Again, if you'd like to enjoy these places in their more normal states, avoid Saturdays. Try lunch here or, better still, visit in the late afternoon before the evening rush.

The Broome Street Bar

If you're planning on photography it's best to get here in the morning when the sun is bright and fresh and the shadows most pronounced. Cast-iron-architecture devotees will find Greene Street between Spring and Broome (turn right at Craft Caravan—a bazaarlike store of African imports) one of the most prepossessing areas, filled with revival masterpieces by Henry Fernbach and Jonathan Snook. The elaborate French Renaissance structure at 72–76 Greene Street, known locally as "the King of Greene Street," is an Isaac Duckworth creation and in contrast to many of the others has a pronounced three-dimensional façade topped by a magnificently ornate cornice. Another Duckworth, the blue-painted "Queen" at 28–30 Greene Street, is the best example in Soho of the Second Empire Style and comes complete with mansard roof and ornate dormer windows.

Turning east on Broome Street we head back toward Broadway. Look out for Global Village, a second video media center with regular public showings, and farther along, Patsy's Barber shop, a classic emporium. We're approaching the black Haughwout Building, the "Parthenon of Cast Iron," on the northeast corner of Broome and Broadway. It was styled by John Gaynor as a Venetian palazzo in 1856. Surprisingly, this sophisticated structure was one of the earliest cast-iron buildings in the city and the first to use Elisha Otis's steam-powered passenger elevator.

Back on Broadway we leave the cluttered streets behind—the crashings of grimy machines in dim workshops, the boxes of leather pieces, the clothes drying on fire escapes, the glimpses of elaborate loft spaces through palm-fronded windows, the long conversations at café tables, the vast white-spaced galleries, the snarled traffic, the barking of truckers, the obliviousness of artists, and the chitter of fur-coated trend-setters. At Broadway we return to the wider, brighter spaces and the long lines of austere business frontages. By comparison—it's rather dull.

The Queen of Greene Street

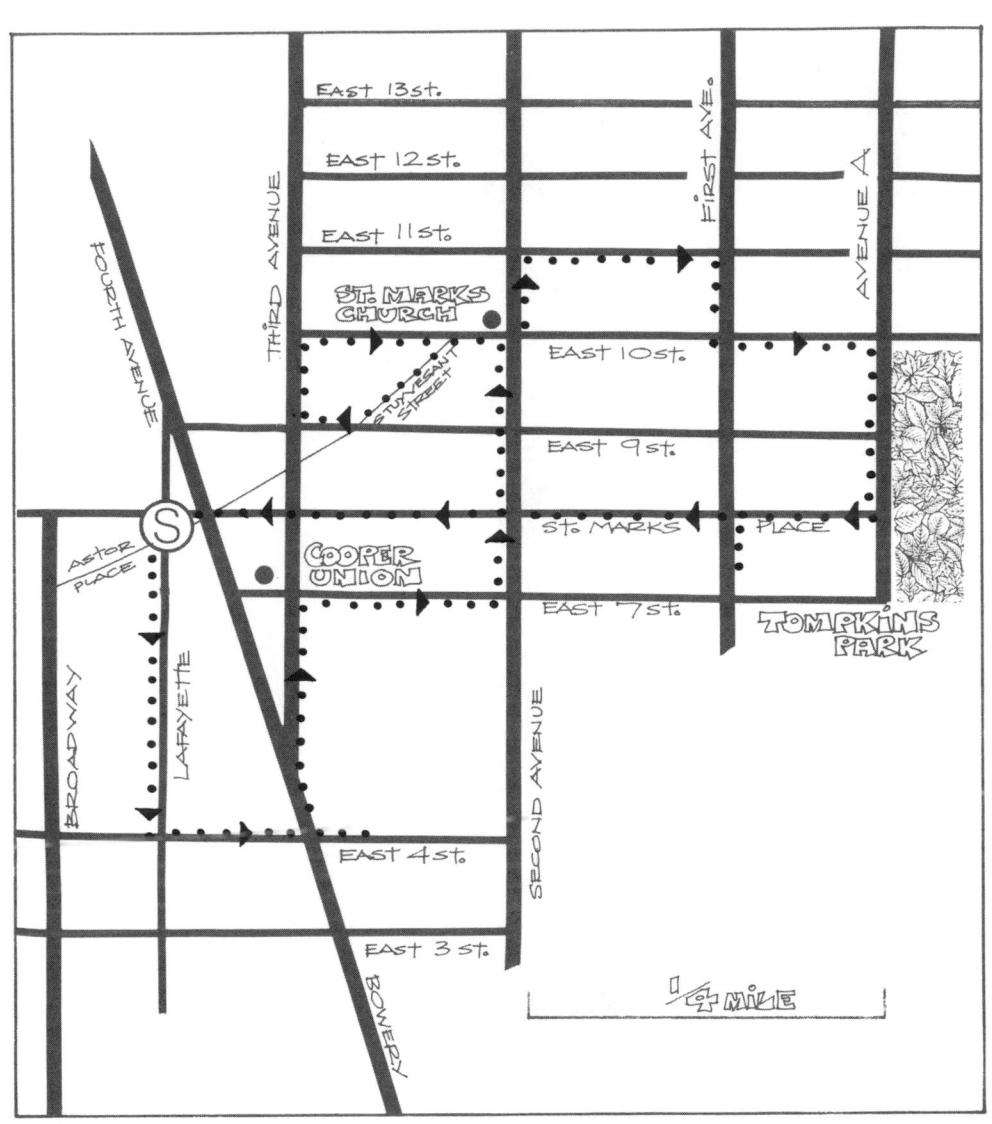

3

THE EAST VILLAGE

"Surely you're not doing the East Village?" asked a dear friend. "No one wants to walk down there. That neighborhood's gone, it's finished." His sentiments are shared, I'm sure, by thousands of New Yorkers who associate the district with Bowery bums, beatniks, hippies, and a braggadocio life-style that rejects societal norms with the singlemindedness of a mainlining addict. And to some extent the image fits the reality. The psychedelic sixties was the era of Bill Graham's Fillmore East, the Electric Circus, Ed Sanders's Peace Eye bookstore, the Phoenix, and a score of high-flying taverns and coffeehouses. During the fifties, Ginsberg, Kerouac, and LeRoi Jones established the abrasive literary tone of the neighborhood. St. Mark's-in-the-Bouwerie was home for the free-floating New York Poets and budding Timothy Learys gave guru sessions on stoops to spaced-out admirers tripping away on LSD. "That was the best time," a frazzle-haired girl told me as we stood chatting near the Kiwi II Bar. "Haight-Ashbury and here. They were the only places worth being."

But the era faded. The Fillmore closed; Ratner's enormous kosher dairy restaurant next door, hangout of the hippiest of the hippies, vanished; and the once-glorious beatnik bookstores became thrift centers and machine-repair shops. LSD tripping was

─────── DIRECTIONS ───────

Subway: IRT 6 to Astor Place/Fourth Avenue
Bus: M13 (east/west), M101, and M102 (north/south),
  M1, 2, 3, 5, 6 (north/south)

replaced by more serious addiction to the hard drugs. The neighborhood became known for vandalism, muggings, rapes, break-ins, and an occasional murder, and outsiders stayed away. Newspapers stopped reporting the crimes and landlords stopped collecting rents. Even the police were reluctant to patrol certain blocks deep in the district. "Things got about as bad as they could," an ex-city cop told me. "In the early seventies you kept away from this place. That's the way most people still see it. You mention 'East Village' and people think of drugs, murder, winos, slums, mugging—the lot. Most of them haven't been down here for years, though, maybe not since the flower-power days."

But Manhattan neighborhoods have an ability to bounce back. The East Village still has its problems—some serious—but there are abundant signs of improvement. Recent restoration of finely detailed nineteenth-century townhouses on St. Marks Place, 9th Street, and along the north side of Tompkins Square has revealed new potentials in old blocks. Improvement associations abound. Sidewalks have newly planted trees, and the vandalism rate is low. Off-Broadway theaters flourish in an atmosphere of mutual support and the pub restaurants along the notorious Bowery—Phebe's, the Tin Palace, Hisae's, the Great Gildersleeves—reflect a new confidence in the locale. I always remember a Sunday stroll I took along the Bowery just below the linerlike bulk of Cooper Union. It was a warm day, and quiet until I noticed a crowd of some twenty or thirty people standing in line outside a rather nondescript restaurant with iron grilles over the windows. There were all kinds in the crowd—furred folk bedecked in mink and ocelot, bearded hippie-style characters complete with headbands and beads, a few professional types, and a lot of everyday New Yorkers queueing quite happily, ignoring the requests of Bowery bums for loose change. The place was Hisae's. The menu in the window featured a pleasant range of chicken and fish dishes, but nothing strikingly unusual. I wondered if some special gimmick was being offered—free meals for the first thirty customers or something. "Oh no," one squirely gentleman told me. "It's just an excellent restaurant with excellent food. This is the only way we can be assured of a seat." His wife joined in. "If you don't come before it opens you hardly ever get a seat. You have to wait for hours." So here, just before five o'clock on a Sunday afternoon, this devoted group stood on a grubby Bowery sidewalk waiting to be fed—just one more sign of life returning to the East Village.

We begin the walk at Astor Place and pause first at the Astor Place Liquor Store, which features one of the largest selections of foreign wines in the city—a veritable library of labels. Astor Place was named after John Jacob Astor, who arrived in America in 1784 with less than twenty dollars in his pocket. At the time of his death in 1848 he had not only accumulated an immense fortune but had earned himself a series of notorious nicknames, not least of which was "landlord of New York." Following his first land purchase in 1789, a small plot of land between the Bowery and Elizabeth Street, he went on to acquire enormous holdings that assured his family a permanently prominent place in metropolitan society. When he died he bequeathed almost half a million dollars and land for the construction of "the finest library in the nation" on Lafayette Place. The Astor Library was designed in Italianate style and opened with great ceremony in 1854. Today as the New York Shakespeare Festival Building, better known as Joseph Papp's Public Theatre (five separate theaters at last count— telephone 677-1750 for more information), it remains the cultural nucleus of the district. The architect Giorgio Cavaglieri supervised its restoration for this purpose beginning in 1967 and one wishes his commission could have included the nearby remains of townhouses called Colonnade Row (La Grange Terrace). Here along with the Astors lived the Vanderbilts, the Delanos (FDR's grandfather), and other prominent citizens of the day. President John J. Tyler was married on the second floor of one of these magnificent colonnaded townhouses, and Washington Irving, Dickens, and Thackeray all stayed here for brief periods. When originally developed by a wealthy speculator, Seth Greer, in 1832, the row consisted of nine Greek Revival townhouses and was named La Grange Terrace after the Marquis de Lafayette's Chateau de la Grange just outside Paris. Plans originally called for pergolas and elaborate roof gardens but these were never realized. In fact the project has a history of constant abuse. Even before its completion, stonecutters in the city threatened to demolish the emerging structure unless the builders stopped using stone quarried and cut by Sing Sing inmates. Then early in this century John Wanamaker demolished five of the houses for a delivery-truck garage. Tasteless protruberances have been added to the roof to increase rentable floor space, the garden and its terrace have gone, and much of the refined ornamentation is missing. The only recent occurrence of a positive nature was the opening of Robert Ogden's Lady Astor's restaurant with its rich nineteenth-century decor. At least here one can begin to imagine the true character of these residences during their heyday.

Of course, it was not all opulence and tranquillity in those early years around Astor Place. On the evening of May 10, 1849, one of the bloodiest riots ever recorded in the city erupted outside the Astor Place Opera House (near 8th Street at Lafayette), where the British actor William Macready was giving his famous rendition of Macbeth. At the time there was strong resentment of the influence that England seemed to have over this nation's affairs. Poor Macready was hardly to blame, although ill-concealed bitterness between the actor and his American "rival," Edwin Forrest, had been sensationalized by the press. Throughout the play the audience hissed and booed whenever Macready appeared on stage. The climax came as Forrest shouted out the fiery line "what purgative drug will scour these English hence?" Pandemonium broke loose. The audience went wild, destroying the seats, the wall lamps, the curtains, and the great crystal chandelier. Outside were several thousand more rioters. The police were quickly outnumbered and on more than one occasion only escaped with their lives by firing point-blank into the crazed mob. The mélée lasted three days, the theater was almost destroyed, and at least twenty-three people (some sources estimate thirty-one) were killed. Macready somehow escaped with his life and returned to England to be personally welcomed by Queen Victoria. He never came back to New York.

Lafayette Street south from Astor Place contains some splendid nineteenth-century structures including the Durst Building (409–411), a powerful blend of brick with cast iron, and the Romanesque-flavored De Vinne Press Building (393–99), named after the renowned author of books on the art and history of printing, Theodore De Vinne. Then abruptly, as we turn the corner onto East 4th Street, the mood changes and we find ourselves facing the diminutive Old Merchant's House (29), thought to be one of the last complete Greek-Revival houses in the city (Tuesday–Sunday

The Old Merchant's House

tours 2, 3, and 4 P.M. Telephone in advance 777-1089. 50¢). At one time the whole street was lined with similar structures and must have matched Washington Square North in character. Built in 1831, the house was purchased in 1835 by Seabury Tredwell and remained in his family until 1933 when a distant relative, George Chapman, managed to ensure its preservation as an example of late-nineteenth-century life in the city. Everything is intact. Most of the objects—the beds, chairs, tables, paintings, clothes, and trinkets—were accumulated by the Tredwells during their century-long residence here. One feels like a guest in the home of a family of refinement. Trunks upstairs in the bedroom still contain the Tredwells' clothes and shoes. It's a captivating glimpse of yesteryear.

Then abruptly we're out on the Bowery itself, a brash, battered street full of character and history. It was named after the road built in the 1600s from the city to Peter Stuyvesant's "bouwerie" or farm, which included all land presently east of today's Bowery between 4th and 7th streets. The governor located his stone house on what is now the corner of 7th Street and Second Avenue, erected the first St. Mark's-in-the-Bouwerie Church, and encouraged the settlement of Dutch pioneers in the adjoining Bouwerie Village. After the British takeover of New Amsterdam in 1664 Stuyvesant retired permanently to his estate and following his death in 1672 was buried in the graveyard of his own church.

For almost a hundred years Bouwerie Village remained unchanged, a pleasant pastoral enclave. Even when Seth Greer was busy building his La Grange Terrace the more conservative New Yonkers considered this area still "country" and ridiculed any attempt at land development. But by the mid-1800s, as the city expanded northward, the Bowery had become a burgeoning entertainment strip of theaters, taverns, and beer gardens. The opening of Sperry's Botanical Gardens, later Vauxhall Garden, near Astor Place was followed by the establishment in 1826 of the Bowery Theater on the site of the Bull's Head Tavern. It was here that Washington had paused to quench his thirst with Bowery Ale on Evacuation Day in 1783. Later came the Windsor Theater and for a while the finest actors of the time strolled the stages of a dozen or more opulent establishments. Then, in typical Manhattan fashion, the tide of fashionable residences continued up the island taking with it the finer cultural facilities and leaving in its wake a flotsam and jetsam of sleazy ale houses, rotgut liquor saloons, and a plethora of gangsters, beggar-girls, card sharks, and ladies of the night. By 1898 the Bowery had ninety-nine houses of entertainment, of which only fourteen were classed as respectable by the police. Here's the reaction of a Southerner who made his first visit to the street around this time:

> These places (theater and bars) were jammed to suffocation on Sunday nights. Actresses too corrupt and dissolute to play elsewhere appear on the boards at the Bowery. Broad farces, indecent comedies, plays of highwaymen and murderers, are received with shouts by the rag-pickers, begging girls, collectors of cinders, all who can beg or steal a sixpence, fill the galleries of these corrupt places of amusement. There is not a dance hall, a free-and-easy, a concert saloon, or a vile drinking-place that presents such a view of the depravity and degradation of New York as the gallery of a Bowery theater.

By 1930 there were hardly a dozen theaters left, and most of these were devoted to burlesque and movies. The vast beer gardens seating fifteen hundred customers at large trestle tables were gone, along with the odd mélange of characters that gave the Bowery so much of its notorious color. The Bowery sank into a virtually total decay which has lasted for almost half a century. Even today it's still a pretty miserable place with its Salvation Army centers, wholesale restaurant-supply outlets, and flophouses, but recently promising signs of a renaissance have appeared. The new bars and restaurants are hectic night-life places. Theaters flourish again after a long absence. La Mama's, the Truck and Warehouse, the New York Theatre Ensemble (all on East 4th Street just past Phebe's), Theatre Genesis, the WPA, and the Amato Opera Showcase Theatre are only a few of the off-off-Broadway establishments in this cultural niche. The Bouwerie Lane Theater is housed in an exquisite example of cast-iron architecture in the French Second Empire style on the corner of Bond Street and the Bowery. In places where the detailing is missing a talented artist has supplied effective two-dimensional replicas.

There are other promising signs of neighborhood revival—cooperative food stores, block-association headquarters, storefront legal centers, and offices providing information on property renovation. McSorley's Old Ale House at 15 E. 7th Street (near Third Avenue) is little changed since it was first opened back in the 1850s and is the neighborhood's bastion of permanence. Everyone who was anyone in New York has drunk McSorley's dark rich ale here and munched the cheese-and-onion sandwiches. Peter Cooper's chair and mug are preserved without fanfare and the old-timers point with a grin at Brendan Behan's favorite corner near the pot-belly stove. And towering over it all like a stern but kindly father is the chocolate-colored Cooper Union Foundation Building. The view north of this famous college devoted to science and art is one of the most impressive in the East Village. Fourth Avenue continues north past the remnants of Book Row (the Strand is the only bookstore of real significance still left) and disappears into a shadowed canyon topped by a skyline of golden towers and the majestic Empire State Building.

Of course when the Cooper Union was first established, this was still a pastoral enclave of rolling fields dotted with a few select mansions. Peter Cooper himself, philanthropist, reformer, and inventor, was determined to found a center for free technical education and for the open expression of opinions on crucial issues of the day by significant spokesmen. (He was also curious to see if his railroad rails, produced in his Trenton plant, could be used effectively in building construction.) In 1860, shortly after the opening, Lincoln made his important "might makes right" address here, which established his reputation as a powerful orator and potential presidential candidate. Henry Ward Beecher, William Cullen Bryant, and William Lloyd Garrison also used the stage of the Great Hall to deliver major speeches against slavery and in defense of the Union. Even today the building remains an important center for education. Free public lectures, seminars, and concerts continue to attract large crowds to the Great Hall, and inexpensive courses in a wide variety of subjects range from Western Philosophy and Graphoanalysis (handwriting analysis) to Comparative Religious Mysticism and Assertiveness Training. (The Cooper Union Museum, once also housed here, is now located at the Cooper-Hewitt Museum at 9 East 90th Street in the Andrew Carnegie Mansion. Telephone 860-2011.)

Augustus Saint-Gaudens's prominent statue of Cooper in the little triangular space south of the Union shows a stately, powerful man sitting kinglike on a high-backed chair. Saint Gaudens was slightly biased, of course. He, like many of America's leading artists, had received a free education at the Union and had enormous respect for the farsightedness of its founder. Other contemporaries, however, described him in more familiar terms as "a kind man, full of ideas and fun" and called him "the leprechaun."

At Third Avenue and East 7th Street we pass into a little world of onion domes and painted eggs, finely embroidered blouses, and Slavic music dancing out from diminutive stores. The Bowery and the cultural monoliths around Cooper Square and Astor Place seem far behind. We're abruptly in the heartland of the Ukraine. That ornate, mansard-roofed building on the corner of Third Avenue is no longer the Metropolitan Savings Bank but is now the First Ukrainian Assembly of God. The domes and Byzantine bulges of the two churches, nestled together like an ill-matched married couple, reflect the strong traditions of the neighborhood. The old St. George's is a dark, romantic place with glimmers of gold mosaic in the gloom. The new one, white and fat, was opened in April 1978, and has a bright interior full of light. Both are massive constructions with thick walls and heavy arches. They reflect the unchanging solidarity of the sixteen hundred inhabitants of this Little Ukraine. The new church is an expression of permanence to many of the neighborhood residents. Taras Schumylowych, an architect and artist who worked on the plans for Independence Plaza and the Rupert Houses in downtown Manhattan, told me, "It's the best thing that's happened to us in years. It's a reminder to others—and to us sometimes—that we're still here." Sixty-five-year-old Irene Kmetyk feels the same pride for the district. She's the local expert in "Pysanky," the painted eggs you'll see in the stores throughout this part of the East Village, and she gives classes in the art at the little-known Ukrainian Museum at 203 Second Avenue between 12th and 13th streets (Wednesday 1–5 P.M., Friday 3–7 P.M., Saturday and Sunday 1–5 P.M. Adults $1, children 50¢. 228-0110). "Our crafts, our culture, are different. We try to keep it alive," she told me. Talk with the people as you wander down East 7th Street and north on Second Avenue. Szonksz Rusych, owner of one of the exclusively Ukrainian stores opposite the church, loves to chat with strangers. "We're proud of our background. We like to talk about it—or about anything else too. You get a Ukrainian started and you'll have a problem stopping him—unless you feed him!"

North on Second Avenue we pass the Ukrainian Mission, the Ukrainian Sports Club, the headquarters of the Ukrainian Liberation Front, and the Ukrainian National Home with its famous restaurant offering such East European dishes as borscht, pirogi, blintzes, goulash, stuffed cabbage, and so on. The Orchidia at 9th Street is a well-loved oddity professing to be the only Italian/Ukrainian restaurant in the city ("pizza, piroghi, and pilsner!"). The Public Library (Freie Bibliothek u Lesehalle), next door to the white ornateness of the Stuyvesant Polyclinic, retains a complete room of German books on the second floor left over from the days when it created exclusively to a German-speaking population.

But Second Avenue is far more than just a Ukrainian stronghold. Look closely at the stores and buildings as you walk north toward St. Mark's-in-the-Bouwerie. Chinese and Indian restaurants abound and Abe Wohl's Second Avenue Kosher Deli near the church has been a popular neighborhood hangout since 1954. Abe himself believes in "when-you've-got-it, flaunt-it," and the windows are crammed with photographs of visiting celebrities and shots of Abe on the Bill Boggs show producing his famous matzoh balls. "Hell," a customer told me, "you wanna succeed in this neighborhood, you gotta use everythin' you got."

Until quite recently, Ratner's store and restaurant were next to the old Fillmore East between 7th and 8th streets. Farther up, there's the Gem Spa, famous for its egg custards, and west on East 9th Street peep into the tiny Montana Palace, where Naomi Schechter produces her incredible cheese boereks, taramsalata, spinach pie, moussaka, and a dozen other carry-out dishes. Recently she added a selection of "Little Rich Cakes" and her reputation is now such that her delectables grace the counters at Bloomingdale's and Balducci's. The *New Yorker* has followed Naomi's progress since she arrived in the city a few years ago, penniless and very determined. Her story is pure Horatio Alger.

At this point in the walk we're deep in the heart of what used to be the old Yiddish Rialto, a second Broadway of theaters offering productions almost exclusively to a Jewish population living in the Lower East Side. In its heyday it stretched all the way from Houston Street to 14th Street and many famous Jewish actors, including Edward G. Robinson, Paul Muni, Maurice Schwartz, and Stella Adler, pranced the boards to the delight of audiences who loved the "immigrant-makes-good" themes of many of the productions. Today it's all gone, with the exception of the Hebrew Actor's Union opposite St. George's Church on East 7th Street. Even the famous Café Royale at Second Avenue and 12th Street, forum for the Jewish intelligentsia and theatrical critics, has vanished. The Jewish population, in typical Manhattan fashion, "made good" and moved north. The durable "Eden" managed to keep going longer than the others, offering fine progressive theater, but even that has gone now.

Fortunately there's one enclave around St. Mark's-in-the-Bouwerie that reflects, in a relatively unmolested state, the earliest history of the neighborhood—long before the Bowery bums, the Jewish, Ukrainian, and Polish immigrants, and the flower people. Sadly, St. Mark's Church itself, built first as a Dutch chapel in 1660 and rebuilt in 1799, was badly damaged by fire in July 1978. The church has begun a fund-raising program in the hopes of raising three million dollars for restoration, but for the time being no one can say when it will be able to reopen.

The church was long renowned for being somewhat unconventional. In 1878 the remains of A. T. Stewart, millionaire founder of Wanamaker's, were removed and held for a ransom of $250,000. Two years later the body was finally relinquished after Stewart's widow had paid out $20,000. Then in the 1920s Dr. William Norman Guthrie shocked the less-enlightened members of his congregation by introducing a church ritual expressing the essential unity of all religions, which included American Indian chants, Greek folk dancing, and Eastern mantras. He also established a Body and Soul Clinic aimed at providing combined physical and spiritual treatments, a most advanced concept of healing in those days.

Later, particularly during the flower era, the church became a focus for the new wave of poets and playwrights and until the fire the Monday and Wednesday poetry readings (8 P.M.) were an integral part of neighborhood culture. In the cemetery, which still contains the bodies of Governor Peter Stuyvesant and Commodore Matthew C. Perry, the area around the graves has been paved over to enable more intensive use by nearby residents. Spend time here under the shade trees, reading the old headstones and admiring the sculpture around the portico. The two weathered Indians were the work of Solon Borglum, who spent much of his early life traveling the Sierra Madre. His statues depicting the characters and flavor of the Old West can be found in museums throughout the country, including the Metropolitan in New York City. On either side of the main door are two chunky lions, both of Florentine marble. Toom Dupuis's sculpture of Peter Stuyvesant peers somewhat indifferently over the graveyard (a gift from Queen Wilhelmina of Holland in 1915), and at the opposite side is Daniel Tompkins, governor of New York from 1807 to 1817, famous for his complete abolition of slavery in the state.

To the east of the church is the delightful "triangle" of sixteen Italianate houses on Stuyvesant and East 10th Streets. Because of the splayed angle of the street (one of the few true east–west streets in Manhattan), it's easy to miss. With the exception of the elegant Federal-style Stuyvesant Fish House at 21 Stuyvesant Street (built by a great-grandson of the governor in 1804 as a wedding gift for his daughter), all the other townhouses were conceived and constructed as a group in 1861. Stanford White was born here, Dwight Macdonald lived nearby on East 10th Street, and W. H. Auden, who was a parishioner of St. Mark's, spent much time in one of the Stuyvesant Street houses. During the fifties this became the territory of Ginsberg, Kerouac, Mailer, Frank O'Hara, and LeRoi Jones. The local coffee shops were the focus of the "beat" culture—Mickey Ruskin's 10th Street Coffee House, Les Deux Magots on East 7th Street, and Cafe Le Metro. How pristine the triangle must have seemed against the kaleidoscope of the avenues and the frantic party-paced life of the times. Kerouac gives this brief description of the neighborhood in his book *The Subterraneans:*

> The wash hung over the court, actually the back courtyard of a big 20-family tenement with bay windows, the wash hung out and in the afternoon the great symphony of Italian mothers, children, fathers BeFinneganing and yelling from stepladders, smells, cats mewing, Mexicans, the music from all the radios whether bolero or Mexican or Italian tenor of spaghetti eaters or loud suddenly turned-up KPFA symphonies of Vivaldi harpsichord intellectuals performances boom blam the tremendous sound of it.

Down East 11th Street, heading toward First Avenue and eventually Tompkins Park, the pace changes. (First though, don't forget to take a detour to the Ukrainian Museum on Second Avenue between East 12th Street and East 13th Street.) We enter an Italian mini-neighborhood, leaving behind the pirogi and borscht for a while. The Veniero Pasticceria near First Avenue brims with trays of the most tempting sugary delectables. Locals sit inside on the soda fountain chairs drinking espresso. At the far end the great chrome-plated coffee machine gleams like an altarpiece. Next door are the Black-Forest Bakery and Russo's, famous for its homemade mozzarella and pasta. Then on First Avenue there are the all-day, all-night vegetable and fruit stands, De Robertis' Pastry Shop (ice-cream-parlor-like with white tiled walls), John's restaurant, and Lanza's, with its dimly lit dining room and oil paintings browned with age and the smoke of strong cigars. Peter's Spice Store (and Everything Nice) is perfectly at home in this redolent section of the avenue.

Down East 10th Street the flavor changes again. We pass a Russian and Turkish bathhouse and the oddly styled St. Nicholas Carpatho-Russian Orthodox Church on the corner of Avenue A. Founded by the Rutherford-Stuyvesant family in 1884, it was known as St. Mark's Chapel of the Bouwerie until it became an orthodox church in 1925. The rich interior is renowned for its beautifully tiled walls, carved beams, and stained glass. Then we arrive at Tompkins Park, a remarkably well-maintained and shady place to pause awhile. Note the fine town houses bounding the northern edge of the park. Immediately behind, at 519 East 11th Street, is a unique experiment in innovative urban-energy alternatives. Various neighborhood groups including "Adopt a Building" (an organization encouraging the rehabilitation of abandoned apartment buildings using "sweat equity" as a prime resource), the Energy Task Force, and the 11th Street Movement cooperated in the development of solar and wind power systems to minimize fuel costs for low-income tenants. Nearby, at 12th Street between Avenues A and B, another group has initiated a community garden project with promising results. "We have no vandalism problems at all," Mary Christianson, a member of the Energy Task Force, told me. "There's too much of the community invested in these projects."

Over on the south side of the park, not far from the band shell, is a favorite forum for the Eastern European residents, mainly males, who gather daily in every kind of weather to discuss the state of the world. Scores of them, most of them in hats and dark coats, stand in tight groups gesticulating and arguing in their native tongues. Appropriately, the nearby statue of Samuel Sullivan Cox, "the letter-carrier's friend," shows a stern-bearded gentleman in a frock coat waving his finger in a grand oratorical gesture. "They're here every day," a young man told me as we watched the fiery discussions. "You think sometimes they're going to massacre each other, it gets so noisy. But then they go away and come back the next day, all smiles and handshakes."

We return to First Avenue past George Proko's Pipe and Tobacco store at 130 St. Marks Place. Mixed with bits of the Italian district to the north we find Guiffre's Fish Store, a pirogi maker, and a couple of Ukrainian meat stores, windows brimming with smoked sausages and hams. Michele Tostanoski took over Tron's Meat and Poultry store (119 First Avenue between 7th Street and St. Marks Place) when her father died a few years ago. "My first love was art," she told me as we chatted inside the store, "but I thought I'd give the business a try. It was either that or sell it. I didn't like the way many butchers cured their meat, though, so I decided we'd do it here without nitrites and all those other additives they use so freely nowadays." So in partnership with Frank Glowacki, Michele introduced new policies of meat curing, using salt as a primary ingredient. "At first it was difficult. People didn't always understand what we were trying to do. Now, though"— she smiled and looked at the line of customers ogling the array of meats in the glass cases—"it's different. People care more about what they eat."

Across the street at 124 First Avenue, the aroma of smoking meats wafts out over the sidewalk from E. Kurowycky and Son's butcher shop, mingling with the smell of fresh loaves from a nearby bakery. Nostalgia hangs heavy over this part of the neighborhood and, indeed, is given pride of place at Theatre 80 on the corner of St. Marks Place and First Avenue (254–7400). Here Howard Otway presents his nightly double-billing of early movies featuring such notables as Fred Astaire, Rita Hayworth, Rosalind Russell, Paul Robeson, Orson Welles, John Barrymore, George

Theatre 80

Raft, and other latter-day super-stars. Note the handprints and signatures on the sidewalk, à la Grauman's Chinese Theatre in Hollywood. Inside an old speakeasy bar now functions as a candy counter and in the foyer there's a memorial niche to Joan Crawford. "She was a good friend" is all Howard will say about her. I asked him if many of the old stars visited the theater. "Oh yes, quite a few. Miss [Gloria] Swanson comes quite often. She's a lovely person."

If you peer to the top of the building that houses the theater you'll see the year 1772! I thought I'd made an astonishing historical discovery until Howard told me it was placed there by members of a Polish Social Club, in honor of General Pulaski, who arrived in the country around that time and later helped General Washington in his struggles against the British.

St. Marks Place between First and Second avenues is a splendid indication of the renovation potentials of the neighborhood. Admittedly some of the remodeling of the townhouses has been a little overdrastic as exemplified by an almost callous removal of elegant steps and wrought-iron railings. But the street has an air of new life to it, the spirit of a fresh start. There's a Polish Club here, a Montessori School, a number of refined churches that blend perfectly with the terraced townhouses, a ballet school, and a group whose motto is "Aid to the Feeble, Comfort to the Aged." The neighborhood is alive with clubs and organizations, the threads that hold the web of community together.

As we complete the final leg of our walk, we pass through the heart of the East Village. St. Marks Place between Second and Third avenues is a riotous summation of all the East Village has been and possibly will be. The street blazes with color and noise. Radios blast from open apartment windows, a rooster crows from a purple fire escape, residents hang out of windows carrying on conversations with passing friends. The bright blue building on the north side of the street was originally a well-known Polish club, the Dom, then later became the Electric Circus, and today contains a beehive of craft classes and activities. The East Side Book Store was the center of the neighborhood's counter-culture, featuring a wide selection of poetry works by New York poets who appeared regularly at St. Mark's Church, and a comprehensive selection of Marxist/Third World publications. The trinket-laden window of a "Reader and Advisor" nestles among stores with such bizarre titles as Manic Panic, Trash and Vaudeville, Conscious Decision, Happily Ever After, and A Place in the Country. People walk at an almost Californian pace and the air is rich with incense and other more illicit aromas. Two children, completely naked, romp together on the sidewalks as their smiling mother, dressed in a sarilike outfit, chats with a companion on a stoop. A young man with a beard to his navel strolls along the sidewalk singing Dylan and strumming a battered guitar. An ice cream parlor features such flavors as Panama Red and Acapulco Gold. Everywhere there's construction going on—stores being remodeled, townhouses being renovated. A few years back it seemed the area was almost too bad for reclamation. Now one can sense a new confidence, a new purpose. There's still much to be done, but at least things have started. It's a great place to explore.

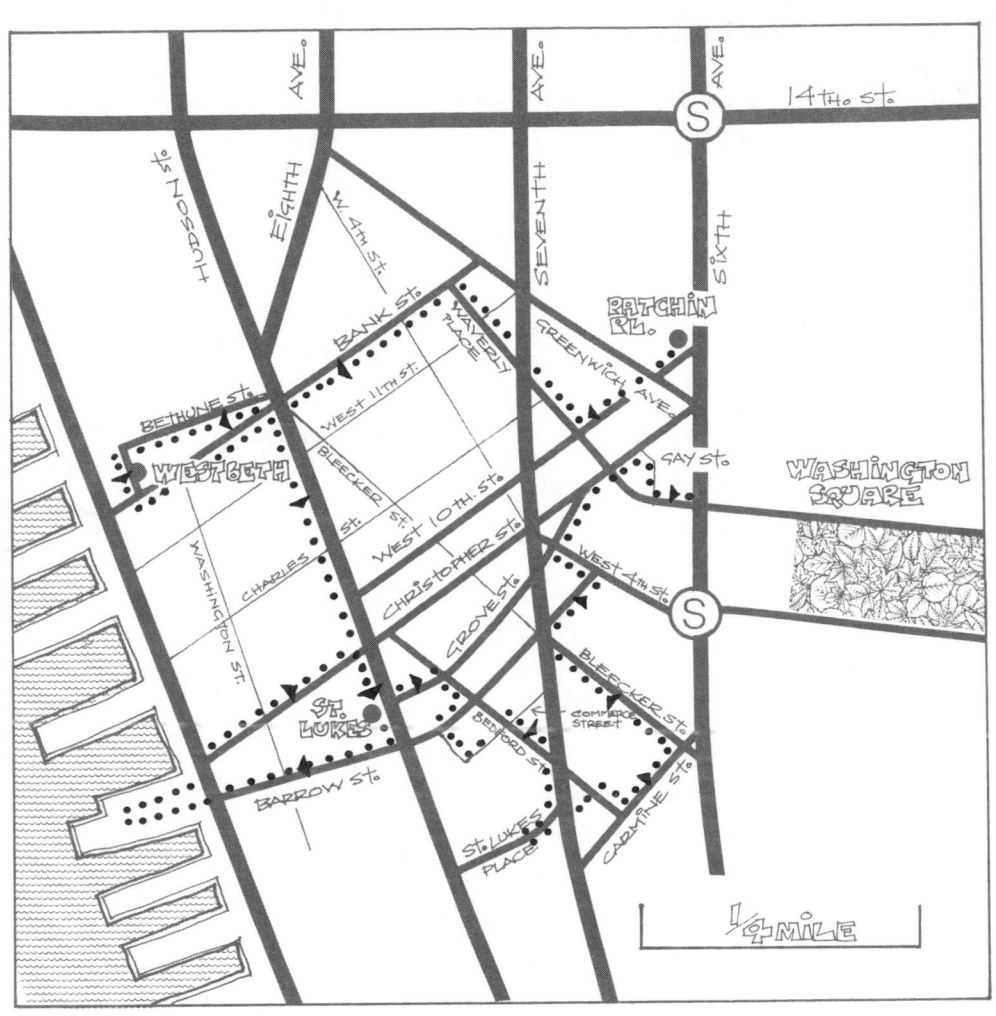

4
THE WEST VILLAGE

Where else could a tour of the village begin but at the base of one of its best-loved landmarks, the Jefferson Market Courthouse, now a public library, at Sixth Avenue (Avenue of the Americas) and West 10th Street. Its architecture, both formal and frivolous, is an apt expression of village character. Our walk will take us along some of the most restrainedly dignified streets in the city, where mellowed façades and delicately pruned shade trees reflect a pace of life that is entirely nineteenth century. The village has always had its quiet corners. We'll explore most of them on our walk.

It all began rather quietly in the 1790s. The verdant pre-Revolutionary estates, rolling acres of grassland, woods, and marshes that characterized this portion of the island were gradually divided up and sold off in modest lots to craftsmen carpenters and sailmakers looking for a base close to the Hudson River, away from the heat and congestion of the New York docks. Then, following a series of smallpox, yellow fever, and cholera epidemics that plagued the city around the turn of the century, anxious citizens fled north to the balmy, breeze-blown meadows of Greenwich. Many regarded this as a temporary expedient and the fragmented proliferation of streets reflected a lack of concern for

DIRECTIONS

Subway: Shuttle (BMT/LL) on 14th Street to 14th Street and Sixth Avenue or IND AA, CC, E, A to West 4th Street/Washington Square and Sixth Avenue
Bus: M5, M6, M10 (north/south), M13 (east/west)

overall community structure. Some streets merely followed previously used cowpaths. Plans for parks and open spaces—more than 170 acres of them—were conveniently bottomed-drawered as the expansion continued. By 1830, however, Washington Square had been transformed from a parade ground into a fashionable residential area, and the later founding of New York University on the east side bestowed formal sanction on the village.

Then, as occurred in every part of the city, the whims of fashion and the continuing northward scramble of the population led to a series of declines in the village around the beginning of the nineteenth century. Tenements and noxious industries along the Hudson cast a pall over the more refined enclaves, whose sensitive occupants hurriedly left. Rents fell, attracting the "huddled masses" from the lower city—the Irish and Italians particularly. Similarly, writers, artists, and others of bohemian persuasion were charmed by the quaintness of the place and moved into the small apartments and mews cottages. The roster of residents reads like a Who's Who of the American arts—Twain, Poe, James, O. Henry, Greeley, Whitman, Dreiser, Millay, Bret Harte, Saint-Gaudens, Hudson River School painters, proponents of the "Ashcan School" Glackens and Sloan, and the painter Edward Hopper.

The village remained at the forefront of American culture, or anticulture, depending on the prevailing attitudes of the times. The "bohemians" became the "beatniks," jazz and folk music flourished in a score of famous cellar clubs until the emergence of the honky-tonks, the porno palaces of the fifties, and increasingly inflated rents led to a gradual emigration of its more creative spirits to such neighborhoods as Soho and the East Village.

Today this disjointed patchwork of fragmented streets, hidden courts, odd bars, famous clubs, tourist strips, and quiet sparrowed parks continues to reflect almost every stage of its own growth. There are still plenty of artists and writers here. Not everyone has moved to Soho (in fact, there's a distinct movement back). The literary bars still attract the literary types and the gay bars have their own distinct clientele. Little old ladies struggle up the steps of elegant townhouses. Coffeehouses are returning. Health-food restaurants flourish. Behind the Italianate, Federal, neo-Georgian, and even "Fairytale" façades the village life continues. Sometimes crass, sometimes crazy—always captivating.

The key on this walk is—keep your eyes open. Immediately to the north of the Jefferson Library, for example, peep past the splendid Bishop's crook lamp post into the diminutive Patchin Place. If you walk too fast on West 10th you'll miss it. Built in the mid-1800s as inexpensive apartments for the Basque waiters at the elegant Brevoort Hotel on Fifth Avenue, this tiny court of off-white townhouses has housed many famous litterateurs—John Masefield, England's brilliant poet laureate who once made a living polishing the floors of village saloons, Theodore Dreiser, Eugene O'Neill, and e.e. cummings. A row of delicate ailanthus trees, a species indigenous to India and once thought to absorb "bad air," provides welcome shade from the sear of summer streets, and there's a little-known view of the Jefferson Library from the far end of the cul-de-sac. I paused one warm afternoon to make a sketch. An elderly lady peered at the drawing and beamed at me. "You should," she said. I looked at her questioningly. "You should draw that view. I've been looking at it for thirty years and I think it's the nicest in the village. It's right to share it." We chatted together about the city. "There's so much that's changed," she told me sadly. "I think people should be reminded there are places left like this." I finished the sketch while drinking the cup of tea she brought me.

Just around the corner on Sixth Avenue is the even more concealed Milligan Place, deep in shade behind its wrought-iron gateway. The houses you see were built in the 1850s for Samuel Milligan, who acquired the property in 1799. Eugene O'Neill spent many long hours here working with Susan Glaspell and her husband George Cram Cook (founder of the Provincetown Playhouse) on his play *The Emperor Jones.*

Up the block, cross the road for another hidden gem on West 11th Street just east of Sixth Avenue. The tiny Second Cemetery of the Spanish and Portuguese Synagogue is all that remains of a larger plot, paved over when 11th Street was extended to join Sixth Avenue in the mid-1800s.

Back on 10th Street continue west across Greenwich Avenue to Waverly Place. Note the elaborately painted doorway on the 18th Engine Firehouse, a masterpiece of the "comic book" style, and pause at the nearby Gallery 10 (also at 21 Greenwich Avenue, just around the corner). Director Marcia Smith normally exhibits the work of at least five artists, including the popular body-sculptor,

Patchin Place

Phil Hunt, whose molded nude forms, complete with pubic hairs and erect nipples, attract a constant stream of window gazers.

The dimly lit Julian pub on the corner of Waverly Place is one of the oldest bars in the village and a popular hangout with the gay crowd. Like most pre-Prohibition establishments, it possesses a generous repertoire of hidden booze and sliding panel tales. Fats Waller once gave impromptu concerts here, and later admirers Truman Capote, Tennessee Williams, and Rudolf Nureyev reaffirmed its reputation as one of the village's more important watering holes.

Across Seventh Avenue, past the well-loved Village Vanguard and the Caffe da Alfredo, we pass St. John's in the Village, an unusually diverse grouping of religious and community facilities. In addition to the church itself, specially designed by Edgar Tatel for performing arts presentations, there's the Richard Morse Mime Theatre, a courtyard area used for theatrical and musical productions, and a charming hidden garden originally developed in the early 1900s as part of the St. John's Artists colony, by clergyman John Armstrong Wade. Access to the garden is through an old "horse walk" and visitors are welcome to call at the Church Office (224 Waverly Place, 9 A.M.–5 P.M. CH. 3-6192) to obtain an entry key.

Approaching the north end of Waverly Place, where it joins Bank Street, we enter the true West Village, an intimate neighborhood of narrow tree-lined streets, terraces of elegant townhouses, and tiny restaurants. The Waverly Inn offers traditional American fare in a genuinely Elizabethan-tavern atmosphere of high-back seats, fireplaces, and mellow candlelight. Along West 4th Street the Café New Amsterdam and La Chaumière are typical of the high quality and restrained dignity of the eating places in this part of the city. Down Bank Street the Hudson River sparkles between the large waterfront buildings. A young girl wheels her bicycle along the sidewalk with a loaf of crusty French bread tucked under her arm. An elderly gentleman dressed like an English squire in plus-fours, tweed jacket, and a deerstalker hat pauses on the corner to gaze at the river. Great billows of smoke from his black briar pipe swirl around his face. His silver mustache, slightly yellowed, and his ruddy cheeks stand out prominently. He whistles a short sharp note, a very gentlemanly whistle, and a frizzled Yorkshire terrier leaves his lamp-post sniffing and bounds along the sidewalk to stand panting at the squire's side. The two continue slowly down the street to the river.

At Hudson Street a broad expanse of park and play area is filled with children and snoozing mothers. On the other side are the first restaurants and taverns of the burgeoning Hudson Strip. The nautical-flavored Benchley's Pub was the home of a sea captain during the mid-1800s. At that time the blocks down to the river were a riot of dockland activities and related antics of a more recreational nature. Houses of ill-repute flourished. Hole-in-the-wall gin palaces sent sotted sailors tumbling into the streets. Brawling and braggadocio produced a night-long bedlam in the narrow cobbled streets. "It was a hell of a place down here," Jack Herbert, owner of Benchley's, told me. His grandfather designed many of the liners that steamed the Great Lakes, and Jack has long been fascinated by sea life. "There were street gangs. The Hudson Dusters were the worst. Gave the penny-dreadfuls plenty of material for their lurid stories. It's pretty quiet now, though. About the only activity you'll find down by the river is at Westbeth." So if you don't mind a short detour away from the sedate streets, stroll down Bethune Street to this interesting complex of artists' studio space and living quarters housed in the old Bell Telephone Laboratories, an austere monolith near the waterfront.

Long before Westbeth was conceived, the Bell Laboratories had developed a remarkable reputation for creativity in the electronics field. The first "talking" movie, Al Jolson's *Jazz Singer*, was produced here on a sound stage that still exists within the complex. Later developments came in the form of TV experiments and transistor research. In 1967, sponsored by grants from the Kaplan Fund and the National Council on the Arts, the laboratories were refurbished to provide 383 apartments for New York artists and space for public-related activities including theaters and workshops. Since then the complex has had its high moments and its doldrums, inevitable in an environment of this nature. At the time of writing there are ambitious plans for increasing interaction between Westbeth's inhabitants and the outside community—talk of new workshops, galleries, festivals, and more theatrical productions. "There's a real renaissance going on," a young resident raved. "There's always a bloody renaissance," muttered one of the older occupants, who'd seen it all before. Still, it's a unique experiment and worth the detour.

Back on the Hudson Strip, it's antique-store time—lots of them all the way down to Christopher Street—antiques, restaurants, and bars along a street that's far too wide for intimacy and far too fragmented architecturally. But there's character and fun here. Dylan Thomas thought so when he frequented the White Horse Tavern on the corner of West 11th Street and that was long before it became an adjunct of the West Village. Afternoons in the tavern are usually quiet, ticking away with the grandfather clock; fly-specked mirrors, yellowed paint, and chipped white horses (the one in the window has lost most of his natural accoutrements) give it the flavor of a true New York bar. But evenings bring life to the street. Conversation flows faster than ale at the Village Green, the No Name, and the Sazerac House. Leather freaks gather in studded groups in the pubs around Christropher Street and a bunch of rolling out-of-towners try to play a tuba dangling over the sidewalk at the Village Stripper Antique Store. Yet a short distance off Hudson, at Charles Street and Greenwich Street, is a cottage so peacefully set in its own garden that it's hard to believe you're still in the city. Also look out for the delightful oasis of plants at West 10th Street and, best of all, the Federal-style St. Luke's church at Barrow and Hudson. Inside the church, all is quiet. The late evening light transforms the stained-glass windows into brilliantly jeweled surfaces of crimsons, royal blues, and deep purples. The colors fall on the oak pews. A young girl with a cello emerges from a side room and sits in the center of the nave, facing the altar. She plays a Mozart sonata; deep, rounded sounds roll down the empty aisles.

The full name of the church is St. Luke's-in-the-Fields, and it was built in the early 1800s as a county church to serve a still rural hinterland. It was here that "sixpenny loaves of wheaten bread" were distributed every Sunday to "such poor as shall appear most deserving" in accordance with the terms of a will and fund set up by John Leake in 1792. In 1890 the congregation had a larger church built way uptown at Convent Avenue and 141st Street, and this diminutive building was purchased by Trinity Church in 1892 and rededicated as a chapel of Trinity Parish. Today it's one of the most delightful places in the West Village. The garden is tiny and tranquil, set behind a group of minuscule Federal-style town-houses. Bret Harte once lived at number 487, the last one on the right.

If you're here before sunset take another brief detour west down Barrow Street to pier 42 and enjoy a stroll alongside the two John Brown ships permanently anchored here and used as a high school. This is a favorite summer-evening haunt of villagers. Even on the most humid days the breezes are cooling at the end of the pier as you stand overlooking the river, the great industrial plants on the Jersey side, the Statue of Liberty in the harbor, and the haze-blue hills of Staten Island beyond. Return to Hudson Street by way of Christopher Street, past the ornate St. Veronica's Roman Catholic Church. Note the elegantly massive bulk of the U.S. Federal Building at Washington Street, built in 1899. There are plans to convert it into a five-story "galleria" of shops and restaurants.

At Grove Street, east of Hudson, we return again to the tranquillity of the West Village, to the delicate Federal-style town-houses and the narrow, intimate streets. Pause at Grove Court, one of my favorite hidden niches. Residents in these delightfully shaded rowhouses, originally built in the mid-1800s as workers cottages, are generally tolerant of intruders exploring the walled courtyard quietly. O. Henry is said to have conceived his short story "The Last Leaf," here, and many subsequent authors, sculptors, and artists have found that this enclave provides just the right amount of seclusion from the occasionally overbearing social whirl of village life.

The odd fairy-tale structure at 102 Bedford Street (a lovely pink idiosyncrasy) was remodeled as "an inspiring home for creative artists" by philanthropist Otto Kahn in 1926 and aptly named "Twin Peaks." Adjoining the structure is the 1822 clapboard workshop of William Hyde, a sash-maker, and a diminutive "slaves' quarters" with canary-yellow shutters. This is surely the oddest collection of structures in the village. Appropriately enough, a little farther down Bedford Street, number 75½ is the "narrowest house," boasting a 9½-foot frontage (just wide enough for a horse and carriage). Edna St. Vincent Millay lived here briefly during the early 1920s.

You may not have noticed an ancient wooden doorway complete with iron grille as you walked down Bedford Street. Well, look again, at number 86, or better still, turn left at the corner of Barrow just past the community bulletin board and enter the first courtyard on your left (number 70). Walk to the far end, open the large door facing you and lo, you're entering one of the best-hidden and most notorious speakeasies in the city, the famous Chumley's. It was here, during the thirties and forties, that the literary notables of the village met to drink, talk, or do whatever literary people do in cozy places away from the hoi polloi. John Steinbeck, Ring Lardner, James Joyce, and John Dos Passos were all regulars. Look at the displays of browned book jackets along the wall. Little has changed since Joyce scribbled segments of *Ulysses* in the corner table by the far door. Saturday afternoons

Grove Court

around 2 P.M. the tradition continues with poetry readings. It's a delightful way to spend an hour or two, assuming you can find the place next time.

This corner of the village is full of surprises. Behind Grove Court, for example, on Barrow Street, is a diminutive courtyard of bushes and fountains surrounded by a dark rustic brick apartment building and, if the doorway at 34½ Barrow Street is open, stroll through the tunnel to the shaded backyard where a lovely wooden cottage sits by itself in a little garden.

The short Barrow/Commerce Street loop, takes us past a most unusual duo of mansard mansions adjoining the Cherry Lane Theater. They were built in 1831 by a sea captain for his two unmarried daughters. Why not one house? Well, it appears that the daughters never spoke to each other and refused to live together, so the captain arrived at this unusual architectural compromise, leaving the garden between the houses open to encourage an eventual rapprochement. Alas, the sisters became more and more indifferent to each other and the garden was allowed to grow wild—a totally appropriate tale in this tiny fantasyland deep in the heart of the village. And, talking about fantasies, number 11 Commerce Street (near Seventh Avenue) is said to be the house in which the darling of the village literati, Washington Irving, wrote his beloved "Legend of Sleepy Hollow."

A brief detour down Seventh Avenue takes us to St. Lukes Place, a street that appears unprepossessing at first. But continue around the corner and you'll discover one of the most sedate terraces of Italianate townhouses in the city, shaded by a row of unusual ginkgo trees. Jimmy Walker, mayor of New York during the boisterous Prohibition days, lived at number 6; Sherwood Anderson spent time here in 1922; and Theodore Dreiser put the finishing touches to *An American Tragedy* at number 16. It's a lovely backwater whose tranquillity is marred only by occasional teen-age bawlings in the park across the street. But even the park has its own bit of history. Before 1890 it was a graveyard and, so 'tis claimed, the long-lost body of the Dauphin of France was buried beneath a stone with the simple if somewhat misleading inscription "Leroy" (Le Roi?).

Across Seventh Avenue, on Carmine Street, we enter the remnants of a once-flourishing Italian district. At the southern end the Chez Vous, believe it or not, is a well-loved Italian restaurant and at the other end, across from our Lady of Pompeii Catholic Church (St. Francis Xavier Cabrini, the first American saint, often prayed here) is the mecca of minestrone lovers, the Bleecker Luncheonette. In between is an interesting array of neighborhood stores and the lovely Aphrodisia, with its amazing array of herbs, spices, and aromatics—dried lily buds, Oberon's summer, Crane's Bill, Ladies' Rising, Lovage root, white willow bark, and pink mint. Up Bleecker the mood continues with Faicco's pork store (homemade sausages and fegatinni), the Bleecker Street fish market ("If it swims, we have it"), Zito's Italian bakery, a butcher shop featuring venison, pheasant, suckling pig, and quail, and Uncle Willie's Flea Market with its old records, battered encyclopedias, pockmarked percolators, and all the flavor of a country jumble sale.

Following Barrow Street to Sheridan Square, we pass the secluded 1 if by Land, 2 if by Sea, a lovely transformation of Aaron Burr's carriage house into a refined restaurant. The creators, Armand Justin and Mario de Martini, have many tales to tell about their experiences during renovations. They discovered two tombstones and vaults under the basement floor and also found a segment of a tunnel that ran all the way to the Hudson (the river was once much closer) and was part of the ingenious "underground railroad" used for transporting Southern slaves to freedom in New England and Canada. In contrast, Jimmy Day's, at Barrow and West 4th streets, is a boisterous Irish-flavored tavern, and on the north side of Sheridan Square itself the Lion's Head attracts the literary crowd (more book jackets) in addition to a highly unlikely neighborhood bunch of "Jewish drunks, Irish lovers, and Italian intellectuals" (according to Al Koblin, one of the owners).

The diminutive Gay Street, off Christopher Street, was originally a secluded niche for black residents and during Prohibition a popular speakeasy strip. Today it has regained its tranquillity and provides a little respite before we emerge once again into the bustle of Sixth Avenue, our exploration of the West Village complete. If it's a warm day the street vendors will be active by the railings on the other side of the street. They're a reminder of the "other" village, the tourist village that we've studiously avoided. Well, the culture trip's over now, so why not join in the hullabaloo for a while?

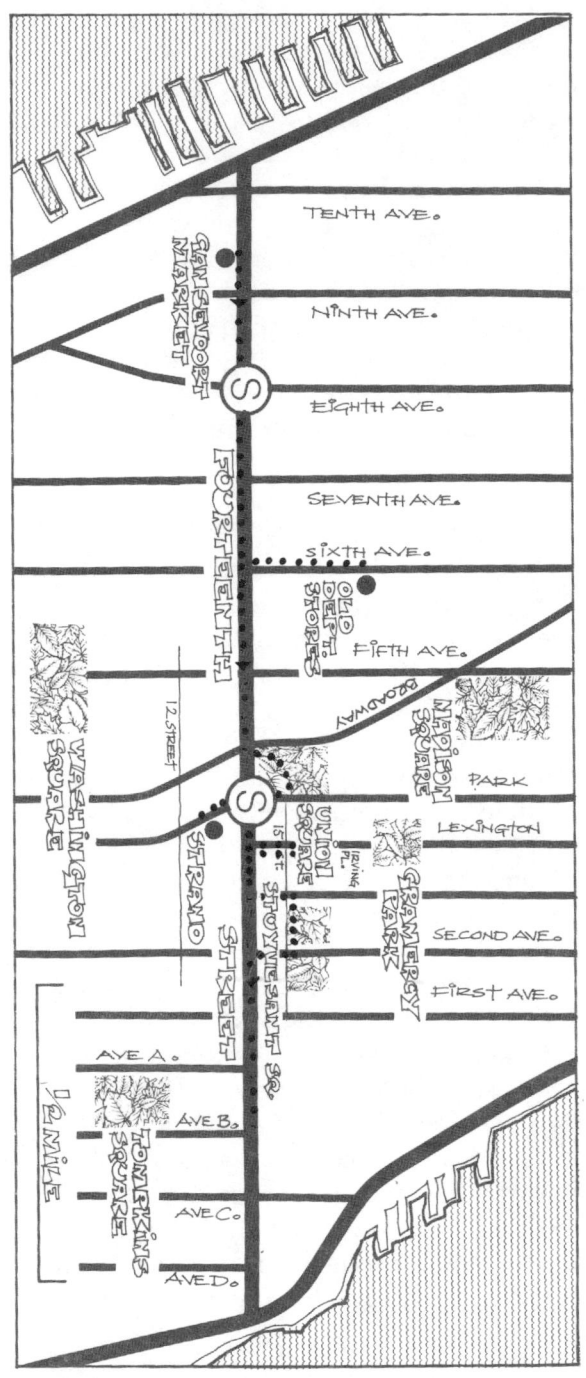

5

14th STREET— A SLICE OF NEW YORK

Fourteenth Street is often regarded as a kind of no-man's land separating midtown from the restrained streets of the village. To the north are the frenzied anthills of the garment district, the flower district, the fur district, the diamond district. To the south, boutiques mingle with outdoor cafés, avant-garde theaters, bistros, health-food stores, and exclusive residences in a jumble of streets which form tributaries of "the valley"—a term used to describe the dense, low-rise blocks stretching southward to the canyons of downtown.

To those who pause awhile, however, 14th Street is more than just a vague demarcation line or a convenient subway interchange. It tingles with life from the early hours of dawn down in the Gansevoort meat market to the latest hours of night around Third Avenue. During the day it booms. The street is a raucous open-air market, a bazaar, a souk. Even Macy's on Christmas Eve

────────────── **DIRECTIONS** ──────────────

Subway: Union Square is a major interchange point, but if you intend to start at the far west end of the street, take the Eighth Avenue subway (IND A, E, AA, CC to 14th Street) or take the BMT LL shuttle from Union Square to 14th Street and Eighth Avenue
Bus: M10 or M11 (north/south), M14 (east/west)

hardly compares with the frenzied push and tumble of the crowds as they churn between Union Square and Seventh Avenue.

It's a street of fun, of contrasts, of life. It's a street worth exploring and, more often than not, a street worth liking.

At six in the morning the stores are closed tight. Crumpled paper and cardboard boxes litter the sidewalk or rest in piles against the steel shutters. Thick padlocks catch the dawn light as it glows over the buildings and silhouettes the chimneys of the Con Edison plant at the far eastern end of the street. An occasional bus

Gansevoort Meat Market

rumbles along one of the avenues. The sound of its engine echoes against the dark walls.

Walk westward to where the street ends at Pier 56. The change is abrupt. The meat market is open and sidewalks are black with grease. Red refuse cans stamped "Inedible" brim with chunks of fat, kidneys, heads, pieces of feet, and an occasional unblinking eyeball. A steel door opens with a blast of refrigerated air and a line of carcasses emerges and hangs limply over the sidewalk, dripping a little. A truck pulls up under the canopy in a cloud of blue exhaust smoke. Men in white coats and little white hats tug at the meat with hooks. Inside are more men in white coats along a wide table. Chop, chop, chop, chop. Shapeless slabs become neatly trimmed shell steaks, filets, and London broil. Someone in a white hardhat scribbles in a looseleaf folder.

Outside, a group of men are gathered around a small fire, their faces bright orange in the glow, eating thick sandwiches and drinking from a bottle in a paper bag. The market snack bar is packed, standing room only. A silver Mercedes-Benz squeezes in between two tractor trailers, and a gentleman in a tweed suit and alligator shoes tiptoes between little dark pools to a white-coated man. White coat and tweed suit disappear behind a stainless-steel door. Another slice of cold air cuts across the sidewalk.

It's only a small area, this meat market, but until lunchtime it's the busiest part of 14th Street. Scores of workers scurry and bawl around the warehouses, throwing great sides of beef, whole lambs, and pigs into the waiting trucks. The din increases throughout the morning; trucks roar away in clouds of smoke, white aprons get bloodier and bloodier, and the cans of "inedibles" crowd the sidewalks.

By early afternoon, however, the hubbub ceases. The tractor trailers, the Mercedes, the burly army of white-coated men, the carcasses, the fires in the street, the scattered bones on the sidewalk—they're all gone. It's very quiet. The black awnings cast deep shadows across the narrow streets and the doors are padlocked.

A few yards across from the market is a topless bar in a local motel (surrounded on all sides by streets and nestled up against the piers of the West Side Highway, it's hard to believe anyone actually sleeps here). The action really starts around midday and—

surprise, surprise—even though there's a near-naked lady dancing along the bar top in the seductive half-light, the place turns out to be one of those dockside S&M bars. Painted in luminous white on black walls are erotically posed Herculeses in tight trousers with bulging crotches. Leaflets pinned on the wall advertise famous gay spots in Manhattan and Chicago. It's too much—the dainty dancer with her siliconed breasts surrounded by men from the meat market in bloody overalls and little hats which read "Buy Beef," backdropped by a decor of jock pictures, chains, and motorcycle parts. And this is only one of the local lunchtime R & R centers in the market. On Little 12th Street in the shadow of an old railroad bridge is a second topless place serving near-beer and raunchy sex shows for the hamburger-chomping meat men. At Ninth Avenue is a third, just across the road from an odd triangular tavern done up in old-time western decor.

Of course, there are other ways to celebrate the lunch hour and the end of a meat-man's day. Just up Ninth Avenue is the Homestead restaurant, an ancient institution in the area, with its brown awnings and ornate wrought-iron work. Here in the chintzy dining areas gather the meat lovers of Manhattan. They come for the filet mignon and those enormous prime-rib platters matched only by Durgin-Park pub in Boston, an equally venerable institution. It's amazing to see the same men who have been working with meat in every shape and form since the early hours of the morning launch themselves with gusto into one of those gargantuan Homestead meals.

Until recently the meat market was exclusively a place for the trade. The public rarely ventured into the area except for the "cattle rustlers" (junkies who occasionally try to run off with the odd side of beef) and "institutional representatives" requesting handouts for a good cause—usually their own stomachs. But not too long ago a couple of wholesale/retail places opened up at the east end of the market near Ninth Avenue and have attracted devotees who flock to buy (at some of the best prices in town) bulk meats, whole salamis and hams, twenty-pound cans of beans, gallon jars of ketchup, and whole cheese wheels. Items are available in smaller amounts but the price tends to be higher—so wait till you're about to throw a big barbeque and then come down here and enjoy yourself.

Between the meat market and Eighth Avenue is one of the more restrained sections of the street—an area of churches, convents, funeral homes, and strange little shops. There's the tiny Church of the Beloved Disciple, which claims to be the first gay church in America. Most of the week it's a quiet place, easy to miss, but on Sunday after the morning services, gays from every part of New York pour out into the sidewalk and gather in groups, glowing with the spirit of discipleship. Nearby are two equally unusual establishments. The Fang and Claw normally displays in its window a grizzly selection of lizards and an occasional tortoise for family trade. Its catalog includes such creatures as African pythons, boa constrictors, yellow-rat snakes, chameleons, salamanders, and tree frogs. Then there's a delightful Dickensian kind of place with a neatly painted shingle, "Almost Everything, Your Little Shop." Who knows, it really may be Dickensian. The master of poignant satire was a frequent visitor to the Academy of Music on 14th Street when he made his reading tour of America, and he often dined at the famed Delmonico's Restaurant, once located at the corner of Fifth Avenue and 14th Street. This is truly "The Olde Curiosity Shoppe" brimming with Victorian knickknacks, trinkets, and bric-a-brac. It's the kind of place you can spend an hour browsing and leave enchanted, the proud possessor of a battered two-dollar snuffbox.

Stroll farther up the street and climb the steep steps to Iglesia Católica Guadalupe, a delightful little church set in a Georgian-style row of townhouses (recently converted into apartments). The street sounds are muffled and a great fan hanging from the frescoed ceiling wafts incense into every corner. A few dark figures huddle in the pews, rosary beads clicking like watch beetles, and a short man with a face as gnarled as an olive tree kneels at each of the stations of the cross. A sign over the confessional reads: "Father Dennis—speaks Spanish, English, French, Portuguese and Dutch"(!) Two shafts of sunlight gild the baroque carvings on the altar. It's all very still and beautiful.

Back on 14th Street again, continue eastward into a section famous for its Latin/Spanish restaurants, where one can dine on great platters of bacalao (salt cod) à la Biscania, paella Valenciana, varied octopus and squid concoctions, Pepitoria de Gallina (chicken in egg and saffron sauce), and delicious tripe dishes, including one splendid creation using a filé-based sauce with chick peas. Or try some of the authentic Chinese dishes at one of the local Cuban-Chinese establishments.

Whether you're in the mood for eating or not, don't pass by Casa Moneo, which is on both sides of the street just before Seventh Avenue. The store on the north side is the more recent and is filled with Spanish and Latin-American products—guitars, flamenco hats, great woolen shawls, records, perfumes, tapestries, and a wide selection of plaster madonnas, three-dimensional Christs in plastic-baroque frames, and garlands of rosaries. The other store is a must for lovers of make-it-yourself Spanish and Mexican cuisine. At the far end there are chilies of every type and temper, tortillas (corn and flour), or the masarina in case you have your own tortilla oven, magnificent orange chorizo sausages, real Monterey Jack cheese (a must for authentic chili rellenos), nougat, quince paste, and all the cooking equipment you'd ever need for classic Castilian dishes (and a lot of canned equivalents in case they don't work out). For real enthusiasts there are also San Miguel, Carta Blanca, Bohemia, and Portena beers, and sparkling Spanish and Argentinian ciders.

Approaching Sixth Avenue we meet the 14th Street bazaar. Stores spill out onto the sidewalks in a welter of trestle tables, upturned drawers, and packing crates smothered in cuddly teddy bears with bright orange fur, clockwork trains clicking and hooting endlessly around circular tracks, Spanish LP's with glossy photographs of overendowed young ladies, mounds of plastic sandals, Japanese dinner sets with paisley decorations, boxes of price-slashed toothpastes, mouthwashes, and bug-killers, and even an occasional stack of galvanized scrubbing boards. Clothing stores, which from their signs always appear on the verge of bankruptcy, feature absolutely the "last and final closeout bargains" in nylon double-knits and the best 99¢ jeans in town. A young salesman, very sweaty, scrubs violently on an oil-stained square of carpet: "Ladies, look at these typical household carpet stains, see how easily [puff, puff] this specially formulated cleaner, developed exclusively for this store, removes oil, soot, and grease [puff, puff] and makes your carpets like new again." A long silence as he scrubs, then a final puff as he removes the last dark specks and straightens up.

He's very nervous. A small crowd of plump matrons have gathered around him and he keeps talking at the store window. Someone makes a clever remark and the crowd giggles. The poor man blushes and, still with his back to the customers, proceeds to cover the little square of carpet with an obnoxious black liquid (presumably a "mixture of typical household carpet stains"). After a hurried glance at his watch, he begins again: "Ladies, look at these typical household stains, see how easily [puff, puff] . . ."

Pause briefly at Sixth Avenue and walk northward to the Old Tenderloin District. Although there's little left of its vigorous past, you can stroll between 18th and 22nd streets and see the grandiose remnants of what used to be Manhattan's Department Store Row (part of the famous "Ladies' Mile") during the early years of this century. The most extravagant of all is the old 1896 Siegel-Cooper store between 18th and 19th streets with its triple-arch entrance and classical trimmings. Once considered "a city in itself," this edifice is rusting and paint is flaking from its great pillars. The building is currently used as a warehouse. The others, such as Altman's, Simpson-Crawford's, O'Neill's, Adams's, and Cammeyer's, have all suffered similar indignities, but if you ignore the miscellany of tiny businesses occupying their lower floors, they still possess enormous charm and character. What a street this must have been in the year 1900!

But back to the 14th Street bazaar between Fifth and Sixth avenues, where the real professionals are at work in the appliance stores. The window displays are masterpieces of material abundance—brimming with televisions, cameras, stereos, binoculars, lighters, clock radios, watches, slide projectors, tape recorders, and calculators. Show the slightest sign of really wanting something and the price soars. Wander around casually. Start by asking about things you've no intention of buying—work up to what you want slowly. Be bored and appear to be on the verge of leaving. Then, as you're walking up to the door, ask the salesman for a price on the item of your choice. (Be very uninterested.) Whatever price he quotes, turn, murmur total incredulity, and make for the door again—slowly. Invariably he'll panic. "Hey, how much you wanna pay?" Don't answer. Let him follow you. "Hey, okay, I'll make a deal . . ." At that point, pause. Go back and take another look. Twiddle knobs, push buttons or whatever, but let him do the talking. Start to look skeptical. Whatever price he suggests, offer him thirty percent less. (It's always best to find out beforehand what the item sells for at more reputable stores.) At this point you might lose him, but it's unlikely. If he stays, you can relax a little. Bargain as long as you want. Start to finger your wallet (but don't open it). If he doesn't play ball, get impatient and look at your watch. If all goes well you'll walk out with a good piece of equipment far cheaper than anywhere else in town.

To bargain successfully in the bazaar is cause for celebration. So, either have a leisurely lunch at one of those Spanish restaurants we passed a while back or snack your way down the street nibbling tamales, plantanos fritos, pasteles, papas rellenas, and legua and empanadas at the tiny sidewalk counters. Or, there's the square itself—Union Square—a great place to munch on a hot dog from the red and gold Hebrew National stand if you don't mind sharing a bench with a guy in three raincoats drinking laced-wine or inhaling air rich with the aroma of Colombia Gold and other equally aromatic brands of marijuana. The square is a haven for the street people—an exclusive club for the downers. An old woman with a lopsided wig sits huddled in a blanket, nestling a dog and surrounded by bags of possessions—newspapers, old shoes, books, umbrellas, and a bunch of dead flowers. Close by, a bearded black gentleman complete with topless top hat and the remnants of a bow tie holds court with a bunch of cronies. The bottle, cloaked in its traditional paper bag, passes mechanically from mouth to mouth. (Ironically, Hugh D'Arcy's famous "Face on the Barroom Floor" was written at a tavern on the southern corner of the square, later occupied by Klein's store.) At the next bench a young man with cavalier hair and bare feet threads out the semblance of a song on a guitar with four strings. He keeps losing the melody and looking at the sky through red eyes.

Union Square was once described as the "social center of Knickerbocker society, first home of opera, theatrical rialto, authentic Bohemia, platform of patriots, rostrum of liberals and communists." Tammany Hall and the Academy of Music were located where Con Edison's "Tower of Power" rises to a tall embellished point. Macy's once had a department store close to the square that was famous for its revolving toy displays. Tiffany's also flourished nearby, and down Broadway as far as 8th Street was a continuation of the famous "Ladies' Mile" with John Wanamaker's department store and James McCreery's Dry Goods Emporium at the corner of 11th Street. Billy Watson and his Beef Trust (a famous chorus line of two-hundred-pound damsels) appeared from time to time in one of the burlesque theaters adjoining Tammany Hall, and close to Third Avenue "Good Old Doctor Grey" (a VD quack) opened his grizzly "Museum of Anatomy" to a curious public.

Union Square itself, once a private enclave for such residents as the Roosevelts, Van Beurens, and Pennimans, found its true vocation as a center for political rallies in the 1860s following the outbreak of the Civil War. In 1870 the iron railings were removed and the square became truly public—a meeting place for such groups as the Anarchists and the Wobblies. On the night of August 22, 1927, a vast crowd gathered to express indignation at the execution of Nicola Sacco and Bartolomeo Vanzetti. The police, fearful of riots, mounted machine guns on what was the roof of Klein's department store. Although the guns were not used, dispersal of the crowd was unusually rough and subsequent gatherings, supported by the Communist newspaper *The Daily Worker*, vigorously protested police brutality.

Following the crash of 1929, the square saw scores of unemployment rallies. A particularly large meeting of 35,000 people on March 6, 1930, was again broken up by police. More than a hundred people were seriously injured, but with the impending threat of total civil disruption the police repented and finally recognized the square as an official meeting place for dissident groups.

By this time, however, the area was declining. There was a brief flicker of bohemian life in the thirties followed by a long period of stagnation as the flourishing midtown area leeched businesses away to more prestigious locations and the street people made the square their home.

But nearby there's still much of interest. Past the superbly ornate Moorish structure at 33 Union Square West (it once boasted a minaret-type tower, but this was deemed unsafe a few years ago and dismantled) there's a budding nucleus of bookstores consisting of Rizzoli's Language Center (an excellent range of language textbooks and general publications); Barnes and Noble (on both sides of Fifth Avenue at 18th Street and possessing a sales annex guaranteed to keep you enthralled for at least half a day); a large center for French and Spanish books just north of Barnes and

Noble, and various other smaller stores in the area where trade is becoming progressively book-oriented.

Union Square has a long history of association with books and publishing. Brentano's first store was situated at the top end of the square, and many left-wing newspapers and magazines were produced in adjoining buildings. The *Daily World* in fact still exists nearby on 19th Street. Farrar, Straus, & Giroux has its offices at 19 Union Square and the Arco Publishing house is located across from the square on Park Avenue South.

Perhaps the most memorable feature was "Book Row" on Fourth Avenue, a string of dusty stores selling used books south of the square, where devotees could browse for hours among floor-to-ceiling shelves in search of some elusive first edition (something missed by the hectic store owner, something for the price of a cheap lunch). Although much of Book Row has gone, a few stalwarts remain on Fourth Avenue, on Fifth Avenue (Dauber and Pine), and at 828 Broadway where the Strand's tiny frontage disguises ten thousand square feet of display space (bigger than the average suburban supermarket) and eight miles of shelves. What a treat awaits first-timers here. This is no marginal establishment with an indifferent owner and an even more indifferent collection of books. This is a venerable institution, a haunt of famous authors (one of the managers, Bert Britton, has produced a book of caricature self-portraits by the hundreds of celebrities who have browsed the stacks over the years), loved by students, and a source of nourishment for reviewers who regularly supplement their income by selling their review copies to the store. Come here with time to spare and, for the sake of your sanity, with some specific field of interest in mind (customers have been known to leave in a state of tearful confusion after hours have been lost through the constant distraction of tens of thousands of books).

Even those allergic to bookstores (I have known individuals threatened and psychologically belittled by these impressive repositories of information and learning) should venture down Broadway and its side streets and explore the clusters of antique stores, mainly wholesale, that have become a distinct feature of the neighborhood. Watch out for public auction sales—they can be fun.

But—have you eaten yet? If all that talk about Spanish food

failed to stir the gastric juices, then how about the nation's first complete natural-food restaurant, first vegetable juice bar, and creator of the original salad bowl? I refer, of course to Brownie's, just west of Union Square on 16th Street. Or consider Lüchow's, that magnificent center of Germanic cuisine and beverages, a favorite with Lillian Russell and Diamond Jim Brady, and once frequented by that master of pianos William Steinway, whose Steinway Hall was directly opposite the restaurant. Lüchow's is the only remaining link with an era when Union Square and vicinity was a nucleus of the German culture. Beer halls flourished everywhere; Tuesday's (Scheffel Hall) on Third Avenue and 17th Street, for example, used to be the famous Joe King's Rathskeller. But if wursts, dumplings, and sauerkraut is too heavy for lunch, turn north up Irving Place, one of the most attractive streets in this part of town. Here you can sit in Pete's Tavern, an old speakeasy, opened in 1864 and loved by O. Henry, who wrote his "Gift of the Magi" in a booth by the door. Farther up the street on the left there's Sal Anthony's, an excellent Italian restaurant that occupies what was once the front parlor of a sedate townhouse and another favorite haunt of O. Henry. (For those fascinated by New York's literary heritage, Irving Place and the Gramercy Park area offer a wealth of past associations with Washington Irving, Mark Twain, Theodore Dreiser, Horace Greeley, Herman Melville, and Henry James.)

Back on 14th Street continue east to Third Avenue, the Times Square of that area. Lines of flashing lights and badly drawn silhouettes of naked ladies pinpoint porno stores and theaters showing various kinds of erotica. The Jewel, a couple of blocks south, is entirely gay, whereas Panascope 35 boasts the largest porno screen in the city. A couple of others are more traditional—cramped, sweaty pleasure-pits showing badly scratched editions of *Schoolgirl Capers* or *Swedish Swingers* with dubbed soundtracks, full of groans and sighs of simulated ecstasy. For the hard-core clientele anxious for live action there is normally an interesting selection of suitably dressed ladies of the street around Third Avenue. Occasionally a police shut-down sends the girls scurrying up Lexington Avenue for a few days and brings a minor period of financial hardship to the seedy hotels down the side streets. But things get back to normal quickly.

How about another diversion, north on Third Avenue to 15th

Pete's Tavern

Street and Stuyvesant Square? Like Union Square, the two lovely sections of park on either side of Second Avenue seem to have been taken over by the street people, yet still retain the dignity of a well-proportioned urban space. At the western end of the park is the Rutherford Place Friends' Meeting House (1861), a good example of refined Quaker architecture, and farther east, beyond Second Avenue, are a number of major medical-related facilities including Beth Israel Hospital, the New York Infirmary, and the infirmary's Center for Independent Living, one of the first programs in the country to develop rehabilitation techniques exclusively for the older blind.

At Second Avenue and 14th Street, a neighborhood feel begins to emerge again. Churches reappear, along with bakeries and small supermarkets. Opposite Hammer's Dairy Restaurant, a well-known kosher establishment, is the Tifereth Israel Town and Village Synagogue, complete with Russian-style domes, which offers to the public a wide range of lectures and films on Jewish culture. Next door is the Emanu-El Midtown YM-YWHA where non-members are welcome to visit the exhibition gallery and attend theatrical productions, many of which are revivals from the old "Jewish Rialto" days (see chapter 3, "The East Village"). Recently there was a presentation of Hy Kraft's *Café Crown*, in which homage was paid to that famous meeting place of Yiddish actors and actresses, often known as the "Sardi's of the Jewish Rialto."

Farther down the street the Botanica San Rafael is a marvelous little store, its window crammed with plaster virgin madonnas in garish colors, Christ figures with golden haloes, curled plaster cobras, and cuddly kittens. Nearby, the charming Roman Catholic Church of the Immaculate Conception provides a richly carved drinking fountain for "everyone that thirsteth"! Unfortunately, it never works. Inside is that smell of incense and the flickering half-light of a thousand prayer candles. A chapel, set to one side, has been Hollywooded into an artificial cave complete with running water and life-size statues.

To the south along First Avenue are the remnants of the old Ukrainian area with its splendid pork butchers and, up the side streets, tiny stores selling religious icons, traditional Ukrainian costumes, and those magnificent hand-painted and carved eggs (see chapter 3, "The East Village").

Across the road the brick bastions of Stuyvesant Town rise up behind a thin, low line of maple trees. A little Jewish bakery, Kossar's (a branch of the famous Grand Street establishment near the Orchard Street Market) sells bialys and displays a window full of round, fresh-baked loaves. Inside, a group of large ladies, recently emerged from the nearby bingo hall, pick and choose cautiously.

The street is ending, coming closer to the East River and the vast Con Edison plant. Behind the little stores is the last great ghetto in this part of Manhattan—a dense neighborhood of dark buildings, part of the old "Gashouse district," and ominous even on a sunny day. It's time to turn around and start back.

No one word can really describe 14th Street. It's a kaleidoscopic strip, full of contrasts, full of ironies. A few yards away from large, plush apartment complexes the street people drink their Ripple or bourbon from greasy bottles. It has more churches than almost any other street in the city, yet at the same time vice is flagrant and porno shops flourish. The great Centennial Memorial Temple of the Salvation Army, west of Sixth Avenue, has an entrance framed by the immortal words of General William Booth:

> While women weep, as they do now
> I'll fight. . . .

The temple is hemmed in by cheap appliance stores and discount cosmetic outlets. Not far from Lüchow's, where executives descend from limousines and scurry hastily into its paneled dining rooms, crowds crush outside the unemployment offices. In Union Square old women in torn overcoats huddle around the base of the flagpole on which are carved the famous lines of the ever-optimistic Jefferson:

> How little my countrymen know what precious
> Blessings they are in possession of and which
> No other people enjoy.

A young man lying on a bench and smoking a joint gives a loud "Right on" and a gaggle of secretaries crossing the Square with their lunch bags giggle softly.

Fourteenth Street, for all its brashness and contradictions, possesses links with almost every facet of Manhattan's history. It's truly a "slice of New York."

6
THE GARMENT
AND FUR DISTRICTS

"So where's your hat? You come to talk to me 'bout makin' hats an' you got no hat. Okay, okay, so sit down. Wad y'wanna know? C'mon, c'mon I ain't got all day—hey, Irv, you seen this guy, he ain't got no hat and he comes to talk to me 'bout hats. Thas'a trouble today—the goyim don't buy hats no more, so why do we bother? Oy, it could be worse. Maybe I could be dead—I should be so lucky. So wad y'wanna know, I'm sittin' here waitin' an' you ain't opened your mouth yet. Here, have a cigar. You don't want one—hey, Irv, this guy don't smoke cigars. You wanna talk to Irv? Hey, siddown, siddown—Irv's no use, he don't know nothin'. But least he wears a hat. Hey, Irv, show him your hat." Irv solemnly brings out a shiny Chassidic hat, broad-brimmed and very black. He doesn't smile. It's some kind of ritual. The large man with the cigar slaps the desk with stubby fingers and bursts out laughing. "Now there's a hat for you." He gasps for breath between the chortles. Irv replaces his hat, still unsmiling.

I'm getting nowhere with the interview and loving every minute of it! At least it's a respite from the streets, although maybe *street* is the wrong word. They're really outdoor corridors, extensions of the cramped workshops that fill every corner and niche of

———————— DIRECTIONS ————————

As no specific walk is planned, any subway or bus stop between an area bounded by 28th and 40th streets and Fifth and Eighth avenues will place you within the garment and fur districts.

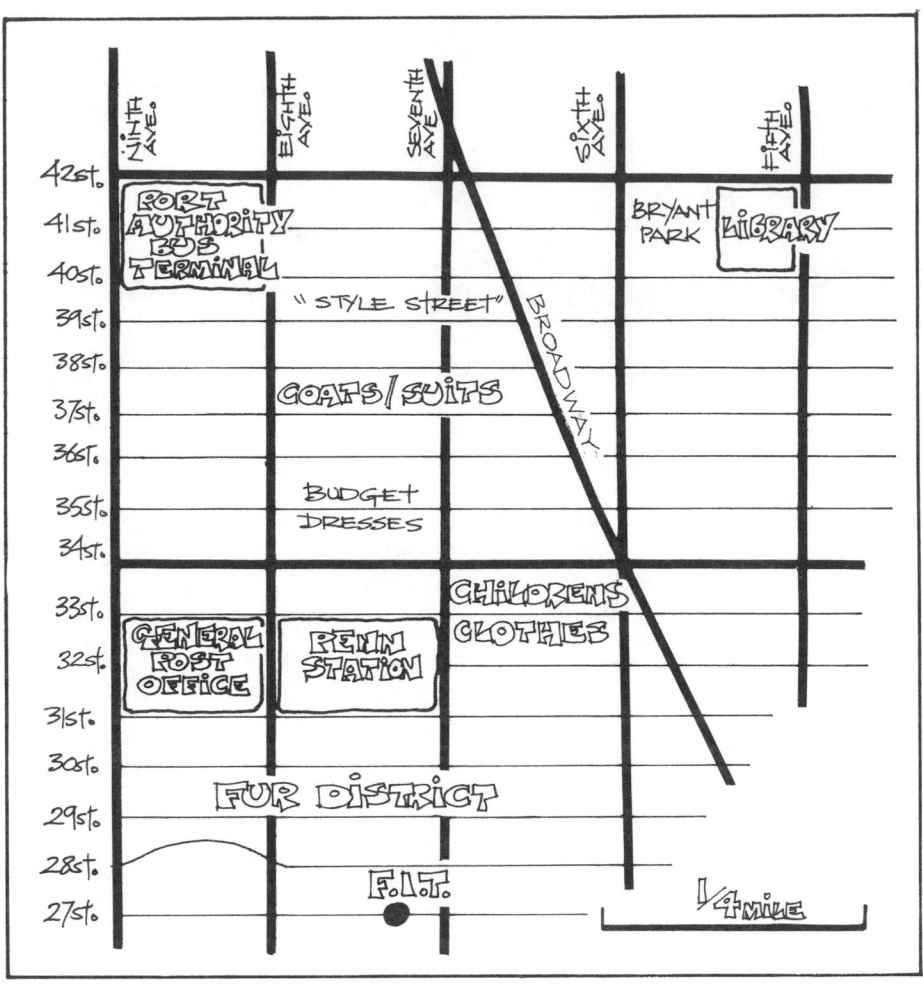

floor space in the gray, grimy buildings of the garment and fur districts between 28th and 40th streets and Fifth and Eighth avenues. Certainly through traffic has no business here. Anybody trying to negotiate his way in a car across this area on a typical weekday should be quietly led away in a straitjacket. He probably would be anyway. People have been known to collapse, suffer nervous breakdowns, and burst blood vessels just trying to get between Seventh and Eighth avenues on 38th Street. Vans on both sides of the street are double-parked, sometimes triple-parked. Tiny pushcarts laden with bolts of cloth and large cardboard boxes or piles of garment pieces emerge without warning from between the double-parkers. The "pitchmen" (pushcart pushers) seem totally oblivious to the confusions of the street. They'll nip and twist between cars as nimbly as a squirrel climbing a thorn tree. Salesmen dressed with a touch of flash maneuver their wheeled suitcases between fenders. Sleek female models, aloof and apparently lifeless, float along the sidewalks, their vacant eyes staring over the churning heads and squealing carts. A rack of half-finished dresses suddenly runs amok down a ramp out into the street, cartwheels, and spins a dozen flimsy satiny things in all directions. The boy frantically scoops up the garments, picking one off a windshield, another off an old lady who doesn't quite understand what's going on, slams them all back on the rack, and scurries down the street. The drunk on the corner, who has perhaps wandered down from 42nd Street for a change of scene, bawls out, "Hey, take it eeeasy, man, jus' take it eeeasy!" slaps his thigh, and does a little dance. "Hey, was' all the rush, I say was'-is-all-the-rush, fellas? Wow! Jes' look at 'em go." He drags out a pint bottle from a deep trouser pocket, takes a long drink, and turns tail. "Wow, man, I jes' gotta get outta here. They's all crazy roun' this part of town."

In a way he's right. There is a craziness that pervades the area, but it's the craziness for which New York is so well known—and loved. It comes from a concentration, a distillation of energy, talent, money, and mutual interests. It comes from the need for contact and communication—direct and continuous—in every phase of the business. "You couldn't move the garment industry. It's far too complex," I was told by the owner of a small high-fashion house. "It took me twenty years to understand how really complex it is. I'm still learning. We all live out of each other's pockets. We curse about conditions, about labor rates, about the city, about the congestion—about everything. But not one of us would move. We need one another. We spy on each other, we play games, we bargain and barter, try to outguess one another, try to find out what's new before anyone else does—even try to drive each other out of business. But it couldn't work any other way. We're not like one of those conglomerates making long-range decisions in ivory towers. We're right in the middle of the marketplace—and it's a hell of a fickle market, let me tell you—and there's hundreds, thousands of tiny businesses all trying to get their piece of the action. Talk about competition being true capitalism—well, this is where it started!"

Garment manufacturing is still one of New York City's leading industries. Between Fifth and Ninth avenues and 34th and 40th streets is the heart of the "rag business." Fashion Avenue (Seventh Avenue) is the center of the most glamorous of all garment trades—women's clothing. Within or on the fringe of this area are the "kindred needle trades": the furriers, shoe makers, and glove manufacturers. The millinery industry can be found between 36th and 39th streets and Fifth and Sixth avenues—30th Street is known to many in the trade as "style street." Window-peering is interesting, although most stores serve the wholesale trade only, and it's usually impossible to get inside to see the manufacturing processes. The furriers (between 27th and 30th streets) are especially nervous. At each shop and loft buzzers sound to admit every visitor and worker, and closed-circuit cameras are a familiar sight. Major crime is fast becoming a serious problem, and the area is gradually shrinking, due to early retirement, fear of robberies and break-ins, and a generally dwindling trade. Today there are about three thousand workers in the fur district; ten years ago there were eight thousand.

Down the dark side streets are grubby storefronts brimming with muskrat, raccoon, beaver, and mink pelts. The narrow workshops are dingy affairs. Paint flakes off the walls and the only light comes from a few random low-watt bulbs dangling on long wires from the ceiling. Old men and old-looking young men huddle in the shadows over sewing machines, rarely pausing. In the center of the floor is a coat rack on wheels, full of fur creations. Even in the most meager workshops along 28th and 29th streets around Eighth Avenue there's often more than $100,000 in furs lying about. Occasionally one of the workers will leave the shop carrying a magnificent $5,000 creation to one of the Seventh Avenue showrooms. There's hardly a more disconcerting sight in Manhattan than little wizened men scurrying along the gloomy sidewalks of the fur district with minor fortunes in coats bundled under their arms.

While you're in the area you may find it fun (and educational) to visit FIT (Fashion Institute of Technology) at 227 West 27th Street (760-7760). Here at the Shirley Goodman Resource Center there are three galleries providing fashion-related exhibits for both students of the college and the general public. Pick up the *Revelations* paper from the information desk and see what's happening in the business. It's fascinating reading.

Continue up Fashion (Seventh) Avenue past the children's-wear manufacturers on 34th Street (No. 112 houses scores of showrooms where buyers from all over the country come to check out the latest trends in child fashions), up to 35th Street, where numerous loft showrooms and popular-priced dresswork shops fill the area between Seventh and Eighth avenues. Note the synagogue on the corner frequented by many of the garment workers. Services start at 7 A.M. and there are even lunchtime and going-home celebrations at noon and 4:30 P.M.

After passing 498 Seventh Avenue, one of the elite coat-and-suit manufacturers and showrooms, you may be ready for a snack. So nip around the corner to 226 W. 37th, through the freight-yard entrance, to Al's Sandwich Shop and rub elbows with the garment workers—the seamstresses, cutters, pressers, and clerks. Listen to their lunchtime "schmooze" talk. You may get some useful hints on upcoming fashion trends or alternatively may discover whose daughter had a baby only last week or whose son has done what to which girl. If you'd rather rub shoulders with the bosses, try Lou Siegel's at 209 W. 38th. It's more expensive than many of the other restaurants in the area, but I'm told by regulars that the food is well worth the price. Another hangout, perhaps the most famous, is Dubrow's Cafeteria, a gargantuan place famous for its bean soup and high-calorie desserts. Next door you'll find the Bagel Nosh (501 Seventh Avenue), its fashion-decor interior bulging with the garment industries' clerical and administrative staff, and an occasional buyer from out of town. If your craving is for kosher food take a walk over to Sixth Avenue and visit Jerusalem 2 (would you believe kosher pizza!) or the House of Taam for kosher Chinese food and snacks. There's also a splurge restaurant in this area—Keen's English Chop House at 72 W. 36th—where lamb chops are the specialty of the house and clay pipes signed by satisfied customers hang in jovial rows from the ceiling. The Artist and Writers Restaurant just around the corner at 213 West 40th Street is a great place for a quick toddy (especially on a cold, windy day) or a leisurely chicken pot pie. Here you'll mingle with the famous, as the place tends to attract a gregarious crowd of columnists, fashion-world celebrities, and Broadway stars. It's unlikely you'll starve while touring the garment district.

Although it's usually difficult to bluff your way into the trade showrooms, there's plenty of movement and life in the area. Just walking the streets and bobbing into the occasional lobby, one can sense the excitement—and the uncertainty. Everyone seems to be wondering: "Is this the year to make that million, or is this the year we bust . . . !" Everybody watches the fashion barometer and hangs on their fingernails. Not too surprisingly the rate of bankruptcy is high: twenty percent among the manufacturers and thirty-three percent among contractors (the people who make up the garments).

If you're interested in learning more about the fashion world, tuck *Women's Wear Daily* under your arm and head off to the Burlington Mills exhibition at Sixth Avenue and 54th Street, where a moving walkway transports you past actual cloth-producing machinery, dye vats, spinning frames, circular doubleknit machines, hosiery knit machines, and a tufting machine for carpets. Then skip over to the International Ladies Garment Workers Union Education Department at 1710 Broadway (at 54th Street). If you call a few days in advance (CO. 5-7000) you can arrange to see a forty-five-minute film entitled *With These Hands* (a history of the development of the garment industry and the union), hear an interesting talk about how the area functions, and take a guided tour of the district with a representative from the union. You'll even visit one of the clothing factories, where, believe it or not, you'll finally see clothes under construction. The two visits combined—

Burlington Mills and ILGWU (make sure to call and make arrangements well in advance)—are excellent introductions to the industry. (Pick up the ILGWU's paper, *Justice*, subtitled "Out of the Sweatshop"; it occasionally makes enthralling reading.)

The sweatshop era stems from the mid-1800s when many German-Jewish refugees began arriving in America. For generations these people had dealt in new and secondhand clothes in their own country, and here they began as peddlers or fringe merchants, eventually finding their way into garment manufacturing. More and more refugees came—entire families from Poland, Italy, Czechoslovakia, and Russia. They settled in the Lower East Side, which inevitably became an enormous sprawling slum and the subject of published protests such as Jacob Riis's *How the Other Half Lives*. Women and children could be seen striding through the mud with bundles of "piece-work" on their heads, and men carrying sewing machines on their backs to the dimly lit, disease-ridden sweatshops. Signs outside reminded the workers who was boss: "If you don't come in Sunday, don't come in Monday" (signed "Management"). Thousands had made their way via Ellis Island to work twelve hours a day, seven days a week, and take home a pittance.

Then came the strikes, particularly the general strikes of 1909 and 1910, which were both milestones of the American labor movement. There were vociferous demands for factory regulations, decent working conditions, hours, and wages. There was also a new sense of brotherhood among the immigrant workers, which ultimately led to the formation of the powerful ILGWU. As the union anthem explains:

> We cut a dream within our head
> And then with needle and with thread
> We fashioned something great and good
> A union seamed with brotherhood.

Gradually the industry moved to more spacious and better located workshops. Searching for an area to establish a complete "garment center," the industry followed the theaters and newspaper offices uptown toward Herald Square, to an area known then as the Tenderloin district, full of dance halls, restaurants, bordellos, and bars and offering ribald frolicking fun—just what visiting salesmen and buyers needed. In 1904 the Pennsylvania Railroad began to thrust its way under the Hudson and in 1930 came the Lincoln Tunnel. Both helped to clear the slums that had characterized the Hell's Kitchen area to the west of the Tenderloin district. These transportation links also put the area well and truly on the map as an established stronghold for the garment workers—an ideal central position for commuter-labor and access to the newly developed department stores and hotels.

Today the garment industry is much less uniform than it was thirty years ago, although this tiny sector of Manhattan is still the hub of trade and activity. The lunchtime crush of workers in the street has in no way diminished, but the ethnic origins of the labor force have altered considerably since the early days when East Europeans made up the bulk of the sweatshop populations. There's also a larger proportion of designers and salesmen than before, and the actual assembly of garments is now often performed elsewhere—in small towns somewhere in Pennsylvania or South Carolina.

But there is still a ghetto—three hundred hidden sweatshops in Chinatown where Chinese immigrants live and work in conditions little different from the pre-ILGWU days, before the industry left the Lower East Side.

Meanwhile each manufacturer prays that "this time" he'll have a "hot number" or at least be able to produce some effective "variations" if his line doesn't sell. That's the spirit that holds this little world-within-a-world together as the push boys crash their carts along the sidewalks, workers gather by the thousands at the street corners, models flit like fragile butterflies through the roaring confusion, and the drunk on the corner bawls out his words of reason: "Hey, take it eeeasy, man, jus' take it eeeasy!"

7
MANHATTAN MARKETS

When the Washington Street Market was unceremoniously removed to make way for downtown's pristine twins, the World Trade Center, there were dour predictions about the fate of Manhattan's other markets. There were (and still are) plans to bundle the Fulton Street fish merchants up to Hunts Point in the Bronx along with all the other dislocated produce people. They say that as soon as 42nd Street is revamped and the new convention center built, Paddy's Market will bid a final farewell to Ninth Avenue. They say the secondhand book market on Fourth Avenue around 14th Street will soon be gone. They grumble about unsanitary and unsafe conditions at the Gansevoort Meat Market at the west end of 14th Street in the shadow of the West Side Highway and threaten yet one more transplant to Hunts Point. (They now gleefully point to plans for "Westway" and can't wait to see the wreckers' ball swinging gaily into the old brick warehouses around Little 12th Street.)

They've got plans to get rid of every market in Manhattan or lock what little remains into sanitized brick boxes and gloat at the silence of the streets, the absence of odors, the smoother-flowing traffic, and the docility of once-tumultuous neighborhoods.

But "they"—the planners, highway engineers, federal specialists, land peddlers, and great construction conglomerates—are finding the process of removal harder than they'd thought. Markets are not idle appendages stuck randomly on the body of the city. Each has a reason and a purpose and is linked to the city by vital arteries through which flows the very life blood of New York

87

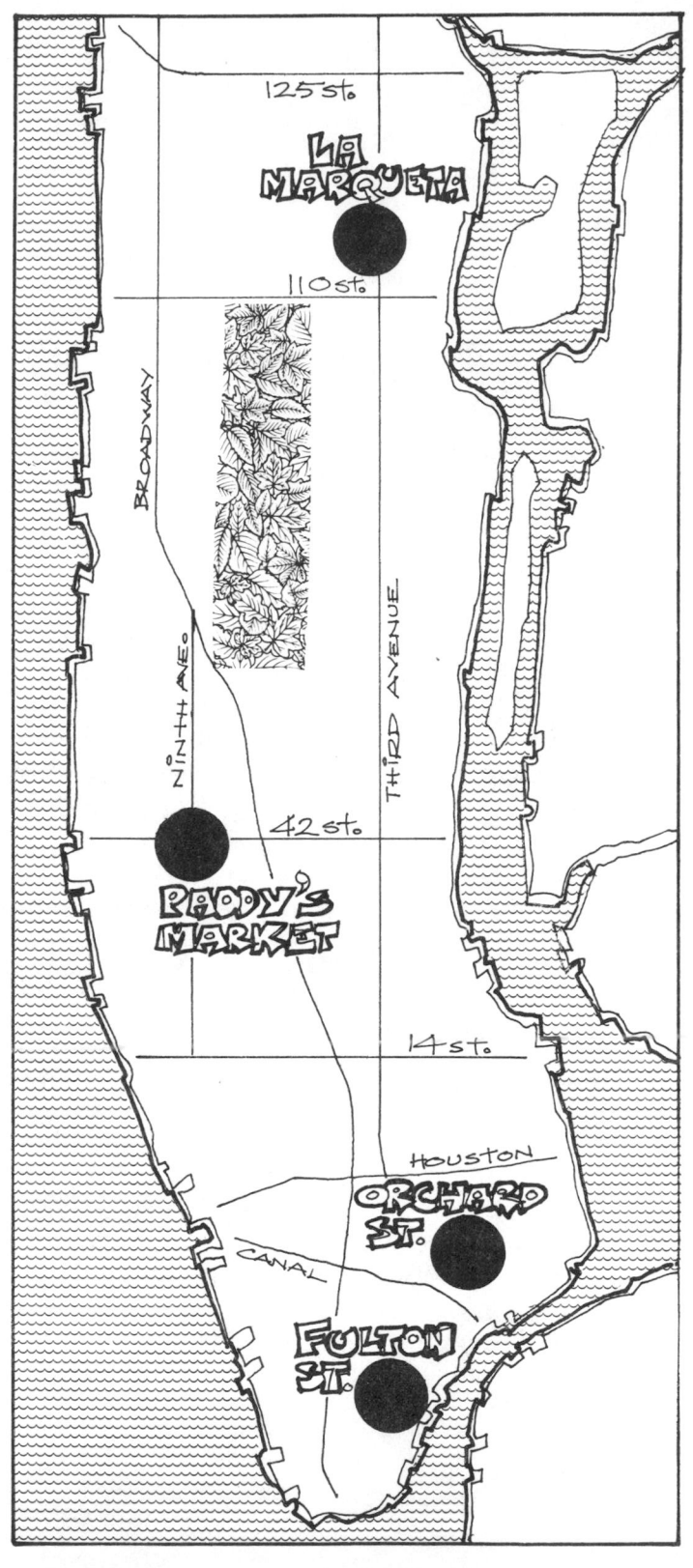

and its people. What would the Lower East Side be without Orchard Street? Where would the people of Clinton shop if Paddy's Market died? What about the Ukrainians around St. Marks Place and their tiny stores reflecting crucial aspects of an ancient culture? And how about the grubby, raucous, impromptu "thieves market" at the east end of Canal Street, long considered an unnecessary annoyance by the "city-beautiful" people? Where would the Bowery boys and the street people go to exchange clothes, trinkets, and gossip if some enlightened idealist decided to remove "this unpleasant eyesore"?

The city is for people, not for planners. The city is the city—grandiose, brash, secluded, litter laden, sweaty, tranquil, smelly, breeze filled, silent, and so damned loud it makes your head spin. Markets are concentrations of needed activities. If they weren't needed, they wouldn't be there. So the message is really very simple—let them be.

We're going to explore four of Manhattan's markets—the Fulton Street Fish Market, Orchard Street, Paddy's Market, and La Marqueta. Other markets are discussed elsewhere in the book: the Gansevoort Meat Market and the secondhand book market can be found in chapter 5 (14th Street); the Ukrainian district is described in chapter 3 ("The East Village"); and the Flower Market, the Sixth Avenue Flea Market, and the "oddments" market along Canal Street can all be found in the "Mini-Tours" section.

FULTON STREET FISH MARKET

The market is located around the junction of Fulton and South streets.
Subway: BMT J, M to Fulton and Nassau streets;
IND A, E to Broadway and Nassau Street;
IRT 2, 3 to Fulton and William streets;
IRT 3, 4 to Fulton Street and Broadway;
Bus: M15 (South Ferry); Culture Bus II, stop 30

At dawn the masts and funnels of the old ships at the South Street Seaport Museum are silhouetted against the dim orange glow over Brooklyn. It's chilly. A breeze full of the Atlantic ruffles across the piers and down the dark streets. It's a time of day most New Yorkers never see—but it's the best time to visit Manhattan's Fulton Street Fish Market.

The deep chasms of downtown are silent. Only a few lights glimmer in the windows of the Southbridge Towers apartments. An old man wrapped in greasy blankets and newspapers is curled like a mouse in one of the dark doorways. His feet rest on a pile of empty liquor bottles.

The unmistakable odor of fish creeps up the narrow streets between the low brick buildings. The light from a single street lamp illuminates the rusted shutters and streaked windows of an old warehouse. Somewhere down by the river a truck trumpets its exhaust, and a group of men, huddled around the orange glow of a fire in an oil drum, turn briefly and then move in closer to the warming flames.

Suddenly, around the corner it's bright and bustling. Down one side a line of tiny stalls displays their wares on tables and in tanks—shrimps, scallops, scungilli, clams, and mussels. Mounds of gray, green, and blue crabs thrash in buckets and boxes. Lobsters, their claws closed with wood wedges, churn in shallow sinks while buyers prod warily. The stall owners, fat and flushed, shout at customers as burly men in caps and rubber aprons trundle carts laden with boxes of pink fish with gaping mouths. Bright bulbs under the canvas canopies of the stalls reflect on the slippery sidewalks and cobblestones where buyers move in a continual throng—a hubbub of mumbles, barterings, and bawlings.

Across the street, under the elevated highway, is the big-time market where the *real* fish can be found—tuna, mackerel, dogfish, halibut, catfish, eels—you name it. A one-hundred-sixty-eight-pound jewfish, its scales as long as a man's thumb, lies by itself on a large wooden bench. A card tied through its dorsal fin reads: "From Florida, for Mr. Mariano."

"Charlie, get these fish outta here." A large man, presumably Charlie, ambles over with a steel hook, spears an enormous prong-tailed tuna just under the gills, and hoists it, dripping, on his back. He half drags, half carries the creature across the wet floor and with a deft flick of hook and shoulder sends it bouncing and slithering into the back of a refrigerated truck. Charlie returns several times to repeat the process with even larger fish, then, satisfied, he clips the hook over his shoulder and wanders outside into the street for a smoke.

"Charlie, where the hell are you going? Charlie . . ." The small

m
ti
o
p
b

c

B·O·O·K·S
& Co.

939 Madison Avenue
Three Doors South of the Whitney

New York City 10021

212/737·1450

nds of mackerel, ges-
ith the stained sleeve
by notebook into his
Charlie, almost tum-
the floor.

Slip, the Paris Bar is
en huddle over tight
e and brandy. Others
iling are yellowed with
tleman with cheeks as
mechanically without a
the mottled mirror on
so tired, stained porters,

All that remains are the
oken boxes, odd bits of
ell—the smell that hangs
the almost deserted bars

gone. There are plans to
he Bronx, and what's left
ng museum," part of the
In a way it's a shame. For
d to some eyes, ugliness,
f the last living links with
le the Seaport project will
his once-vibrant little area,
he fish market, and Fulton
again.

ORCHARD STREET AND ESSEX STREET

Subway: BMT J, M
Bus: M9, M14, M15, M21

(Avoid coming by automobile. The Bowery boys will hassle you at every
step along "desolation row," parking is virtually impossible, and the
local traffic police are the most alert in the city.)

If you prefer window-browsing and buying in relative calm (remember the word *relative*), come to Orchard Street during the
week. There may even be a spare table at Katz's Deli at East Hous-

ton and Ludlow and only a short line of waiting customers at Guss's Pickle Emporium. Alternatively, if you'd like to experience the real Orchard Street scene come on Sunday when the top end, from East Houston to Delancey, is closed to traffic, and people—thousands of them—take over for the day. If you can, find a place to pause briefly. It's a narrow street full of grim buildings, unwashed windows, and a filigree of fire escapes silhouetted against the sky. Bearded Chassidim scamper past the hundreds of tiny stores selling the widest, cheapest (and occasionally the best) variety of dresses, coats, shoes, handbags, shirts, jackets, blouses, and underwear in the city. Little square signs, all about the same size and all painted in the same reds, yellows, and blues, hang over every store. The better places (look for the credit-card signs) have neat window displays and electronically controlled doors to limit the number of customers inside at any one time. Lines of anxious ladies wait outside. The other stores are less restrained. Their doors are flung wide open and clothes and bolts of cloth and assorted boxes of socks and handkerchiefs tumble across the sidewalk on a profusion of trestle tables. The owner's outside stalking buyers with the subtlety of a Central Park mugger—"Hey, you—you, yeah the one with the pimples, c'mon over here, let me show what I got here. Hey, you seen a blouse like this before? It's real silk. Touch it. Go on, just feel it . . ."

A bald man of gigantic proportions takes up most of the sidewalk with himself and a large box full of packs of razor blades. "Three for a dollar, you can't beat it . . ." Lower down, an old, rather crumpled lady wrapped in a gray shawl sells handkerchiefs from a supermarket bag to sympathetic customers.

The Orchard Street area is the last real remnant of the Lower East Side and still possesses all the flavor of a Jacob Riis photograph. Nearby Grand Street was once the wealthiest shopping street in New York. Lord and Taylor had a large establishment at the corner of Chrystie Street, and Ridley's ran special coach services to bring customers from the Debrosses Street ferry on the Hudson side and the Grand Street ferry on the East River. At that time Hester Street and Orchard Street were a peddler's market. Hundreds of pushcarts lined the sidewalks. Their Jewish and Italian owners sold everything a local resident might need—wines, chicken, freshly made horseradish, fruits and vegetables, olive oil, cloth, eyeglasses (sold by the "glimmer men"), newspapers in every Eastern European language, suspenders, candles, candy, "broken chocolates," sweet potatoes, hot corn, nuts, halvah, umbrellas, pickles, bread, strange sweet drinks, and a wide array of hot snacks to be gulped down while peering and poking in the peddlers' carts. That was the era of penny knife grinders, "sniff cartes" (installment plans to buy steerage tickets for relatives back in the homeland), elaborate shoe-shine parlors, and bartering sessions unmatched outside the bazaars of the Middle East.

It all ended rather abruptly in 1938 when Mayor Fiorello La Guardia authorized the construction of the enclosed Essex Street market for the street traders and transformed peddlers into merchants overnight. The market remains, between Broome and Delancey streets. Inside the dull red brick buildings (open Monday–Saturday 7 A.M.–7 P.M., closed Sunday) the Spanish influence is pronounced, and many of the meat and vegetable stalls resemble those at La Marqueta up in El Barrio (110th–116th streets on Park Avenue). But somehow it seems a sad remnant of the old peddler-and-pushcart days.

Essex Street itself, though, still retains its distinct character. Guss Pickle Emporium ("Eat Guss's Pickles and Stay Young and Beautiful") just around the corner on Hester Street, next door to the H&M Skull Cap Manufacturing Co., seems to have provoked a flurry of competition. There's the Pickleman ("All our Pickles are Straight and not Crooked") with a mouth-watering display of pickled eggplants, olives, tomatoes, peppers, dills, cauliflower, and just about any other vegetable capable of being doused in vinegar. Then next to a kosher cheese shop is Hollander and Sons, a third pickle establishment which, for all the color of its display, lacks the solid authoritative appearance of Guss's with its line of gray pickling vats and gallon jars of sour tomatoes.

Kossar's bialy bakery, hidden away in a line of small stores on Grand Street just east of Essex, is famous for its bagels, onion breads, poppyseed and onion boards, and its delicious bialys. Of course, as might be expected in this touchstone of the American Jewish culture, there is constant debate over the relative merits of the food in the area. Some claim that the Ratner's at 138 Delancey Street is the only place for bagels, but there's general agreement that the tiny Yonah Schimmel's at 137 is the best knish bakery in

Guss Pickle Emporium

New York, that Russ and Daughters at 179 East Houston Street has the finest smoked fish and pickled herring, that the Economy Candy Market at Essex and Rivington has the best selection of confectionery around, and that Moishe's at 181 East Houston Street excels with its Russian bread. Finally, patrons insist that Bernstein's-on-Essex with its kosher-Chinese cuisine is not half as bad as it sounds. Their kreplach, potato pudding, kashavarnishkas, and goose dishes (during the November kosher goose festival) are particularly outstanding.

Which brings us back inevitably to noisy Katz's Deli (205 East Houston Street), decidedly nonkosher, but serving generous pastrami and corned beef sandwiches with plenty of chutzpah thrown in with the mustard and dills. There's a kosher place next door with a more restrained spirit, but most visitors seem to prefer the plastic tables, the yellow walls, the din and chatter, and the spirit of "eat, eat!" that is Katz's. After all, the place caters to those who enjoy the push and shove of Orchard Street, the waiting in line outside a store to buy a handbag, trying on clothes behind a blanket held by clothespins to a length of string, being shanghaied into stores and dragged out again by frustrated companions, and suffering the final indignity of being told "you're too fat, dearie." If you come to Orchard Street—come prepared for the fray.

PADDY'S MARKET

Subway: IND A, E, AA or CC to 34th Street and 8th Avenue (Penn Station) or 42nd Street and 8th Avenue (Port Authority bus terminal)
Bus: M11

If you're hungry, start at Manganaro's (488 Ninth Avenue between 37th and 38 streets). It's a good idea for two reasons. First, you'll get one of the best hero sandwiches in town. Second, you'll buy less later if you're not hungry, and along this short section of Ninth Avenue, within the shadow of the Port Authority bus terminal at 40th Street, it's very hard not to go through a month's food budget in a couple of hours, mumbling clichés like, "Well, it'll keep and it's so cheap," "I've been meaning to have a party anyway," or the classic "Well, I'm down a few pounds, so . . ."

It's a pretty shabby area really—just as a good market should be. Fire escapes cast lengthy gray shadows on blocks of grubby buildings ranged along the avenue like the smashed teeth of an Irish bar-brawler. Traffic, avoiding the crush of Times Square or swirling around the ramps to the Lincoln Tunnel, surges by constantly. Packs of dogs chase one another across vacant building lots and buses roar overhead up the ramp to the terminal. But along the sidewalks and in the crammed stores everyone is oblivious to the hurly-burly. There's one focus of interest, one torchlike beam of enthusiasm and conversation—food. At Manganaro's Grosseria Italiana the old wood floor boards creak as customers mingle, peer, and prod at the hams, sopressata, and long, pear-shaped provolones dangling from the yellowed tin ceiling. On a table opposite the counter there's a display of cheeses all ready for cutting. High above, on bent shelves, are boxes of pastas—spaghettini, capellini, perciatelli, bucatini, mezza zita, cannaroni rigati, lumache medie, pennoni. It's not the kind of place to pick up a pound of any old macaroni. Perfectionists come here to buy their own ravioli makers. Gourmets come here to vie with one another. Gourmands come here to gush at the mounds of prosciutto, mortadella, pancetta, salamis (the finest Sicilian), pepperoni, and cotechini. Coffee lovers leave with espresso makers tucked under their arms and trundle up to the nearby Empire Coffee and Tea Company to select an Italian roast from a score of blends which include the real Jamaican Blue Mountain and green beans for do-it-yourself roasting enthusiasts.

What's the secret of Paddy's Market? Well, it's not a "fancy-foods at fancy prices" kind of area like some of the more elite streets on the East Side. It offers instead the best in meat, seafood, Greek, Philippine, and Oriental foods, rare Italian delicacies, herbs and spices, cheeses, breads, and vegetables at some of the best prices in town. It does this without affectation, without snobbery, and with a respect for the knowledge and taste of the customer. There's the assumption that if you're not already a gourmet, you certainly soon will be and you'll obviously be coming back.

Of course, there may be many types of food not quite to your taste. Well-dressed West Siders frequent the little bakeries with windows full of golden fresh-baked loaves, but hurriedly pass by the butcher shops displaying racks of smoked pigs' heads, rabbits, brains, hoofs, trotters, tripe, and testicles. But it's hard to bypass

Giovanni Esposito and Sons' pork shop on the corner of 38th Street, with its dry-cured Smithfield hams and its homemade sausages—parsley and cheese pork sausages, Italian links with fennel, and those pungent garlic sausages.

On both sides of the street there's Vinnie's, with its encyclopedic array of fruits and vegetables, and a little higher up on the west side of Ninth Avenue (between 39th and 40th streets), stores spill out onto the sidewalk with boxes and burlap sacks of paprika, crushed peppers, red lentils, dried fava beans, oregano, bay leaves, fresh tarragon, fennel seeds, and coriander. Slabs of salt cod, buckets of herring fillets and bloaters mingle with baskets of garlics, nuts, dried fruit, and ginger roots.

Don't pass by the Philippine food stores if you like to experiment with your cooking. Many of the products are recognizably Chinese, but there are some unique specialties here, including a remarkable array of dried fish, sweets wrapped in banana fronds, fermented fish sauce, langkas (an odoriferous seasoning made from roots), and unusual fruit jams such as ube, mango, and jack fruit. Alternatively, if these exotic goodies don't excite, visit the stalwart fish and meat stores on the west side of the street and enjoy the largest and freshest selections in the city.

Above 40th Street the market fragments. Much has been lost to redevelopment, but if you don't mind an extended stroll, visit Molinari Brothers between 51st and 52nd streets, home of delicious pâtés (the only other charcuterie I've found to compare with this place is Les Trois Petits Cochons at 17 East 13th Street) or Poseidon Confectionery and Oriental Pastry between 44th and 45th streets, where you can buy phyllo dough to make your own strudel or baklava.

If you skipped Manganaro's at the outset there's a fish-fry store near Vinnie's that offers a tempting array of cooked whiting, porgie, mackerel, snapper, shrimp, scallops, and clams. Or, for splurgers, there's Giordano's Restaurant tucked down 39th Street around the corner from a fruit-and-vegetable store. This somewhat elite establishment was once a true neighborhood Italian restaurant at a time when Clinton, better known as Hell's Kitchen, was a staunch Irish/Italian neighborhood and Paddy's Market was a far larger affair than it is today. But for all the changes in the area, the businesses still flourish, serving both a local clientele and a devoted army of enthusiasts who flock from all over the city, particularly on Saturdays, to prod and poke and sniff and gaze, and go home with bulging bags and beaming faces.

LA MARQUETA

The market is located on Park Avenue between 110 and 116 streets and is open Monday–Saturday 8 A.M.–6 P.M.
Subway: IRT 6 to 116th Street and Lexington Avenue
Bus: M1, M2, M3, M4, M101, M102

"Yessir, yessir—you wanna somma this, mister, *buenos días*—eh! Come 'ere I wanna to show this, *señor* . . . hey, mista, take a look at this tuna—yessir, you wanna pig—hey, how 'bout some chili peppers—hey . . ."

Frantic, loud, raucous, booming with Latin American music, smelling alternatively of abattoir, greenhouse, incense-filled churches, with overtones of the Fulton Fish Market—it's one of the liveliest places in town, deep in the heart of El Barrio, Spanish Harlem.

The main market is located in a series of block-long buildings directly under the tracks of the Penn Central railroad. Trains grate and squeal overhead, their commuter passengers oblivious to the tumult below. Everyone shouts. At the end of the day chaos reigns. The fruit and vegetable stands at the lower end of the market, so neatly arranged at eight in the morning, are a shambles. It's hard to separate the vast array of plantains, mangoes, coconuts, sweet potatoes, persimmons, chayotes, cassavas, papayas, sugar cane, and banana fronds (used for making pastelles, a kind of tamale). Higher up, in the meat sections, the butchers are gesticulating wildly, making last-minute reductions, trying to sell off whole pigs and every conceivable byproduct—ears, tails, snouts, heads, feet, skin, chitterlings—even gallon bottles of blood for making blood sausage.

On Fridays the fish section way up at the top end near 116th Street is the busiest part of the market. The floor is a treacherous mass of ice, blood, and scales. A line of gaping tuna heads frames a pile of contorted black eels. There's red snapper, mackerel, salted codfish, gray gelatinous octopus, conch, lobsters, and huge gulf prawns. If you can put up with the stench, you'll get some of the best bargains in town.

La Marqueta

Hidden among the bustling meat, fish, and vegetable stands are quieter stalls. One sells nothing but religious trinkets—statues, rosaries, brightly colored pictures of Christ on the cross (the eyes blink as you move by), candles, and all kinds of prayer cards embossed with saints smiling under their halos. Another specializes in grossly painted plaster products—purple owls, green dogs, madonnas of every hue, even a Christ figure in fluorescent pink!

Then there are the little hole-in-the-wall places offering strange concoctions of herbs and spices from old glass bottles, cheek by jowl with stands displaying six different types of rice and dried beans of every shape and color—"Hey, mister, I make my own chili sauce—real hot—the hottest." A little man with a greasy mane of curled black hair waves a container of murky gray-brown liquid in front of my face. I can see, dimly, the floating shapes of deadly jalapeño peppers. I smile and quickly pass into the street for some fresh air.

Outside is almost as chaotic as the enclosed market. Along both sides of Park Avenue and much of 116th Street there's a confusing array of coats, suits, shoes, dresses, and shawls, dangling from every doorway and awning or perched and piled on the sidewalks. Salsa music blares out from a score of perforated speakers. Everyone looks so totally enthusiastic. It's almost 100° with high humidity and minimal shade from the elevated tracks and everyone's beaming and laughing—even dancing at the street corner. Let's go and join in. For an hour or so, lose yourself in the infectious spirit of the barrio. You might arrive home with a bag full of "chitlins" or even a pig's ear as a souvenir. You might blow your carefully structured diet in a lunch of fatty snacks—tamales, papas rellenas, legua, plantanos fritos, and empanadas, but so what? It's not every day you go to a carnival—and it's much cheaper than a trip to Puerto Rico.

8

THE UNITED NATIONS AND VICINITY

What I enjoy most about this walk are the contrasts and the unexpected surprises: the little niches, the quiet corners, the hidden places we'll discover as we move along the frantic, bustling streets of central Manhattan.

We begin in the furniture district, roughly defined by 29th to 34th streets between Third and Fifth avenues. It's more diffuse and less immediately spectacular than the Diamond District or the Flower District to the west. Many of the trade showrooms are hidden behind shuttered windows or located high in ponderous buildings closed to the general public. Those places that are open to the casual passerby present a tiny sampling of the district's wares and are usually highly yet delightfully specialized. Deutsch, Inc., for example (196 Lexington Avenue at 33rd Street), is a bright, airy place filled with an extensive collection of wicker and bamboo furniture, and stores along 34th Street, between Madison and Park avenues, display endless variations on the convertible sofa theme. My favorite, and a favorite with anyone willing to invest a lifetime's savings in domestic comfort, is the Roche-Bobois showroom at 35th and Madison. One can quite easily spend an hour here, notepad in hand, brain swirling with design concepts for the ultimate bedroom or singles pad. There's even a bargain basement for limited-budget connoisseurs, although management's idea of low-budget is usually the equivalent of many de-

---
DIRECTIONS

Subway: *Start:* IRT 6 to 33rd Street and Park Avenue
   Return: BMT RR or IRT 4, 5, 6 from 59th Street and Lexington Avenue
Bus: M1, M2, M3, M4, M101, M102

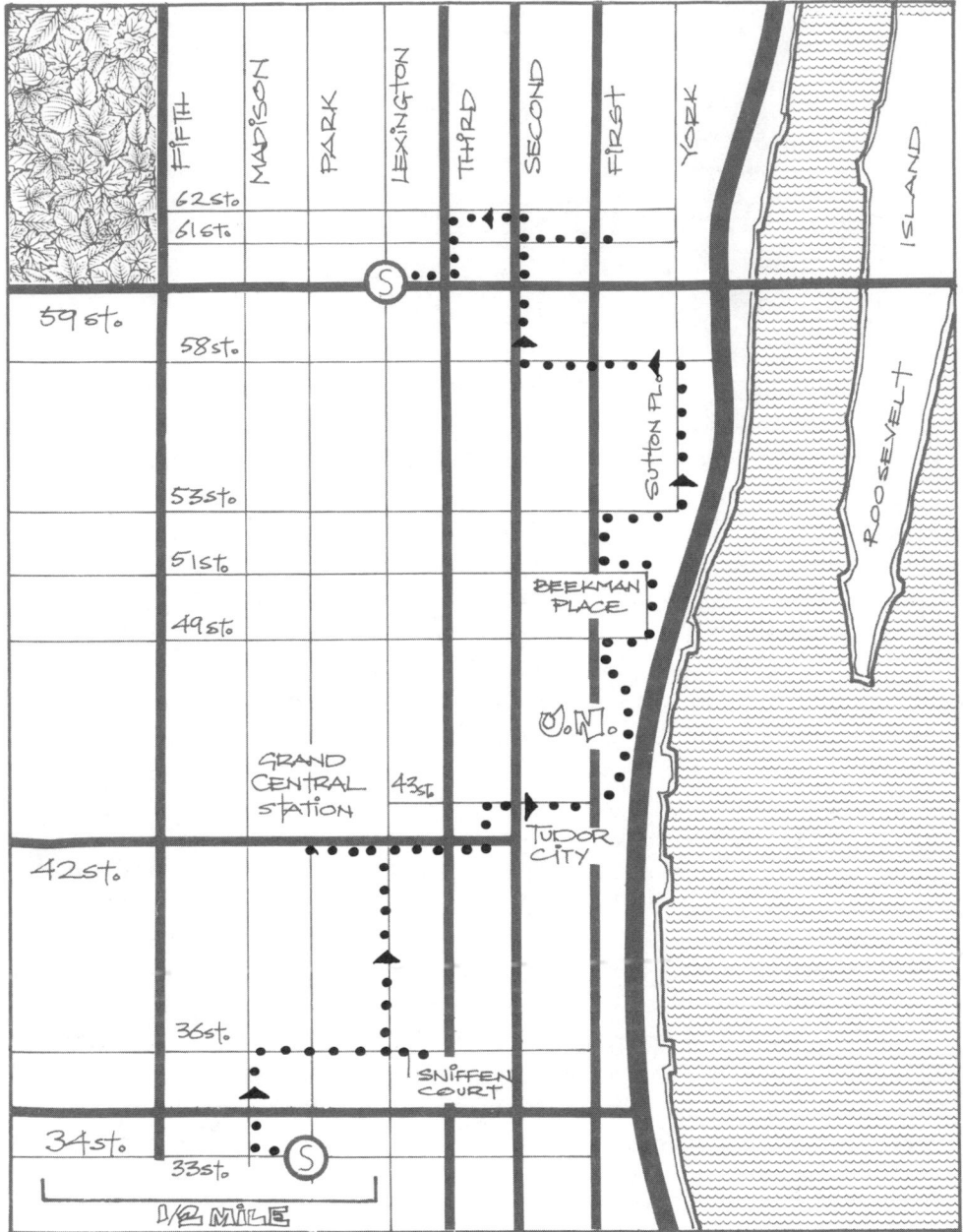

partment stores' top-line offerings. I always leave refreshed knowing that there is indeed fine furniture available in Manhattan but with a vague sense of inadequacy at the thought of my own abode. I used to surreptitiously sketch details of cabinets and tables intending to produce identical pieces at a fraction of the Roche-Bobois price. Somehow, though, they never worked out and I returned to gaze in admiration at the perfect craftsmanship found here.

At the corner of Madison and 35th Street there's the Church of the Incarnation, a delightful place to pause and enjoy one of the frequent lunchtime concerts (preceded by a snack from the nearby delicatessen that looks as if it just arrived from the Lower East Side). Or if your interests encompass a broader range of theological thought, pop into the Anthroposophical Society up the street, in a tiny gray building at 211 Madison Avenue (MU. 5-4618). There are pamphlets galore explaining the concepts of the society's founder, Rudolf Steiner, an Austrian philosopher whose prime interest was in man's ability to obtain objective knowledge of spiritual realities and to use that knowledge to improve the quality of existence both before—and after—death. His ideas, many of which have been absorbed into humanist concepts, are applied in the fields of education (special Steiner schools), architecture, the arts, and biodynamics. Steiner's work is attracting considerable interest at the present time and the society offers regular lectures and presentations for the public. The notice board just inside the door usually gives all the details.

Nearby we come face to face with the presence of another great nineteenth-century man, J. Pierpont Morgan. At the corner of 36th Street and Madison is his library, which became a public institution in 1924. The annex through which one enters the building (exhibition hours Tuesday–Saturday 10:30 A.M.–5 P.M., Sunday 1–5 P.M. 685-0008) is the site of Morgan's house. On the northern corner is his son's house, the J. P. Morgan, Jr., Mansion, now occupied by United Lutheran Church offices, and directly across 37th Street is the incredible DeLamar Mansion, now the Consulate General of the Polish Peoples in New York. This miniature French chateau complete with cherub-adorned entrances was the work of the architect C. P. H. Gilbert and, if you peer in the windows, you'll notice the interior detailing is even more extravagant than

The Polish Consulate

the façade. By contrast, the Morgan Library seems an austere creation, finely articulated in the Italian-Renaissance style by McKim, Mead and White, but lacking the exuberance once characteristic of the homes of the Four Hundred in this elite part of Murray Hill. Morgan had no interest in fleeting fashions. He wanted a structure that was timeless in its design and reflected the finest craftsmanship. The great white marble blocks of the library itself were laid "dry" (without mortar), held together by weight and the absolute exactness of the fit. It's an admirable creation. The tiniest details on the iron railing in front of the library are exquisitely produced and the two cheetahs, on either side of the main entrance, seem ready to spring at the slightest sign of inappropriate behavior from passersby.

I'm surprised how few residents of New York have visited this rich storehouse of literature and art. Admittedly, the library itself can be used only by accredited scholars, but the two public galleries and the exhibition areas contain what, at the time of Morgan's death in 1913, was considered to be the most splendid private collection in the country (in an era when collecting was a popular pastime of the super-rich, that was no mean achievement). There are illuminated manuscripts from the sixth to the sixteenth century, the Book of Hours of Catherine of Cleves, autographed manuscripts of Byron, Keats, and Milton, etchings by Rembrandt, and famous paintings by Tintoretto and Perugino. But those are only highlights. Stroll through the library yourself and experience the solemnity of history, particularly in the east room, where enclosed shelves rise from floor to frescoed ceiling. There's a complete wall of Bibles and two blue leather boxes labeled modestly "Gutenberg Bible." The collection is priceless. One can only gaze in wonder at the knowledge and learning stored within those hundreds of worn leather bindings. In the west room, wonder turns to awe as one stands next to Morgan's carved desk in the tall red room he used as his study. His presence is almost tangible; the aura of unmitigated power fills the room. One of the guards told me how he loved being on duty in this room. "It always makes me feel bigger," he said.

In a haze of culture, continue east on 36th Street until you reach Sniffen Court, one of those unexpected surprises you'll find constantly throughout the walk. This delightful alley consisting of a mere handful of two-story homes was built in the mid-1800s by John Sniffen as a series of coach houses and stables for the gentry of the Hill. They were converted into dwellings in the 1920s; the building at the end was for many years the studio of sculptress Malvina Hoffman. There's also a small theater, an architect's office, and an abundance of decorative additions—lamps, flower boxes, odd chimneys, a lovely triangular bay window, brass bits and pieces, and lots of climbing plants. Unfortunately, an occasional car sits in the court and destroys the illusion of being in some Bayswater back garden or one of those quiet passageways that lace the French quarter of New Orleans.

Sniffen Court

A couple of blocks north on Lexington Avenue, at 152 East 38th Street, is another tiny remnant of nineteenth-century Murray Hill, a delightful townhouse set back from the street behind a flourishing garden. In contrast, at Park Avenue and 35th Street is the J. Hamden Robb House, a solemn edifice of brick and terra-cotta in various shades of burnt siena and umber. The house, once described by a celebrated architectural critic as "an ideal setting for a wealthy young bachelor," was for many years the home of the Advertising Club. Adjoining streets lined with well-maintained rows of townhouses give this section of town an air of dignity and grace—one can almost hear the clopping of hooves on the cobbles and carriages rumbling by, transporting their frilled and feathered occupants on ceaseless rounds of social engagements.

Stroll north along Lexington, past a series of attractive restaurants and pubs, to 42nd Street and into the hubbub around Grand Central Station. Here we can wander and explore the foyers, passageways, and great halls that seem to characterize the architecture of this bustling enclave. Guided tours are frequently available and details can be obtained at the information desk in the main concourse. Take for example the station itself. Tens of thousands of scurrying commuters pour through every day, but how many pause to admire the great 140-foot-high ceiling painted with the constellations of the zodiac, where each star becomes a pinpoint of light after dusk? How many have enjoyed the magnificent New England clam chowder, a meal in itself, served in the refurbished Oyster Bar, or played "whispers" under the vaulted arches outside the restaurant entrance? How many realize that this is one of the few enclosed shopping malls of any significance in the city?

Then on the east side of Lexington Avenue there's the famous Chrysler building, one of the finest examples of Style-Moderne in Manhattan. Everyone recognizes its tapering sunburst tower and its stainless-steel gargoyles, but few venture into its marble and steel lobby, bathed in surrealistic light, to admire the Trumboli paintings on the ceiling (now almost the same color as the marble) and the total unity of design, down to the smallest details—letterboxes, the guard's stainless-steel cubicle, and the elegant elevator doors.

The Chanin building, across from the station on the south side of 42nd Street, is an even more elaborate example of the Art Deco style both inside and outside, although my favorite space in this complex is the Bowery Bank at 110 East 42nd Street. Through the great arch one enters what could be the throne room of an extravagant Renaissance palace. Columns, each of different marble, rise almost seventy feet to an ornate beam ceiling. Voices echo off the intricate mosaic walls and the equally extravagant floors. One feels very tiny in such a space as this. The security guards stand like centurions below the columns, rarely smiling. Palaces are not for smiling in. But they're certainly excellent for singing. I happened to visit here one Christmas when a choir of sixty young girls presented a program of carols. Their voices rang pure throughout the hall, richly reverberating. People came in off the wet streets and stood listening. Everyone paused. The tellers looked out from behind their ornate cages. The customers relaxed a little. The spirit of the season filled the whole building. It was an experience I'll long remember.

But enough of all this meandering. Let's continue eastward and visit two more 42nd Street edifices, noting before you leave the Grand Central area the New York City Convention and Visitors Bureau tucked in under the viaduct, a most useful resource for both visitors and residents.

Past a truly authentic Horn and Hardart cafeteria, one of the few left in the city, at the corner of Third Avenue (slots, flap boxes, and fish-head coffee machines), we come to the self-contained *Daily News* building at 220 East 42nd Street. Unfortunately, the tours, particularly of the adjoining printing plant, have been discontinued, so you'll have to make do with a saunter around the great globe of the world in the lobby (there are occasional exhibitions) and a scan through the Special News publications in the information area. Then if you fancy a complete change of scene, cross the street and enter the ten-story glass-enclosed garden at the Ford Foundation building. Again, public tours of the offices have been discontinued, but visitors are encouraged to lose themselves in the lush terraces, among full-grown trees, waterfalls, pools, and rampant shrubbery. This creation, without doubt one of the most sensitive and imaginative pieces of institutional design in Manhattan, was opened in 1967 and, as critics predicted, became instantly famous. The *New York Times* proclaimed it "one of the most romantic environments ever devised by corporate man." Kevin Roche, of the architectural firm Kevin Roche, John Dinkeloo and Associates, explains his concept as follows: "The conventional office building tends to isolate the individual and store him away in a cubicle with no means of communication other than electronics . . . and with no view other than that of the anonymous cubicles 100 feet away across the street." So Roche decided to design an environment that would allow employees to enjoy fresh and stimulating views and at the same time be aware of the presence of fellow employees—to create the sense of "a family of effort."

Roche's concern was also for the building's relationship to the external environment of the street. "It would have been easy for us to have designed another tower building, but we chose, rather, to keep the building as low as possible and to conscientiously observe the lines and planes created by other buildings which form the surrounding street." Result? The building is modest yet extremely powerful because of the integrity and clarity of the concept. How refreshing to see this kind of restrained statement in a city full of exclamation marks.

Exit on 43rd Street and turn right, into the Tudor City complex, a "self-contained city" developed during the twenties. Here we experience a transition of architectural thought from the sublime to the sublimely ridiculous—multistory apartment towers with such quaint names as "The Cloister" and "The Manor," topped with half-timbered gables, turrets, and water towers disguised as miniature Elizabethan manors. There's also a Tudor-treated church, the Church of the Covenant, next to the 600-room hotel. Fortunately, the complex also has its redeeming features. There are fine views between the towers of the United Nations and the East River; there are two parks, intimate and shaded; there are pubs and restaurants and La Bibliothèque, a small but popular dining establishment overlooking the river.

One could argue, I suppose, that Tudor City is at least an improvement on the Irish slums that blanketed the area in the late 1800s. Not far from here, in 1863, the infamous draft riots began and spread like windswept fire throughout the city. The wealthy, who had been permitted to buy draft exemption for three hundred dollars, scurried out of town while the mob rampaged the streets, burning and looting, lynching Negroes, and fighting with the police. More than twelve hundred people were killed in that four-day insurrection. Later, during the early 1900s the Tudor City area was home of Paddy Corcoran's "Rag Gang," and down in the flatlands by the river, where the real Turtle Bay had been (Poe once described a peaceful fishing expedition on its quiet shores), was the most noxious neighborhood in Manhattan, full of dank, smoke-filled streets, slaughterhouses, glue factories, breweries, rendering plants, and gas works. All this was cleared out for the construction of the United Nations complex in the 1950s, but was still very much in existence when Tudor City was built—hence the lack of windows on the east face of the towers.

Descend the steps near La Bibliothèque Restaurant, cross First Avenue, and enter an area of international territory, home of the UN and a score of other world-oriented organizations along United Nations Plaza and up the side streets. New Yorkers are doubtless familiar with the tours, exhibitions, and souvenir-shopping area in the General Assembly building, but there are two little niches here even frequent visitors tend to miss. The first is just inside the Assembly Building, to the right of the U.S. Moon Rock exhibit. It is the Meditation Room, "a room devoted to peace and those who are giving their lives for peace. It is a room of quiet where only thoughts should speak." Come here and sit in the near-darkness in front of a smooth block of iron ore. A tiny needle of light shines on its upper surface. Behind is a simple mosaic representing the concepts of harmony, freedom, and ultimate balance. The significance of these three elements—the block, the light, the mural—depends on individual interpretation, but everyone seems to leave a little quieter in spirit.

Allow time to explore the United Nations gardens, one of the most refined and carefully conceived spaces in the city. Note how the curve of the riverside esplanade reflects the roof line of the General Assembly building and how, while the massing of the complex always changes as you move about the park, it is always in balance. In the park the knife-edged lines of shaped bushes contrast with the free grouping of trees at the northern end and provide a foil for the two heroic pieces of sculpture, gifts from the USSR and Yugoslavia to the UN.

Hidden in the trees at the far end of the park is a memorial to Eleanor Roosevelt. A semicircular stone seat faces a pink marble tablet on which are inscribed the following words:

She would rather light a candle than curse the darkness and her glow has warmed the world.

Look closely for this secluded niche. It's easy to miss.

Leave the park by the north entrance if the gate is open and continue up First Avenue to Mitchell Place. If you feel like a rest there's a cocktail bar at the top of Beekman Towers with a splendid view over midtown. Next door is Peartree's, a popular place for UN personalities and jet setters.

Beekman Place, just around the corner, is one of those small New York enclaves full of the aura of the old Four Hundred days. Although cramped by tall apartment houses, this row of townhouses still possesses a distinctly aloof and refined character. As Oscar Wilde once remarked, "Breeding can never be disguised."

Many New York notables have lived here—the Rockefellers, Ethel Barrymore, Irving Berlin, Katharine Cornell, and other famous theatrical personalities. The area is named after William Beekman, a contemporary of Peter Stuyvesant. They sailed to America together and his son, James, built his Mount Pleasant Mansion here on the hill overlooking the East River and Turtle Bay. Some of the furnishings of the house are on display in the New-York Historical Society building at Central Park West and 77th Street. (The exhibitions here and at the Museum of the City of New York, Fifth Avenue between 103rd and 104th streets, are excellent and should be a regular part of any New Yorker's exploration itinerary.)

Beekman Place abounds with historical tales: General Howe established his headquarters on the Mount Pleasant Estate, Nathan Hale was captured and hanged nearby, and arrangements were made here by the British to accept the assistance of Benedict Arnold. Today it's all very quiet and restrained. Uniformed doormen officiously watch every stranger on the street. Limousines glide silently to chandelier-adorned foyers, and the only disturbance comes from the occasional overfed poodle, yapping at some other equally pampered specimen in the street.

At the end of 51st Street there's a footbridge over the tiny roadside park, across FDR Drive, to a riverside walk. Here residents occasionally gather to watch the East River scene (those residents, that is, without their own river view) or sunbathe while traffic roars by a few feet away.

Continue northward and take 53rd Street east to Sutton Place.

This is indeed a unique corner of the city. Short cul-de-sacs on the side streets off Sutton Place end in tiny parks and play areas. Select groups of townhouses on 57th and 58th streets nestle together, oblivious to the great blank blocks of apartments nearby and the continuous rumble from the Queensboro Bridge. It's a world apart. One of the rooms above the street on 58th has on display the heads of various types of deer and gazelle. Doubtless there's a tiger skin complete with unblinking eyes on the floor and a gun room off the hall. Two Lamborghinis (his black, hers white) purr outside a gray Georgian-style house with canary-yellow shutters. Little gnomes hide in the shrubbery of enclosed gardens overlooking the river. The smell of pollen-laden flowers wafts over the walls. There's no sign of life in the houses and somehow that too is appropriate. People would seem far too intrusive in this setting of arcadian tranquility.

Stroll westward to Second Avenue. Turn left to 56th Street and visit another antique complex in this neighborhood of antique stores—the Manhattan Arts and Antique Center (Monday–Saturday 10 A.M.–6:30 P.M., Sunday noon–6 P.M.). Here are more than eighty-five unusual stores and galleries displaying all manner of silver objets d'art, Oriental artworks, icons, ceramics, jewelry, crystal, porcelains, wedgwood, furniture, chandeliers, contemporary fine arts—even African sculptures and Tibetan temple ornaments. One can tell just by the Rolls-Royce and Ferrari showrooms nearby that this is a monied enclave. The two lower levels of the center contain some of the most magnificent displays of antiques and art treasures in the city. According to one of the eloquent store owners it's a "veritable vortex of vicarious experiences"!

If you find all this wealth beginning to pall, take a ride in the Roosevelt Island cable car from Second Avenue and 59th Street and regain your perspective on the city. In fact, you'll gain an entirely fresh perspective up here as the yellow wheels turn, sending the little box climbing high above the rooftops and the avenues. Down below, looking north, you can see the Abigail Adams Smith Museum, looking strangely out of place. There's a virtual jungle on the top of a large warehouse nearby (Terrestris)—a hothouse filled with trees and shrubs surrounded by black roofs and odd groups of chimneys. Then comes the East River with its chubby tugboats, views of the Roosevelt Island residential complex, and the descent to the terminal. It's quite a change from subway travel. Everyone seems to know everyone. The operator of the car is on first-name terms with many of his passengers. For most of the journey he discusses the care of azaleas with a distinguished-looking gentleman in a vicuña coat. If you'd like a sidetrip through the growing community here, take one of the jitney buses. Then return to "the mainland" by cable car and watch the apartment towers go by with their hundreds of tiny rooms inhabited by hundreds of cliff dwellers.

By the time you arrive back at 59th Street you'll have a different view of the city. Maybe you'll want to go roaring off to the country to find places where trees don't grow in hothouses on warehouse rooftops. Maybe instead you'll love the city a little more, in which case visit the Abigail Adams Smith Museum at 421 East 61st at York Avenue (Monday–Friday 10 A.M.–4 P.M. $1) for one of the final surprises of the walk. Tucked between a parking garage and a new block of apartments is a 1799 stone carriage house built on the estate of Colonel William Stephens Smith, husband of John Adams's daughter Abigail and aide-de-camp to George Washington. Smith named his estate Mount Vernon in honor of his chief's favorite home but after a reversal in his financial fortunes was obliged to sell all twenty acres. The coach house was subsequently used as an inn, a private home, and a Salvation Army soup kitchen until, in 1924, it was purchased by the Colonial Dames of America. Massive refurbishing was necessary, but today this remnant of Smith's folly, as the estate was once known, is a charming museum of early nineteenth-century life. It's usually quiet here, especially during the week, and guided tours are provided by a representative of the Dames. There are a few reminders of its original function, but the building has been successfully converted into living space tastefully decorated and is full of elegant furniture. In one of the upstairs rooms there are framed letters from George Washington and President John Adams who, in an awkwardly formal letter to his daughter, wrote:

> I have received your pretty letter and it has given me a great deal of pleasure, both as it is a token of your duty and affection to me and as it is proof of improvement in your handwriting and in the faculties of the mind.

Typical Adams sentiments!

This is a most refreshing place to spend an hour or so, and if you're a little foot-weary there's a small garden at the rear of the

Abigail Adams Smith House

house where you can rest. But try to conserve enough energy for a
final stroll up to the Treadwell Farm district, on 61st and 62nd
streets between Second and Third avenues. Here are two of the
most attractive streets in this part of town, so very close to, yet totally divorced from, the burgeoning 59th Street scene around
Bloomingdale's. As one might expect, many of these elegant town-

houses, built between 1868 and 1876 on land that was originally Adam Treadwell's farm, have been occupied by New York notables including Paul Gallico, Gertrude Lawrence, and Eleanor Roosevelt, and continue to retain their dignity and charm despite rampant redevelopment all around. It's a lovely place to end the walk.

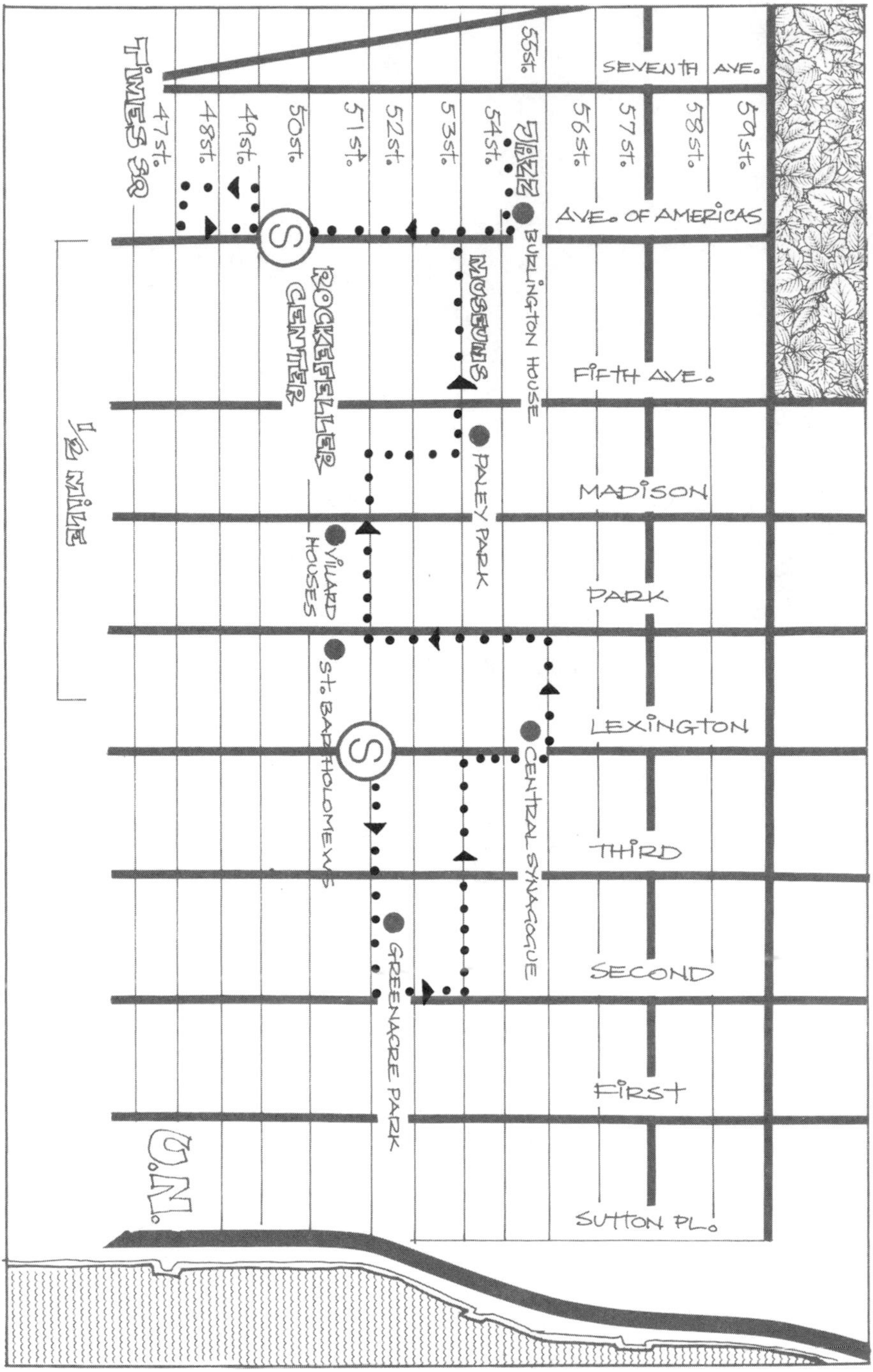
TIMES SQ
47 st.
48st.
49st.
50st.
51st.
52st.
53st.
54st.
55st.
56st.
57st.
58st.
59st.
SEVENTH AVE.
AVE. OF AMERICAS
FIFTH AVE.
MADISON
PARK
LEXINGTON
THIRD
SECOND
FIRST
SUTTON PL.
JAZZ
MUSEUMS
ROCKEFELLER CENTER
BURLINGTON HOUSE
PALEY PARK
VILLARD HOUSES
St. BARTHOLOMEW'S
CENTRAL SYNAGOGUE
GREENACRE PARK
1/2 MILE
U.N.
S
S

9
MIDTOWN

It seems perhaps a little unnecessary to rest in a setting of water-falls and landscaped terraces at the beginning of a walk. However, in the case of Greenacre Park (51st Street between Third and Second avenues) it's impossible to resist a short sojourn in this delightful niche, given by Abby Rockefeller Mauzé to provide "some moments of serenity in this busy world." A refreshment stand near the entrance offers ice cream and sodas, and people sit in dainty white chairs sucking ice cream cones, nibbling sandwiches (the Broodje shop across the street has a delectable array of Dutch sandwiches—cold cuts on soft buttered rolls), and chatting indolently while sparrows and pigeons pick and peck among the feet. Lovers nuzzle at the base of the "waterfall." The sound of tumbling water soothes the frazzled nerves of editors, advertising executives, television producers, journalists, radio commentators, and all the mélange of media people who seem to populate this part of town. Even on warm Sundays, the park is filled with people. (Of course, if the water itself is inadequate to calm disturbed nerves, next door to the park is the Primal Institute, a counseling center that uses Arthur Janov's primal therapy research and techniques.)

DIRECTIONS

Subway: *Start:* IND E, F to Lexington Avenue–3rd Avenue at 53rd Street, or IRT 6 to 51st Street and Lexington Avenue
  Return: IND F, B, D at Rockefeller Center/Sixth Avenue
Bus: *Start:* M101, M102 (north/south), M27 (east /west)
  Return: M5, M6, M7 (north/south), M27 (east/west)

117

There are other equally convenient outlets for rapid relaxation nearby. On 50th Street, close to its junction with Second Avenue, are three of the city's most renowned gourmet establishments: Lutèce, the Box Tree, and the Leopard. You may have to look closely to find them. All possess modest façades and are the essence of understatement. Some of the Lutèce regulars even think the restaurant's diminutive sign a little excessive. "After all," as one dapper client told me, "those who know it, know it, and those who don't, don't need to."

Up Second Avenue between 51st and 53rd streets is a splendid selection of Irish taverns, perfect for the liquid-luncher or boisterous evenings with the boys. Duncan's, Desmond's, the Green Derby, Flanagan's, and Danny Boy's are all within easy beer-drinking distance of one another. The Green Derby in particular seems to have a noted celebrity following, with such notables as Jimmy Breslin, Tommy Makem (of the Clancy brothers), the Irish Rovers, and even Bernadette Devlin passing through occasionally, to the delight of the regulars.

So—we've hardly begun, and already we've had a pleasant sit in a garden, eaten in a fancy restaurant, or blarneyed with the boys at the bars. It seems that this particular part of the walk is not really conducive to walking, and a stop at Morrell and Company (Second Avenue at 53rd Street) merely exacerbates the problem. However, this amazingly diversified wine store should not be missed unless you feel an overwhelming urge to scurry along to the more cultural highlights of the tour.

Inside is a wonderland of wines, an Aladdin's cave brimming with bottles, some sparkling with brightly colored labels, others encrusted with cellar dust. Pick up Peter Jay Morrell's catalog and explore the hidden corners of this large establishment. His descriptions reflect a robust enthusiasm for the prime source of his livelihood: "Can I, in good conscience," he asks on the page devoted to Beaune-Theurons vintages, "recommend an $11 bottle of Beaune? The answer is 'Yes'—and Yes, again, for the rarity of enjoying a truly flawless jewel is a noble and enervating experience for only those Burgundy lovers who know how to truly appreciate one of the finest things in life."

Morrell offers customers opportunities to make special reservations for limited bottlings of rare Bordeaux wines, and although the catalog regularly contains prices in excess of $300 per case, one feels confident that these are fair appraisals of value.

Take a look at his range of California wines too. Rarely does one come across such an excellent array from the West Coast's lesser known vineyards. Many of Morrell's selections are hard to find even in San Francisco.

The nearby store of Wim and Karen contains mainly Scandinavian furniture. Even if you have no intention of buying, it's an exhilarating experience to find evidence of craftsmen whose work in wood, leather, tile, and glass matches the exacting standards of Savile Row tailors. If you feel like continuing your browse through the world of furniture there are always the myriad antique stores nearby, around Second and Third avenues, including the New York Antiques Center at 962 Third Avenue between 57th and 58th streets (Tuesday–Saturday 10:30 A.M.–5:30 P.M., Sunday 12–6 P.M.). If you're really serious, take a stroll north to 56th Street between Third and Lexington avenues and wander through the interior designers' showrooms, filled with a million ideas for the imaginative home decorator.

But we digress. Back on 53rd Street let's head west toward the awnings and colorful façades of a midtown restaurant row between Second and Third avenues. In the midst of a mouth-watering selection of Japanese, Italian, Thai, French, and steak restaurants we find an equally tempting establishment, the Quest Book Shop (Monday–Friday 10 A.M.–6 P.M.). This base of the New York Theosophical Society is renowned for its gourmet fare for the mind—a scintillating array of works on Zen, the occult, ESP, astrology, reincarnation, witchcraft, metaphysics, and just about every religion ever practiced by man.

One of the prime aims of the society is "to encourage the study of Comparative Religion, Philosophy and Science." Regular public programs are offered to familiarize nonmembers with the society's efforts to trace the common links and bonds among all major religions and bodies of philosophical thought. Lectures with such titles as "Marriage: A Zen Viewpoint," "Atlantis in the High Andes," and "Plato and Divine Ideation" attract a varied group, and the meditation workshop has proved to be one of the most popular sessions (call PL. 3-3835 for details). Even the casual book browser will find much of interest in the shop. On hot summer

Garden of the Theosophical Society

days the garden courtyard at the rear is a delightful place to rest a while with books selected from the shelves. How about *Satan and the Celtic Religions* or *The Secrets of Pyramid Power?* It's possible the aura of power radiates from the store. Nearby at the Maria Sin Sin restaurant, table eight is said to have the remarkable capacity to bring wealth and good fortune to its occupants. The comments of the man behind the counter at the bookshop when I gave him this piece of local folklore are unprintable.

On the corner of Lexington and 53rd Street are two notable institutions, the YWCA with its array of public courses, programs, exhibitions, and "events," and the Citicorp Center, about which so much has been written that its inclusion here seems almost superfluous. The former has been with us for many years. It's part of the fabric of the midtown "neighborhood." Citicorp, of course, has been a feature here only since 1978 when it opened to a great fanfare of editorials, critical analyses, and local TV "specials," and somehow survived all that to establish itself rapidly as the prime nucleus of eastern midtown. To do the place appropriate justice, a complete walking tour of its very unique nooks and crannies would be necessary. Suffice it here to suggest that you explore "the market" yourself—wander through the various levels of Conran's "everything-for-the-modern-home" store, sample the wares at the six lower-level restaurants, watch boules and baguettes baking in see-through ovens at Au Pain, sun yourself in the central glass-enclosed courtyard, meditate in the meditation room adjoining a chapel where jazz mingles movingly with religion and passersby peer in at the activities. Regular events and shows are staged in the atrium (Monday–Thursday 6–8 P.M., Saturday 11 A.M.–noon, Sunday 3–4 P.M.) for the enjoyment of everyone. There are even—wonder of wonders—clean, graffiti-free, no charge, rest rooms for the needy, an almost extinct facility in Manhattan. Nyborg-Nelson is here with its wonderful selection of Scandinavian foods, "Slotnick's Daughter" offers a bountiful array of coffees, teas, and spices, and the Doubleday Bookstore is a perfect place to browse after a languorous lunch.

The same might be said of the 1871 Central Synagogue (Lexington Avenue and 55th Street) except that this odd "Moorish revival in Gothic arrangement" structure is normally closed to the public. Nevertheless, it's worth making the short detour north to admire its octagonal towers topped by ornate copper domes and the Cordoba-like character of the lower arches and columns. The architect, Henry Fernbach, aware that the synagogue was commissioned by the earliest Reformed Jewish congregation in the city, decided to use this particular style to reflect the Near Eastern origins of Judaism. He considered the Gothic style, at that time the accepted vernacular for religious buildings, to be inappropriately "Christian." His ideas subsequently formed the basis for a popular school of synagogue design.

Friendship Park, another one of midtown's vest-pocket parks, is immediately adjacent to the synagogue and is usually one of the quieter niches for a brief rest.

Around the corner on 55th Street between Lexington and Park there's a fascinating array of architectural styles containing lesser-known places of interest in the district. At the Folio Society, for example, the public is invited to browse in the gallery of the society's publications (Monday–Saturday 10 A.M.–6 P.M). Here we find some of the finest examples of printed and illustrated books available today. Many are reprints of famous classics; others are more obscure works revived by the British-based society.

Next door is the Central Synagogue Community House, with a permanent exhibition of old Hebrew religious artifacts (Monday–Friday 9 A.M.–5 P.M.) and a gift store. Examples of traditional Jewish theater presented by New York's oldest theatrical company, the Folksbiene, are usually staged here between October and April (call 838-5122 for information).

Across the road (116 East 55th Street) is a remarkable re-creation of a Georgian-style mansion by architect William Laurence Bottomly complete with eagles on the gate pillars, wrought-iron fence, and dormer windows. Built in 1928, the building since 1969 has housed the Allied Bank International, a commercial institution not open to the general public.

At Park Avenue we turn south and peer down one of New York's classic "canyons" containing such notable office towers as Skidmore, Owings and Merrill's famous Lever House, Seagram, Colgate-Palmolive, Union Carbide, the Chemical Bank, and the American Brands buildings. "If only"—moaned one frustrated city planner—"if only we could have used some of the Rockefeller Center ideas here. What a wasted opportunity." Certainly comprehensive development of these vast properties would have enabled coordination of plazas, sunken gardens, pedestrian walkways, and other public/employee-oriented facilities. As it was, each block was developed independently. There are some half-hearted attempts at pedestrian thoroughfares and "plazas," but the results are pathetic—no Greenacre Park with waterfalls and dainty seats, just windswept forecourts and formal fountains. Even Robert Cook's powerful sculpture *Dinoceras* is tucked away down 51st Street and no sidewalk cafés lighten the scene.

Yet for all the missed opportunities here, one can hardly fail to be impressed by the powerful scale of the canyon, a "beehive" of tens of thousands of busy workers scurrying their days away behind the towering curtain wall-cliffs. Public exhibitions of art and sculpture regularly held in the Lever and the Union Carbide buildings dilute some of the aloofness of the avenue. Tours of the Seagram building are provided on Tuesdays at 3 P.M., at least a gesture to a public curious about life behind the million windows. Then of course there are the Racquet Club and St. Bartholomew's Church, both of which help retain the original scale and quality of the thoroughfare and act as effective foils to the monoliths. The former is a 1918 McKim, Mead and White creation designed in sober neo-Florentine style trimmed with rustic-cut granite. Ghostly figures of the elite can be seen moving at a wraithlike pace past the windows facing the street. One can almost smell the aroma of polished leather chairs and expensive cigars wafting across the avenue. The church also is impressive in its urbane Byzantine dignity even though, like Park Avenue itself, it is the combination of the work of many architects. McKim, Mead and White designed the sturdy Romanesque-style entrance porch in 1902. Bertram Grosvenor Goodhue conceived the powerful bulk of the church in 1917–19 and, after his death, the adjoining Community House was added by Goodhue's associates, Mayers, Murray and Philip—altogether a remarkable example of aesthetic coordination. (The great tower rising up behind the church is not, as some newcomers think, part of the structure. Although the ornate crest is quite cathedrallike, it is in fact the old General Electric building.) After passing through beautifully ornate doors we enter the church itself. It has the ponderous appearance of an Istanbul mosque complete with golden domes, thick mosaic-covered arches and vaults, and an almost encyclopedic array of marbles for the columns. Yet here is great majesty. One leaves New York briefly and journeys back to the early days of Christianity when architectural bulk was not only an engineering necessity but, more important, an expression of immense power. A deep golden light fills the whole structure. Whispered voices echo under the great dome.

Outside again, pause in the delightful little side garden with its Roman-style chairs and delicate waterfalls and regain your bearings.

If you enjoyed the brief interlude away from the city, the synergistic grouping of the Daniel Casriel Institute of Dynamics, the Sri Center for Human Growth, the Astrology Counseling Service, and the YOCA Meditation/Astrology Center may also appeal. These are located on the north side of 51st Street immediately west of Park Avenue.

Daniel Casriel, author of *A Scream Away from Happiness* (Grosset & Dunlap, 1972) was the first resident psychiatrist at Synanon in California and cofounder of Daytop on Staten Island. He uses "scream therapy" and group dynamics as components of a "New Identity Process," and informative leaflets can be picked up at the institute.

The Villard House on the corner of 51st and Madison Avenue once more reflects the remarkable talents of McKim, Mead and White. The challenge in this case was to design a unit of four houses to resemble one large mansion complete with carriage forecourt and ceremonial entrance. Using the neo-Italian-Renaissance style they accomplished the task with ease. Henry Villard, a Bavarian journalist and later a railroad tycoon and owner of the New York *Evening Post*, lived in the house on the corner of Madison Avenue and 50th Street. The other three houses he sold to friends. Later, part was taken over by the Roman Catholic Archdiocese of New York and the 51st Street corner mansion became the headquarters of Bennett's Cerf's Random House team from 1946 until 1969. In 1978 much of the entire structure was demolished to make room for a luxury hotel, but preservationists managed to ensure that the south wing and part of the north wing, including the famous Gold Room, would be saved.

Across the street, note what remains of the two wings of the Villard House mirrors a similar arrangement of the two identical buildings, the Rectory and the Cardinal's residence, that frame the French-Gothic–style Lady Chapel at the rear of St. Patrick's Cathedral. Impeccable examples of this level of architectural sympathy are rare in New York where each block, or occasionally each unit in each block, is designed with total disregard for its surroundings. The attitude of "it's my property and I can do what I want

Rear of St. Patrick's Cathedral

with it" (at least in architectural terms) has plagued virtually every effort of town design in the city. Enjoy this gem.

Avoiding Fifth Avenue and the crowds that invariably fill St. Patrick's, stroll through the interior courts of Olympic Place with its waterfall and seating areas and out past the Iranian Handicraft Center (well worth a visit) to Paley Park (53rd Street, just east of Fifth Avenue), another delightful niche for lunchtime sunning.

Next to the park is one of the city's least-known museums, the Museum of Broadcasting (Tuesday–Saturday noon–5 P.M. Contribution $1.50, children 75¢). Here, thanks to the cooperation of the broadcasting networks, is an incredible inventory of significant radio and television programs from the twenties to the present day. The interested visitor can watch and listen to everything from broadcast speeches by all U.S. presidents since Warren G. Harding and early comedy routines by Bert Lahr and Bea Lillie to Judy Garland's radio debut when she was twelve, or a host of carefully indexed commercials.

The museum's most popular videotapes include the Edward R. Murrow and Joseph McCarthy discussions, the Beatles on the Ed Sullivan Show, the TV version of Alex Haley's *Roots*, and Alistair Cooke's famous series, "America." It's a marvelous way to spend an hour or two, browsing through the index cards, selecting the tapes, and sitting at your own console watching your favorite TV shows.

Two other little-known attractions nearby are the Austrian Institute at 11 East 52nd Street (759-5165), where occasional lectures and exhibitions are open to the public, and the Israeli Art Center at the America-Israel Cultural Foundation, housed in a "handsome survivor of an opulent age" at 4 East 54th Street (751-2700). This high-Renaissance townhouse (yet another McKim, Mead and White creation) was built for the industrialist William H. Moore, founder of the United States Steel Corporation, the American Can Company, and the National Biscuit Company. Today it contains an interesting and ever-changing array of Israeli arts and crafts, many of which are for sale.

Pause at St. Thomas's Church at Fifth Avenue and 53rd Street (music recitals are featured here on Wednesday at lunchtime from 12:10 P.M.). Compared with St. Patrick's it tends to be rather quiet, and there's a sense of tranquillity here I find quite extraordinary. It's not unusual to see briefcase-carrying businessmen scurry in, hunched and scowling, and leave after five minutes' silence, walking at a measured pace with an almost bouncy air. (A similar transformation also seems to take place at the Top of the Sixes bar in the adjoining Tishman building as a result of spectacular views over Central Park—and large cocktails!) Like St. Bartholomew's, this oddly asymmetrical church is the work of Bertram Grosvenor Goodhue and is regarded by many architects as his finest creation in the city. Finally consecrated in 1914, it replaced an 1870 structure destroyed by fire in 1905. Its reputation as an appropriate church for fashionable marriages is reflected in the dollar sign carved next to the lovers' knot above the Brides' door (to the left of the main entrance). Inside, the gentle yellow sandstone provides a suitably neutral background for the exquisite richness of the rose window; and the magnificent reredos or altar screen, one of the largest in the world. This symphony of carved niches, pinnacles, and crenelations in ivory-tone Dunville stone from Wisconsin was the work of Lee Lawrie, and a special folder obtainable in the church gives details of the figures contained in the work. In the late afternoon when the sun shines through the sapphire-blue windows behind the white screen, visitors are easily brought to tears. It's a hard place to leave.

But leave we must, and enter one of the city's most popular street segments—53rd between Fifth and Sixth avenues. It's hardly appropriate for a guide to nooks and crannies to dwell at length on the delights of this "museum row." However, even long-time residents must occasionally be reminded that in addition to the famous Donnell Library with its endless lists of events and services (pick up the flyers at the information desk), and the Museum of Modern Art with its sculpture garden and incredible array of contemporary artwork, the street also contains other lesser-known attractions. These include MOMA's bookstore and sales annex (the catalog itself is a work of art), the Museum of Contemporary Crafts (Tuesday–Saturday 11 A.M.–6 P.M., Sunday 1–6 P.M. Adults $1, under 15, 25¢), the Museum of American Folk Art (daily except Mondays 10:30 A.M.–5:30 P.M. Adults $1, children 50¢), the American Crafts Council (useful information on craft shops and galleries in the city; Monday–Friday 11 A.M.–5:30 P.M.), and various other art-related stores. One needs at least a day—preferably two—to enjoy all the riches the street has to offer. And there's even more nearby. The Mill at Burlington House, Sixth Avenue and 54th Street (Tuesday–Saturday 10 A.M.–7 P.M. Free) provides a brief moving-walkway guide to textile production complete with hosiery-knitting machines, dye vats, double knitters, shuttleless looms, and about five thousand color slides flashed to a background of rock music.

But museums and exhibitions, no matter how brilliant and varied, can pall a little after the second day (or hour, for some). So look out for the ticket distributors on Sixth Avenue around the ABC and CBS studios at 53rd Street or at the NBC headquarters farther down the avenue at Rockefeller Center. Of course there's the grand old Rockefeller Center tour, one of the city's classic experiences—adults $2.15, children $1.35.) Although most television shows are now filmed on the West Coast, there are a few soap operas and game shows left in New York. It's the latter that bring the crowds—to be prepped by the prompter man, rehearsed in laughter and applause techniques by the announcer, and titillated by a half hour's high jinks on some curious show. If you've never attended one of these affairs, it's fun (once).

Alternatively, if you can arrange to while away the early part of the evening at a restaurant or show, you may wish to relive a little of the jazz era at Eddie Condon's or Jimmy Ryan's on 54th Street (both start jumping around 10 P.M.). In the mid-thirties this part of the city was the jazz center of the world. Scores of smoke-filled clubs occupied the cramped basements of old brownstones along "Swing Street," featuring such popular notables as Billie Holliday, Count Basie, Billy Daniels, and Nat "King" Cole. Roy Eldridge has been resident band leader and one of the prime attractions at Jimmy Ryan's for more than seven years. "Hell, it's beautiful," he says. "I've got a good rhythm section. The cats are nice and it's like a home, man, after traveling for fifty years." (If jazz isn't your style, the East Fifties, once the home of the Stork Club and El Morocco, still maintain their reputation for night life in the form of supper clubs and discos.)

Of course, you may still be on the culture trail, in which case there are a few points of interest as you make your way southward along Sixth Avenue. The Equitable Gallery (between 52nd and 51st streets, Monday–Friday 10 A.M.–5 P.M. Free) normally has an excellent display of paintings and sculpture on the second floor, and if you're thinking of taking any out-of-town journeys (possibly as a relief from all this walking), then a visit to the travel-information center in the Exxon building will insure you an adequate supply of excellent maps. Farther down, the popular "New York Experience" multimedia show (Monday–Thursday 11 A.M.–7 P.M. on the hour, Friday–Sunday noon–8 P.M. Adults $2.25, under 12, $1.25) is presented in the basement of the McGraw-Hill building at 49th Street (the bookstore is an excellent place for browsing too).

If you're ready for a brief rest in yet another of those delicious little parks that dot this route, stroll to the rear of the McGraw-Hill building and you'll find an idyllic niche of water cascades, shrubbery, and seats. It's a quiet, lesser-known link between 48th and 50th streets, and an excellent place to rest your aching feet.

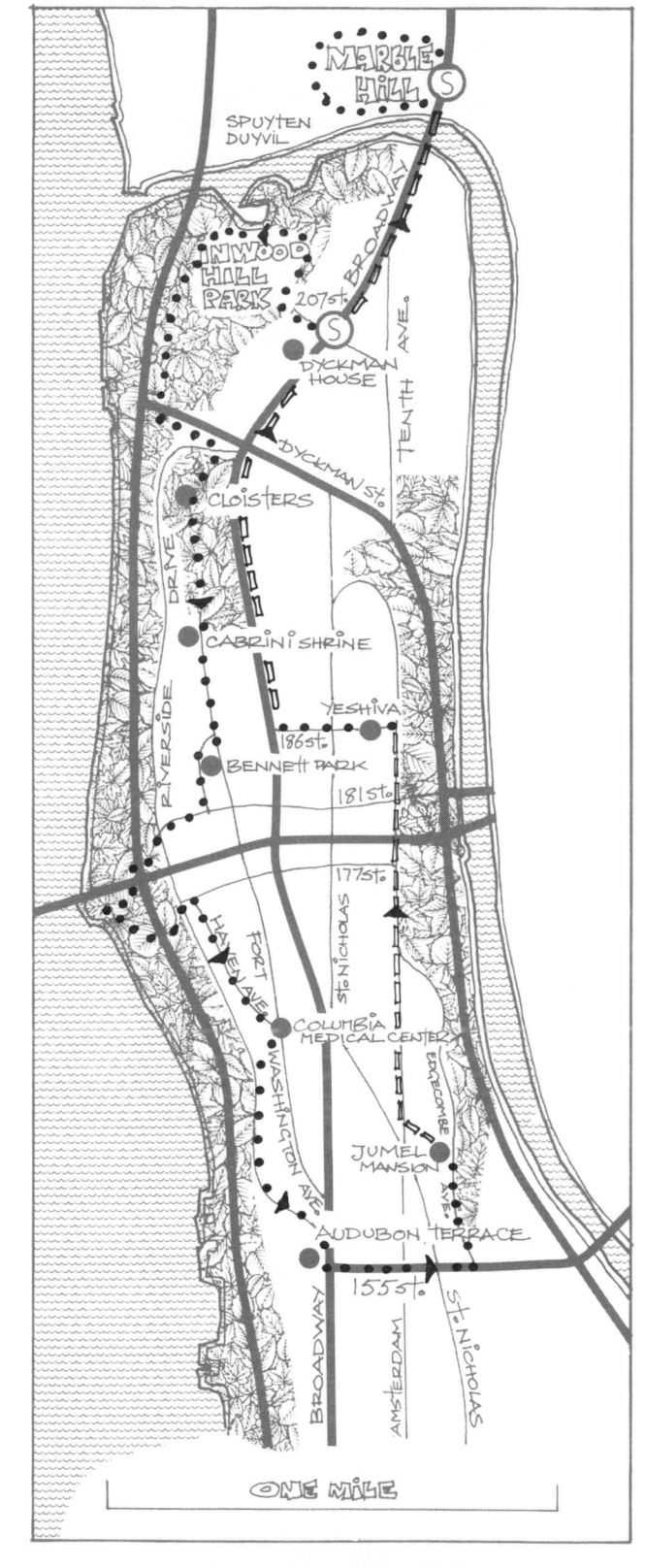

MARBLE HILL Ⓢ

SPUYTEN
DUYVIL

INWOOD
HILL
PARK

207st.

BROADWAY

TENTH AVE.

Ⓢ

DYCKMAN
HOUSE

DYCKMAN ST.

RIVERSIDE DRIVE

CLOISTERS

CABRINI SHRINE

YESHIVA

186st.

BENNETT PARK

181st.

177st.

FORT HAVEN AVE.

ST. NICHOLAS

WASHINGTON AVE.

COLUMBIA
MEDICAL CENTER

EDGECOMBE AVE.

JUMEL
MANSION

AUDUBON TERRACE

155st.

ST. NICHOLAS

BROADWAY

AMSTERDAM

ONE MILE

10
INWOOD—
WASHINGTON
HEIGHTS

The balcony at the United Church, 175th and Broadway, shakes alarmingly as a thousand feet bounce to the beat of "Joy to the World." A large black woman in a gold-sequined hat three times bigger than her head grabs my hand and shouts into my face, "God specializes, God specializes." A man on my right is leaping two, maybe three, feet off the floor, tears streaming over his cheeks, mingling with sweat spinning off his nose and chin. A small girl turns cartwheels in the aisles. Both organs roar out the crashing chords. The drummer bobs and shakes with the rhythm. The choir, full of little bouncing boys, is a gyrating mass of blue and red gowns. Above it all, on a dais, the Reverend Frederick Eikerenkoetter, better known as Reverend Ike, drinks from one of two sparkling silver goblets brought to him by an assistant on a gleaming silver tray, and watches the audience carefully. He raises

————————— DIRECTIONS —————————

The walking tour starts at the Dyckman House, Broadway and 204th Street.
Subway: *Start:* IND A to 207th Street and Broadway
  Return: IND AA, B at 163rd Street and Amsterdam Avenue
  IRT 1 at 181st Street and St. Nicholas Avenue or
  IRT 1 at 225th Street and Broadway in Marble Hill
Bus: *Start:* M100
  Return: M2, M3, M4, M5, M100, M101

131

a hand and the frenzy starts to slow. He raises both hands: "Lift up your hands as high as you can," he cries out to the audience. "Lift them up—up—and say after me: 'You cannot outgive God, you cannot outgive God.' " The response is full and unanimous. "God does not grow feeble with age and neither do I. C'mon," shouts the reverend, "Say it—say it loud, say it after me . . . 'God does not . . .' "

It's just another typical Sunday in the ornate temple, an old Loew's theater, in Washington Heights. Soon Reverend Ike—his curly black hair glistening with pomade, his voice as powerful as Little Richard's, his rings flashing in the spotlights—will begin his message of material wealth and well-being—the gospel of "green power." He'll read testimonials from followers who gave generously to his ministry and were blessed in return with Cadillacs, diamonds, mink coats—and good health. He'll tell them to "Think rich," he'll have them screaming out in unison: "You can't lose with the stuff I use." He'll have them loving him and coming back again week after week.

Not far away, on the line of benches below the old Dyckman Farmhouse, groups of elderly residents talk together quietly and

The Dyckman House

enjoy the silence of Sunday streets. Over in Inwood Park, just past the Columbia Boathouse on Spuyten Duyvil Creek, a couple stroll arm in arm up the hill to the caves in the rock where Indians lived centuries before the first European settlers sailed up the Hudson.

At Audubon Terrace on 155th Street four young students are leaving the Hispanic Museum. "It's fantastic," says one of them. "I never knew this place was here."

In Morris Park visitors stand at the fence and look out over High Bridge Park, and across the river to Queens and Brooklyn. Behind them is the eighteenth-century Jumel Mansion—Washington's headquarters during September 1776—with its great white portico and delicate balcony. Over to the west, down under the towers of the George Washington bridge, a child, hand in hand with his father, stands and smiles at the Little Red Lighthouse. Inside the Mother Cabrini Shrine, near the entrance to the Fort Tryon Gardens, rosaries click and people pray, their eyes fixed on the remains of the saint in the glass coffin below the altar.

"You know, the crazy thing is, if you took this top part of Manhattan and put it down anywhere else, it would be one of the biggest tourist attractions in the country." I was chatting with Carol Silagyi, who with Heather Schweder, constitutes "Arts Interaction" for this northern tip of the island. "There're more than one hundred sixty thousand people living up here, y'know, we're the same size as Syracuse. There are nine major museums, two world-famous universities, all kinds of historic buildings and landmarks, a dozen sites commemorating the Revolution, over six thousand acres of parks—and yet we're ignored. Many people who've lived in Manhattan for years have never been here—except maybe for that one visit to the Cloisters. Even local residents don't know the area."

The aim of Arts Interaction is simple—to put Washington Heights, Inwood, and Marble Hill on the map. Carol and Heather produce poster campaigns and directories, publicize local events, and operate an information hotline (928-8800). "You could spend days exploring these neighborhoods—there's so much going on and so many places to see. Just give me a couple of hours," Carol told me, "and I'll show you what I mean." She did. I was taken on a fascinating journey and was introduced to one of the most interesting, and, in places, most beautiful parts of New York.

We begin at the Dyckman Farmhouse (1783) perched on a rocky garden high above the sidewalk at Broadway and 204th Street (11 A.M. – 5 P.M.; closed Monday). People tend to associate Inwood with somber blocks of gray apartments, the screeching of the el as it twists its way north to the Bronx, or grubby, overused parks devoid of grass. They might be surprised to learn that not very long ago this was verdant farmland surrounded by dense forests. They may also be surprised to learn that much of the natural landscape still remains. On a summer day the garden behind the old farmhouse is full of shade and the smell of flowers. The traffic seems far away. Just down the street there's the great green bowl of Inwood Park with its hidden valley walks and views across to the rocky precipice of the Palisades. Inside the farmhouse it's dark and cool. When the door is closed, you enter a little world of candlelight, of small, simple rooms furnished with eighteenth- and nineteenth-century pieces, many based on Chippendale designs. The ceilings are low, particularly in the basement, which contains the kitchen and a small display of artifacts from the revolutionary period. As you descend, head bowed to chest level, note the intrusion of Manhattan rock on which the farmhouse is built. Many of the objects, the clay pipes, old pieces of stained silverware, wine bottles, and even bone buttons from military uniforms were found in the garden. It was used as a military encampment for much of the revolutionary period, and a replica of one of the soldiers' log huts, complete with log roof, can be found down the path at the back of the house.

The old people of the neighborhood gather daily in ritual fashion at the benches below the farmhouse. They think it's one of the nicest places in the city and consider it their exclusive territory. While I was there a stranger strolled up, selected a bench at random, and sat down. One lady was most upset and murmured to her companions, "That's Mrs. Epstein's seat. He shouldn't sit there, you know." There was a brief flurry of discussion among the ladies. They decided that someone had to tell him that it was one of "their" benches. The ones at the top end, away from the corner, were for "outsiders." Fortunately, a bus came, the man left his seat, and the problem was resolved. Mrs. Epstein, who had gone around the corner to chat with a man friend, hurried back to reclaim her seat and the ritual continued.

Take one of the streets west from Broadway and stroll into In-wood Hill Park—one of the few unspoiled and undiscovered parks in Manhattan. Across the ball fields there's the Spuyten Duyvil Creek and the "new" stretch of the Harlem River. In 1895 a short-ened link was made to improve navigation around the top part of the island. The old arc of river that ran around what is now known as Marble Hill was filled in. Marble Hill was abruptly cut off from the city and became a continuum of the Bronx. The residents, however, were having none of that and demanded to remain Man-hattanites. We visit this strange little fifty-acre parcel later in the journey.

Down by the Duyvil Creek is the Columbia Boathouse, de-murely contrasting with the great apartment towers on the other bank. The rail line disappears behind a slice of hillside inscribed with a huge blue-and-white "C." Painting this creation, the larg-est piece of graffiti in the city, was a popular hazing escapade for Columbia freshmen and is now officially discouraged.

At the western edge of the park's grass fields, where the woods begin, there's a gray boulder set in the pathway. A plaque here marks the site of the largest Indian village on Manhattan, Skorak-kopoch, and claims this as the place where Peter Minuit reached agreement with the Indians for that famous twenty-four-dollar sale in 1626. There's much dispute about the authenticity of this site. Many historians believe the transaction took place at the southern tip of the island where the Dutch settled. But somehow this seems the more impressive location. One can visualize the In-dian village here on the slope of the meadow, canoes lining the river bank and smoke wafting through the woods enclosing the natural amphitheater. Higher up there are caves in the hillside once occupied by the Indians.

Pick a path at random and stroll into the woods. Not many peo-ple come this way, particularly during the week, and there's a silence you won't find anywhere else in Manhattan. As with many of New York's parks it needs some restoration, but the overgrown character of the place only serves to emphasize its sense of sepa-rateness from the city.

When I come here I normally head south through the woods, taking the western ridge with its occasional views across to the Palisades. After half a mile or so the land drops steeply and the path leads out of the park, over a bridge alongside the Henry Hudson Parkway, around the curve of Riverside Drive, and into Fort Tryon Park. It's a nuisance the parks are not contiguous, but the link is short and in no time you're walking up through the woods to the Cloisters (Tuesday–Saturday 10 A.M.–5 P.M., Sunday 1–5 P.M. Contribution). I once made the mistake of taking the shorter route, up the steps. It was like the traditional mountain-climbing experience where the higher you ascend, the farther away the summit appears to be. Only choose this route if you're one of those sweat-suit type of people determined to make /life hard for yourself.

The Cloisters, of course, is a prime New York landmark, amply described in almost every available guidebook and pamphlet. Suffice it to say that it's also one of my favorite not-so-hidden places. I experience different sensations and discover new niches every time I explore its cool rooms filled with medieval works of art— tapestries, altarpieces, icons, sculptures, chalices, statuettes, and, in the treasury, some of the most highly prized medieval religious works in the world. It's hard to imagine a more pleasant way to spend a hot afternoon than sitting in the St. Michael de Cuxa courtyard listening to the ageless Gregorian chants. Unfortunately, most New Yorkers visit Inwood just to see the Cloisters, Fort Tryon, and the gardens and then hurry back down on the 190th Street subway. Those with a more adventurous bent should now join our walk southward into Washington Heights. Before leaving the park, however, pause on one of the terraces of the old fort and enjoy the fine views of northern New York, the Hudson, and the Palisades.

Just outside the park on Fort Washington Avenue is the Mother Cabrini Chapel, named in honor of America's first citizen to be canonized—Saint Francesca Saverio Cabrini, who attained beatification in November 1938. The wall around the altar is covered in mosaics depicting incidents in her life. She was a tiny person, full of energy, who founded orphanages, child-care centers, hospitals, and homes for the aged, and made twenty-five Atlantic crossings establishing other similar centers outside the country. She died, exhausted, in 1917, and her remains are entombed in a glass coffin under the altar. The nuns who run the little relics-and-souvenir stand just down the corridor from the chapel speak of her as if she were still alive. It's a rather touching place.

Continue a short distance southward on Fort Washington Avenue to Bennett Park, site of the original Fort Washington. Built in 1776 by the patriots, it was soon captured by the British and remained in their hands until the end of the war. A wall inside the park is a partial reproduction of a segment of the original structure. The land was later owned by the Bennett family and was presented to the city in 1903 by James Gordon Bennett, Jr., errant son of the *New York Herald*'s stern owner. Known for his passionate indulgence in most of the conventional, and a few unconventional, sensual activities, James finally disgraced himself at a New Year's party given by the family of his bride-to-be. It was an occasion characterized by all the pomp and puffery of high wealth and the affair was a splendid success until Mr. Bennett, hailing the onset of 1877 through a brandy haze, decided to relieve himself in the main fireplace in front of the guests. Shortly thereafter he left New York for Paris, brideless, and returned to the city only when business required and/or to consult with the architect Stanford White about his proposed mausoleum—a 200-foot-high hollow statue of an owl where his body would be suspended in a casket hung on chains inside the owl's head. White was shot, however, before the project come to fruition and Bennett was buried in a far more modest manner at Passy, Paris. All we have left of him is his park, a delightfully urban enclave bounded on the west side by the medieval-style Hudson View gardens. Although there's a "private" sign at the gate of the apartment complex, visitors often stroll along its quaint interior street lined with rockeries and rose bushes, and pause to admire the fine views across the river. Unfortunately, though, for many of the residents, the views are not what they once were. A new complex full of tall red brick towers known as Castle Village was built directly in front of the Hudson View gardens by a Dr. Paterno, on a terrace of land previously occupied by his private castle. According to a plaque on the wall near the office, the doctor was a most philanthropic developer:

> In apartments he built, he lightened burdens with labor-saving conveniences and lifted the spirit with the beauty of gardens.

Some say, however, that he built his village primarily for spite when a close friend was prevented from purchasing a property in the Hudson View complex. But whatever the story, there are certainly some lovely gardens and viewing platforms, although members of the public are not always encouraged to walk here.

Follow Pinehurst Avenue on the west side of Bennett Park south a short distance and then descend a palatial set of steps leading to 181st Street. Here, just briefly, walk up the hill, to Fort Washington Avenue and note the building on the southeast corner. This is one of scores of buildings in this part of town richly adorned with sculpture. The larger-than-life figures here are splendid caricatures—but of whom? No one I talked to in the area seemed to know. Note the one on the corner, with glasses. Not far away at 165th Street and Broadway is the Audubon Ballroom, where Malcolm X was shot. That too possesses some magnificent ceramic details, including an almost life-size Viking ship above the main entrance. Many of the apartment buildings, somber and austere on the outside, contain hidden courtyards, fountains, lobbies rich in Italian marbles, mahogany paneling, stained-glass windows, and in the case of the apartments on the corner of 159th Street and Edgecombe, a complete ceiling of stained glass thought to be Tiffany in origin. Gargoyle-gazing and lobby-looking could become a popular local pastime.

But we digress. At the base of the steps on 181st Street those with energy to spare should continue west to Riverside Drive, take the footbridge over the Henry Hudson Parkway, follow the path through the underpass to the base of the George Washington bridge, and arrive finally at the famous Little Red Lighthouse sitting coyly in the shadow of the "Great Grey Bridge," just as described in the beloved children's story. "This is my fav'rite bridge," I was told by an Irish bridge painter, sitting in the sunshine drinking a lunchtime beer. "Why, I've worked on just about every one in the city, but this one, she's the best, 'specially when you get upstairs. That's a view worth braggin' about. 'Course it attracts the sad ones, y'know. Somethin' about this bridge that attracts the sad ones. A fella this mornin', 'bout seven it was, he jumped. Police came around. Couldn't find a thing. Hardly ever do. But it's still a lovely piece of work." He slapped the base of one of the great piers. "She's built to last, this one," he said.

Take time to explore the area around the bridge. On the north side there are creeks and shallows hidden from the path where you can spend a whole day undisturbed, oblivious to the city at your back.

To the south there's a long riverside walk leading all the way to a footbridge at 155th Street that brings you up alongside Trinity Cemetery and Audubon Terrace. It's beautiful along the edge of the river, accompanied by ducks and sea gulls, but the bridge is not recommended. Instead take the alternative climb back up the Heights, coming out at 177th Street and Haven Avenue. Of course, those who feel the detour to the lighthouse is a bit much just to dangle feet in the Hudson will have slipped down Fort Washington Avenue from 181st Street. Either way, the route now leads southward past the new Long library building into the heart of the Columbia Medical Center and that delightful park at 168th Street, near the Eye Institute and the church. Be careful not to get the parks confused—the one on the west side of Fort Washington Avenue is for resident nurses only.

At 163rd Street there's another choice to be made. Either follow Fort Washington Avenue south to Broadway and on to Audubon Terrace at 155th Street or turn right, walk to Riverside Drive, turn left and follow the curve of the street past groups of ornate apartment buildings and smaller, but richly decorated, row houses. This is one of Manhattan's little baroque backwaters—too mixed architecturally to become a historic district but totally charming nonetheless. Closer to Broadway it becomes a little seedy, but that oasis of culture, Audubon Terrace, is looming up ahead, so scurry into its comforting confines, beyond the huge Indian totem pole that peers incongruously over the refined neoclassic architecture.

Like the Cloisters, Audubon Terrace is a well-loved, well-publicized New York attraction. For some reason, though, its diversity of museums is often ignored and attendance during the last few years has been disappointing. Recently the American Geographic Society (Monday–Wednesday 9 A.M.–noon, by appointment. Free) almost had to give up its premises because of a lack of funds, and there's even been talk of relocating the most popular of the remaining five museums, the Museum of the American Indian (Tuesday–Sunday 1–5 P.M. Adults $1, others 50¢), in some more nationally central site. Certainly it seems ridiculous that only a tiny proportion of its more than four million artifacts can be shown here because of lack of space and limited museum funding. By far the largest part of the collection is in a vast Bronx warehouse, closed to the public.

There are currently four other museums in the terrace. The Hispanic Museum (Tuesday–Saturday 10 A.M.–4:30 P.M., Sunday 1–5 P.M. Free) contains an extravagant collection of Spanish art, sculpture, and crafts from the Visigothic period to the contemporary era. Most noted are paintings by Goya and Velasquez and El Greco, and a series of bullfight etchings by Goya. The library, off the richly decorated main gallery, contains more than 100,000 volumes, including 12,000 published prior to 1700.

Behind the ornate bronze doors of the American Numismatic Society Museum, at the southern rear corner of the terrace (Tuesday–Saturday 9 A.M.–4:30 P.M., Sunday 1–4 P.M. Free) is one of the world's largest collections of coins, paper currency, medals, and medallions. Even those previously uninformed in the subtleties and complexities of money will find the displays well documented and fascinating. Visitors invariably emerge peering at their small change, looking for that rare Lincoln penny.

Finally there's the American Academy of Arts and Letters (Tuesday–Sunday 1–4 P.M. Free) which, with its parent association, the National Institute of Arts and Letters, recognizes and honors the American creative spirit. The National Institute has 250 writers, poets, architects, composers, and artists as members and the even more exclusive academy has 50 members, selected for their unique and enduring contributions to the arts. They include such celebrities as Pearl S. Buck, John Dos Passos, Aaron Copland, Carl Sandburg, John Steinbeck, Andrew Wyeth, and Norman Mailer. In addition to bestowing honors the academy presents regular exhibitions and, on special request, makes available original manuscripts, first editions, and even the scratchpads, notebooks, and doodles of their famous creative members.

Ideally, a separate day should be given over to exploring the museums of Audubon Terrace. The displays and exhibitions are far too impressive and extensive to be enjoyed during a rigorous walking tour of the area.

Across from the terrace, at 155th Street, is Trinity Cemetery, resting place of many New York notables—Madame Jumel, John James Audubon (a tall cross next to a tiny bird box), Clement Moore (there's a candlelight procession here every Christmas Eve for the man who wrote " 'Twas the Night Before Christmas"), and the unfortunate Alfred Tennyson Dickens, son of Charles Dickens, who died abruptly in 1912 of a heart attack at the Hotel Astor while making preparations for his father's centenary celebrations. The cemetery was part of the second-line-of-defense earthworks during the Revolution, hence its rather incongruous undulations. There's a plaque on the corner of the Parish House behind the neo-Gothic Church of the Intercession that illustrates the layout of the earthworks.

The church is an impressive piece of early-twentieth-century architecture complete with cloisters (the entrance to the cemetery is through here), parish building, a crypt, and even a secret "abbot's eye" window above the main altar. The remains of its architect, Bertram Grosvenor Goodhue, are contained in a wall vault adorned with a reclining sculpture of the man and bas-reliefs of his major architectural achievements—an immodest but impressive memorial. While much of the stained glass is disappointingly uninspired ("It was intended as temporary but was never changed," I was informed by an impromptu guide), the wood carvings, particularly around the chapel, are exquisite and the roof, supported by massive wood beams, gives the nave an almost baronial banquet-hall flavor.

The Church of the Intercession is one of several religious centers in the immediate vicinity. In fact, Inwood and the Heights have a remarkable number and diversity of churches catering to a highly varied ethnic population—Chinese, Indian, Greek Orthodox, Armenian, Russian Orthodox, to name but a few. One of my favorite churches—the Church of Our Lady of Esperanza—is just across the road from Trinity Cemetery, along the north wall of Audubon Terrace. This has now become the cultural center for the area's burgeoning Puerto Rican population, and the tiny church, located up the stairs from the small entrance on 156th Street, is strangely restful and contains some lovely groupings of stained-glass windows.

Follow 155th Street eastward beyond St. Nicholas Avenue to a narrow footpath that turns north to join Edgecombe Avenue. Here begins what was once the island's most dramatic open space, the High Bridge Park. Regrettably, vandalism and the apparent lack of interest on the part of the Parks Department have resulted in neglect and abandonment. Few people walk through its wooded terraces. Junked cars litter the hillside and after-dark muggings are

not uncommon. Yet there are still magnificent views across the East River, out toward Long Island Sound, from the park's rocky ledges. It is ludicrous that such a remarkable resource as this is being allowed to deteriorate to the point where it will soon be inaccessible to the public.

Fortunately, there's still the Roger Morris Park and the Jumel Mansion at 160th Street and Edgecombe Avenue. This is one of Manhattan's most notable historic districts, offering a diversified range of late-nineteenth-century row houses, a narrow street of tiny clapboard homes known as Sylvan Terrace ending in a set of stone steps leading to St. Nicholas Avenue, the Roger Morris Park,

and the "Grand White Lady" herself, the 1765 Morris-Jumel Mansion (Tuesday–Sunday 10 A.M.–4 P.M. 50¢).

The district is becoming an important stopping point on city tours. While I was sketching the mansion some Newark residents were being shown the Jumel Terrace by a fiery black woman with an afro, as part of the "Harlem As It Is" tour operated by the Penny Sightseeing Company. She proudly pointed out the house where Paul Robeson lived for many years and went on to describe in lurid detail past housing inequities in the area. The group listened silently but eagerly.

The mansion is a delight. Again, like the Dyckman House, it's one of those places where you can lose all sense of time and place. The large white door closes and you're transported into the eighteenth century, into an era of decorous manners, exquisite craftsmanship and taste, a time of delicate sensibilities which reflect themselves in subtle hand-printed wallpapers, translucent eggshell china, and the restrained tick of perfectly crafted clocks. The mansion has been described appropriately as "a serene home." Washington found it "a most admirable place" and established his headquarters there for a brief month in September 1776. It subsequently became a summer camp for English and Hessian generals, then after the war, a tavern and a farmhouse. In 1810 Stephen Jumel and his wife Eliza purchased and refurbished the house, importing pieces of furniture said to belong to their friend Napoleon Bonaparte. After Mr. Jumel's death in 1832, Eliza briefly married Aaron Burr but the union was a failure and the divorce decree was granted, ironically, just prior to Burr's death in 1836.

My favorite room here is the elegantly proportioned octagonal drawing room on the first floor, furnished in late-eighteenth-century style and possessing a remarkable spirit of dignity and calm combined with a sense of intimacy. Outside in the garden you can watch traffic churning along the expressways far below, planes roaring in and out of La Guardia, subway trains clanking and screeching across the East River bridges. Inside the mansion all remains quiet, and visitors leave looking a little less harried than when they arrived.

If you're now exhausted, there are regular buses on St. Nicholas Avenue or subway trains from 163rd Street at Amsterdam Avenue. Alternatively, if you still feel in the mood for exploring, take a bus up to Yeshiva University at 186th Street, where there's a small permanent museum and occasional exhibitions on aspects of Jewish culture (Tuesday–Thursday 11 A.M.–5 P.M., Sunday noon–6 P.M. Adults $1, others 50¢). Of course, you could walk there along the edge of High Bridge Park and visit the water tower off 173rd Street, adjoining the popular High Bridge pool and play center. This handsome campanile structure once supported a 47,000-gallon water tank and was part of the remarkable sequence of engineering accomplishments that brought water from the Croton River along forty miles of aqueducts, and an aqueduct-bridge spanning the Harlem River, to the distributing reservoir in Central

Park. There has been talk recently of reopening the pedestrian walkway across the High Bridge aqueduct and improving the whole of the park environment around the water tower. We wait (hopefully but doubtfully) for action.

Here's one final pause for those enthusiastic souls who have enjoyed this rediscovery of a forgotten segment of Manhattan. Take a bus north on Broadway across the Spuyten Duyvil Creek into Marble Hill and ramble up the slope to the left, around the narrow curling streets. There are no architectural landmarks here—just the spirit of a small town full of slightly worn Victorian villas and leaning verandas. The wood-shingled St. Stephen's Church overlooks the old course of the Harlem River, now filled in. Just across the street Johannes Verveelen operated his ferry from 1669 over "the waterway of ebb and flow" until the construction of the Kings Bridge in 1693. Behind the church is the site of the American fort, erected in 1776, later known as Fort Prince Charles.

This odd little community, cocooned in its past, is a fascinating reminder of how this area must have looked a hundred or so years ago. Across the river in Inwood it's possible to find an occasional old home with conical turret and high-pitched shingle roof, but most have been replaced by great gray apartment blocks. In contrast Marble Hill looks as if it might stay this way forever. "We're not really as old-fashioned as we look," a young resident told me. "We just like it this way—and d'you know, people have started to come and take pictures and write articles on these old homes now. They get all excited about them. Heck, who'd heard of Marble Hill a few years back? Now we're getting known and—you feel prouder, you spruce things up a bit more."

Great! It's good to see there's plenty of life left in this northern tip of Manhattan.

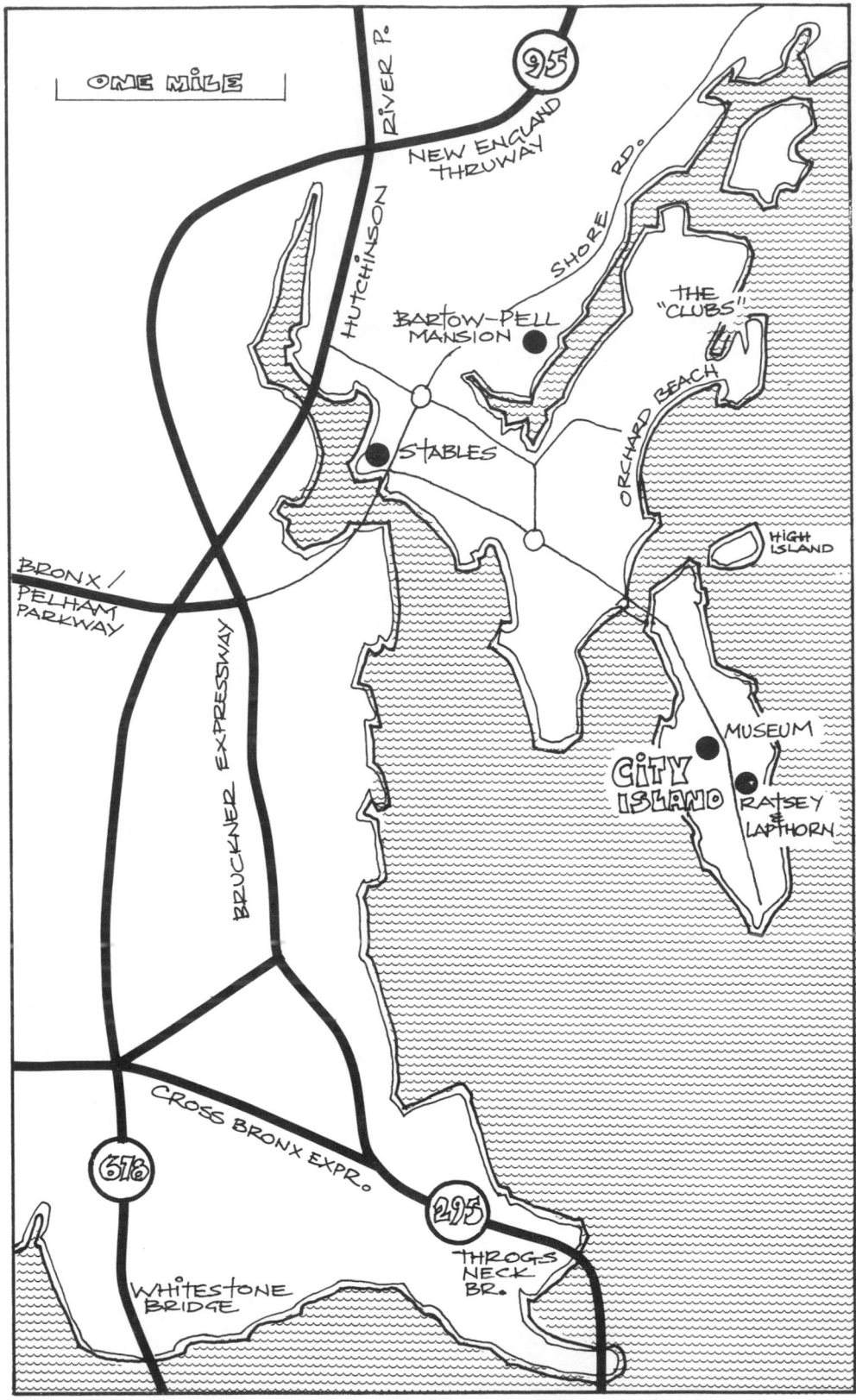

The Bronx

11
CITY ISLAND

To me City Island is always a surprise. I've been there in all
seasons—at the first flicker of spring and when snowdrifts half cover
the Glover's Point Rock, just before the bridge. There's no
buildup. One minute you're traveling the highway, fendered in
by traffic, tall apartment towers as far as you can see, jets screaming into La Guardia. Then there's the exit, a brief drive through
the estatelike landscape of Hunters Island, and finally—the bridge,
the bay, and the island. Church spires rise above the trees. A
launch leaves one of the piers and ripples send a shower of gulls
spiraling. Smoke curls from chimneys. Domes and mansard roofs
rise above porticoed verandas, slightly bowed. There's the smell
of seaweed, the smell of garlic from one of the seafood restaurants,
the smell of resin from the boatyards. There are boats everywhere—lined up two, sometimes four deep along the wharves,
supported on platforms for cleaning, peering between houses,
over houses, out of garages, on front lawns. Red ones with white

──────────── **DIRECTIONS** ────────────

Sailors can tell you exactly where it is—latitude 41° 51′ 0″N, longitude 73°
47′ 30″W. Many visitors do, in fact, arrive by boat—everything from
dinghies to multistateroom launches. Landbound travelers use cars
(City Island/Orchard Beach exit off the Bruckner Expressway or the
Hutchinson River Parkway) or a combination of bus and subway (IND
to Fordham Road/transfer to Bx12, or IRT 6 to Pelham Bay Park/transfer
to Bx12).
NOTE: If you come by public transport it may be best to limit your exploration to City Island itself.

147

stripes, blue ones with black stripes, peeling ones, barnacled ones, upside-down ones, fat porky ones, thin sleek sloops, some with superstructures fifteen feet above the deck, white vinyl fishing chairs, and radar scanners. Richly detailed Victorian villas are surrounded by gaggles of diminutive clapboard cottages. One of these villas was the setting for the film of O'Neill's *A Long Day's Journey into Night*, starring Sir Ralph Richardson and Katharine Hepburn. There are delicate white paling fences and neatly cut hedgerows. A sturdy stone gatepost is embossed with a large "M" marking the driveway to the exclusive Morris Yacht Club with its manicured lawns sloping to the waters of the bay. Its parking lot is full of boats, and the once formal garden is full of boats. Not far away are the other clubs—the City Island Yacht Club, the Stuyvesant, the Olympia—all rigorously defended against the possible onslaught of outsiders. The same with the beaches. The short east–west streets all dead-end at the water, but the tiny beaches are for the use of residents only. "It's the only bit of privacy we have," said an elderly lady at the end of Pilot Street, adjusting her beach chair, on her own patch of sand and pebbles. Visitors must join the crowds at nearby Orchard Beach.

Islanders stroll along City Island Avenue, chatting together ("clam-diggers," they call them, if they've lived on the island long enough). A fisherman, wrinkled as a walnut, peers into a sea-tackle store. Bob Borchers, owner of Thwaites Inn, is on the wharf still dreaming of the day when he'll open up that old ferryboat in the dock across the road as a floating restaurant. He's had plans

City Island

for the *Michael Cosgrove* for years, but things get done rather slowly on the island. This is not New York, even though you can see the towers of Manhattan, way out in the haze, between the forests of masts in the harbor. Many visitors liken the island to a New England village. Others sense a touch of Mexico in its *mañana* pace of life.

The great East Coast entrepreneurs chose City Island as a harbor to keep their magnificent boats and as a place to relax. Here one could find Vincent Astor's *Nourmahal*, J. P. Morgan's *Corsair*, Jules Bache's *Colmena*, and Thomas Lipton's *Shamrock*. Many of the palatial yachts of the wealthy were built at the great yards that lined the shore—Nevin's, Minneford's, Kretzer's, and others.

There have been numerous visionary plans for this tiny 2½-by-½-mile island, known variously as Minniford, Minnewais, Mulberry, Great Island, and the Isle of Man. Before the Revolution there was speculation that it might well overtake Manhattan in importance. Then during the mid-1800s vast fortunes were made from the local oystering industry, followed a few years later by the emergence of the shipbuilding yards. August Belmont conceived a scheme to convert the island into a huge race course, and there have been subsequent projects for casinos and Marina del Rey–type complexes along the waterfront with apartment towers, multilevel malls, seafood markets, restaurants, and all the frolic and frazzle of a Californian ocean-front development.

The islanders and clam-diggers are consistent in their opposition to such glossy projects. They like the island the way it is. In fact,

for many it's already too crowded, particularly on summer week-ends. They blame nearby Orchard Beach, a Robert Moses creation, for the influx of day-trippers. They remember the days before the bridge. An elderly fisherman told me: "Now that was a time. My dad used to fish the oysterin' beds up the sound. Biggest and best oysters you'd ever seen. Why them Ches'peake Bay tooties got nothin' on these creatures. Fifty, sixty bushels a day. M'be more in a big season. Ev'body lived like kings in them days—some of 'em was richer'n film stars. Jes' from oysterin'!"

Another gentleman who'd lived on the island since he was a boy described the arduous process of reaching the island from Man-hattan during the early 1900s: "Subway to 177th Street, trolley to Van Ness, railroad to Bartow, horsecar to t' City Island Bridge, stagecoach to t' police station. Then if you wanted to go onto Hart Island [farther out in the bay] you'd take a rig to t' pier and a launch to t' island. So's as you might expect, it was pretty quiet out here in them days!"

Today it's still quiet, especially if you come out during the week and avoid summer weekend crowds. Take time to stroll along City Island Avenue, peering into the stores selling ship supplies and nautical equipment—the Ship's Tender, the Square Rigger, and the Sailing Bag. Pause in one of the pubs and listen to the locals discussing island affairs. Invariably the conversation revolves around someone's idea for "makin' changes." Beer spills as glasses are thumped on the bar for emphasis. There was a con-troversy raging a while back about whether the main street should be resurfaced. Islanders feared it would encourage more people to bring their cars onto the island. Last time I was there the conflict was still unresolved and the road was as rutted and scarred as ever.

Among the pubs there are antique stores, boutiques, a couple of photo galleries, and the Say Cheese, a delightful flower- and plant-filled wine-and-cheese restaurant featuring fondues, cheese desserts, and at least twenty different kinds of fresh-cut cheeses. Restaurants abound along the avenue. No one will ever go hungry on City Island. For the limited-budget diner there are plenty of snack places and small cafés serving a representative selection of fresh seafood dishes, but if you're in the mood for a splurge try Thwaites, Anna's Harbor, Sea Shore, or the Lobster Box. This

Main Street—City Island

chintzy Victorian cottage (at the far end of the island, overlooking the sound) usually offers a small selection of budget dinners, but its reputation has been built on its lobster creations, twenty-five in all, with such appendages as à la Lemle, Luzianne, Fra Diavolo, and Salsa Verde, Texas-style, and Creole. There's also an authentic bouillabaisse that even residents of Marseilles would relish.

Many of the great boatyards have gone, but occasionally employees at Minneford's or Consolidated will provide an impromptu tour of the wharves. It's mostly servicing work today, though. Boatbuilding is a dying art here. Even at the famous Ratsey and Lapthorn sailmaking establishment off East Schofield Street, the pace of work is not what it was. In England, where the company was founded well over two centuries ago, there were once hundreds of workers stitching, stretching, knotting, and testing the great sails that powered the tea clippers and the towering galleons of the British navy. This was the company that produced the sails for Lord Nelson's flagship *Victory*, and much more recently, for the Schaefer Brewing Company's re-creation of the famous sailing ship *America*, built locally at Minneford's yards. There's a small museum here, and you can watch employees making new sails in the adjoining loft. Brightly colored sail bags are piled high under signs hanging from the rafters: "Sails to Be Gen'l Overhaul and Scrubbed," "Sails to Be Tagged and Put into Work," "Finished Sails Waiting Racing Numbers."

If you enjoy museums, the islanders have recently opened one in the old school up Fordham Street (Sunday 2–4 P.M. Free. 885-1292). Also, a couple of miles to the west, along Shore Road (you'll need a car), there's the austere gray Bartow-Pell Mansion with its landmark interior and a fine formal garden, both open to the public (Tuesday, Friday, and Sunday 1–5 P.M. Admission 50¢). The mansion was built between 1836 and 1842 by Robert Bartow on land acquired from the Indians in 1654 by his predecessor, Thomas Pell. The pamphlet about the mansion contains a copy of the original agreement with the local Indians complete with their "markes," and is full of richly Elizabethan language: "[We] do sell & deliver to Tho. Pell his heyres & assignse to hould injoy improove plant as hee shall see Cause to his Best to be improoved ffor & to him & his heyres fforever w^h out any molestation on our p^t. This Wrightinge was signed & Wittnessed Beffore a great Multitude off Indvans & many English we who are under written do testify."

Few people seem to visit the mansion. It's a lovely place to spend a warm afternoon strolling across the lawns through the woods to the Hunters Island lagoon. There are no apartment towers to be seen, no bridges, no traffic noise to spoil the stillness of reed-edged water. It's a place for squirrels, mallard ducks, sea gulls, and the quiet spirit.

For the more actively minded there's horse riding at the Pelham Bit Stables on the north side of Eastchester Bay, golf on the Split Rock Golf Course opposite the Pell Mansion, miniature golf alongside the road to City Island, and, of course, the Orchard Beach complex itself—that great man-made arc of white sand complete with grandiose bathhouses and snack bars.

City Island is, as you might expect, a fisherman's paradise. The numerous wharves provide ideal places to settle for a few hours with a rod and line or, if you fancy something a little more adventurous, there are fishing cruises out into the sound after the big ones. Boats leave the docks from the west side of the island. One of the favorite sights off the southern tip is the Stepping Stone Lighthouse, said to be named after the tiny rocky islands that litter the bay like stepping stones across a stream. The devil himself is said to have used these when fleeing from the ferocious Indians, to safety on Long Island. Actually, the local Indians were a generally peaceable group. Their only major offense was the massacre of Anne Hutchinson, one of the first settlers to rebel against the strict Massachusetts colony and establish her own base here in 1642, near Split Rock. This courageous pioneer was killed almost incidentally during a reprisal raid by the Weckquaesgeek Indians against Dutch settlers in the area.

At Belden Point at the southern tip on City Island is the old pilot house, once headquarters for the Hell Gate pilots who used to navigate the ships through the treacherous whirlpools of the East River to the docks at South Street. Then a mile or so up the island on its eastern shore is the Pelham Cemetery, with some of the Pell family gravestones dating from the 1740s.

Not far away is the Hart Island ferry, a cheerfully painted craft fulfilling a cheerless mission. Hart Island, east of City Island, has been used since 1868 as New York's potter's field burial ground— home for deceased John Does, stillborn infants, and even amputated limbs. It's not open to the public. George DiLasio, one of the engineers, has been running various New York ferries for twenty-three years. Most of the others have been abandoned—all that is left is this one and the Staten Island run. He works his shift every day from a tiny office-cum-kitchen-cum-lounge-cum-bedroom along with the ship's cat, Boots, and the ship's dog, Brownie. "This ain't the real Brownie. This here's the new one. The other one was a real old whore. Ev'time she was in heat, why them island dogs, they'd come down there in packs justa have a go. She had eighty-six puppies all told. Usta have 'em up under that boat shed. Every time we'd hav'ta crawl under and drag 'em out. Everyone loved old Brownie, though—boy, was she a good watchdog. This one's okay, but a bit too friendly."

George told me about Hart Island. The ferry carries the morgue wagon across twice a week, along with a group of Riker's Island inmates whose job it is to label each pine box coffin and stack it in a shallow trench for interment. Surprisingly, it's a popular prison detail. There's a waiting list to join the "F Squad" (adult burials), the "Baby Ghouls" (infant burials), and the "Ghoul Squad" (disinterment of claimed bodies). George explained: "Well, you gotta see it from their point of view. They get fresh air and good food all day and no chains an' stuff. An' now they got bulldozers so they don't have to dig trenches no more. All they gotta do is put 'em in—and once in a while dig 'em out. Wouldn't fancy that part too much myself, though."

Hart Island is the most densely populated land in New York. Over 700,000 bodies have been buried here on a 60-acre plot— more than 10,000 bodies per acre. And it's well used. After a twenty- to twenty-five-year burial period the land is recycled for new burials and the new trenches are renumbered with stone markers. Bits of bones and parts of skulls lie scattered like seashells among the weeds. At the north end of the island, just beyond the potter's field, is a large square monument with the word PEACE inscribed on it. Nearby there's a granite cross which reads: "He calleth his children by name." No irony was apparently intended.

From the north end of Orchard Beach you can get a good view

of the island and the monument. You can also see the sound and all its tiny islets, the Blauzes (after the Dutch *de Blauntjes*—"little blue ones"). Over on Pea Island is an old radio station—currently disused. The transmitting tower (NBC and CBS) is now located on High Island, linked to City Island by a private bridge.

I like Orchard Beach in the late fall. The crowds are gone; the regulars take over. There are thirty of them at most, many of them East Europeans who live in Brooklyn, the Bronx, even as far out as Yonkers. They meet here most days to talk, play cards, and read. When it's cold they huddle around picnic tables under the great arches of the Orchard Beach Bath House, light fires, and chat until dusk. If the sun is bright and the wind low, they sit out on beach chairs in true Miami Beach style. "Oh yes," one of them told me in a heavy accent, "we have been coming here for many times, we are a group of friends. We sit together and talk and we're always here. Even when it snows we come here. We don't like to be inside. We like to be by the sea and we like to be together."

Stroll beyond the beach, northward across the beautifully colored rocks that roll like lava to the sea—pinks, pastel greens, and curling sinews of quartz—like thick cream swirled in soup. Follow the curve of the promontory until you come to a long set of stepping stones leading across a patch of marshy ground to a small rocky island topped by twelve windswept trees. Here you enter another world—a little enclave unknown to visitors, unknown even to many residents of City Island.

I crossed the stepping stones and met John Johnson. He was sitting in a little rock-built shelter protected from the chilly breeze. There was an old wooden bench, an oil drum with holes in it for use as a fire, a small pile of books and magazines covered by a tarpaulin to keep them dry, a worn pack of cards, and a battered coffee pot. He was waiting for his friends Big Jean and Henry to arrive. They were all in their seventies. They meet here, usually every day. It is their "place," their own special "club": "Yeah, we built this ourselves. I've bin coming here since I was a school kid. We put up this wall 'bout ten years back and these trees—we planted these too, that's an apple tree there. Them two's cherry, at the side there. Usta have a roof too, and tin panels inside, real cozy like but they made us take it down. Said we couldn't have no roofs."

After showing me around the "club" he led me up to the high

point on the island and pointed out the landmarks in the bay—the disused fort on Davids Island, the straggling white bulk of the New York Athletic Club across the lagoon, and the Execution Lighthouse out past Huguenot Island. It was on that island, so he told me, that British captives were tied to the rocks at low tide by their American captors during the Revolution and left to drown. Then he pointed across to the hill on Hunters Island and told me about the great Georgian mansion that once sat on the ridge over-looking the bay. John Hunter lived there in the early 1800s sur-rounded by his magnificent collection of Titians, Rembrandts, Ra-phaels, and Rubenses. Gradually the estate fell into disrepair, and the mansion was eventually razed in 1937. There are still a few remains up there—part of the huge gateposts and flat areas where the lawns used to be. "We get our water from up there, there's an old fountain. Best water anyplace."

John told me more about the Hunters Island and Twin Island "clubs." "Used to be a lot more places like this 'round here—twelve, fifteen camps all along this side of the island. But they all died down, the old people, they died off and the young folks don't wanna bother coming out here on account of their cars—too much trouble for 'em. There's still a few left, though. They're not all gone." He pointed across the lagoon. "There's another gang on top of the hill. They play cards up there. Over on the point, that's the Russians, and there, where that smoke is, that's the Dutch-men's place, we call 'em the Führers, the Heinies. That's Henry over there now." He called out to a man on the far bank but he didn't respond. "We keeps to ourselves, y'know. We don't go in for socializin' much."

I crossed the lagoon by the old bridge to visit Henry (Wag-ner), one of the "Heinies." He was cleaning away the leaves on an old abandoned badminton court and told me how the club began. "Years ago, when we came to this country, all us Germans, y'know, no money, outta work sometimes, and this was the cheapest place. We like nature, y'understand. We used to come and play a Bavarian game—we called it 'plattel'—we used iron plates, we'd throw them, some were three or four pounds, we'd throw them fifty feet or more. Was healthy. Made you sweat." Henry showed me around his club—a bit more refined than John's place. He'd built most of it himself and was very proud of his workmanship: "Well, it's my bungalow," he said. Farther down near the rusted steel barge, beached in the reeds, the "Russians" were leaving their island for home, crossing the marshes on low bridges made from thick timber beams. I waved. They smiled and waved back.

What a strange little corner this is, unchanged for a generation. The same men have been coming here since they were school kids. Their numbers are dwindling slowly, though. More and more of the benches are empty on those bright afternoons. Soon only a few old residents of City Island will remember them.

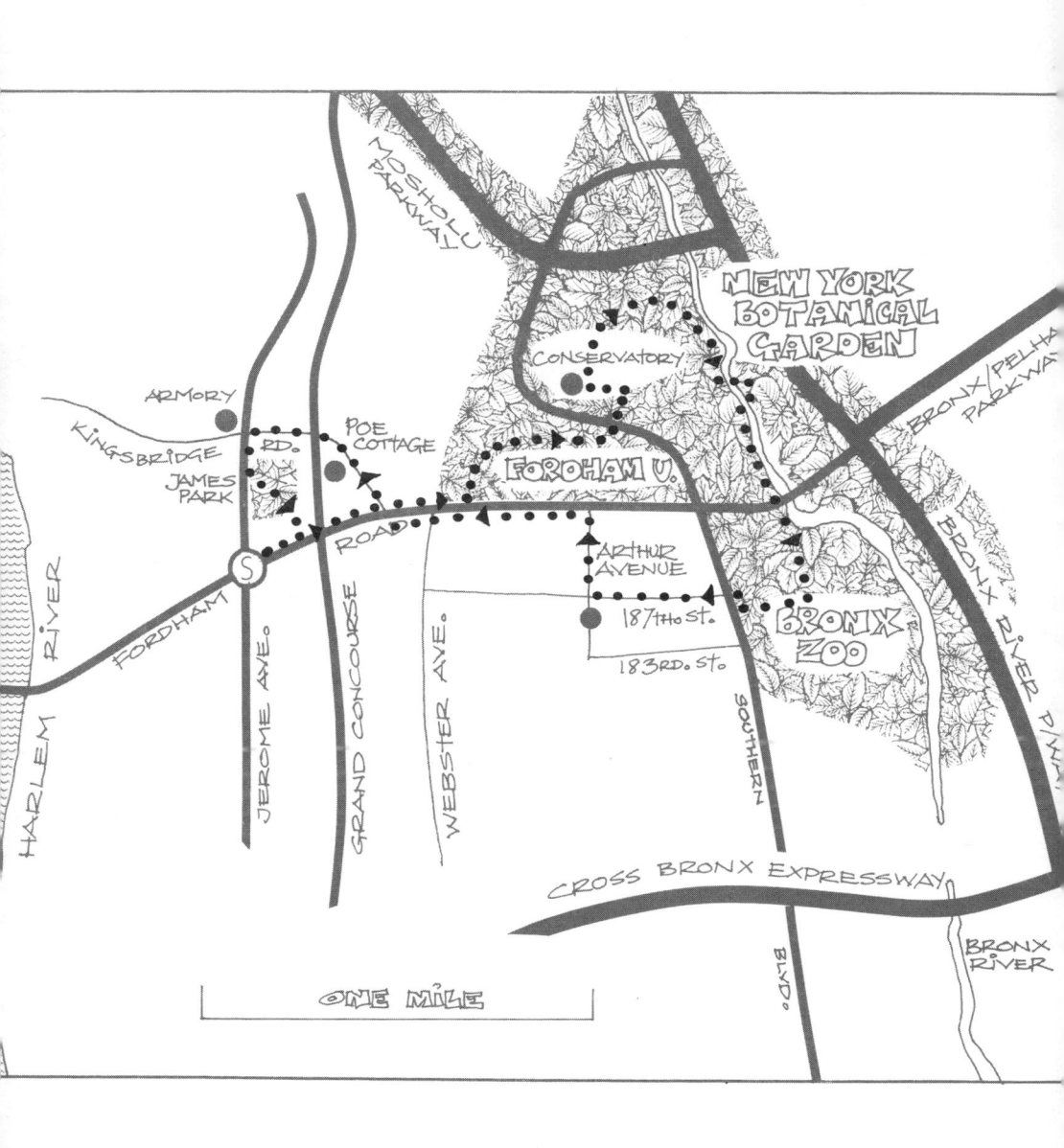

12
THE BRONX—
FORDHAM

To some it's Boogie Alley, a brassy strip bumping and grinding to the thick sounds of a hundred hand-held transistor radios. To others it contains some of the best bargain stores in the five boroughs, a place to barter for fashionable clothes, boots, furs, kids' toys, even oversized outfits for large ladies determined to maintain an up-to-date image. There are always crowds here. Most of the stores stay open late and the throng jostles along from Loehmann's on Jerome Avenue at Fordham Road (an incredible price-slashing garment store since 1921), past Smart Size, Alexander's, Guys and Dolls, Goldman's Yarn Center, and the Tress Discount Center, to McDonald's restaurant near Webster Avenue.

It's Fourteenth Street ten times over. The salesmen are out on the sidewalk "bringin' 'em in." The Palace Deli ("genuine noodle pudding and hot knishes") bulges with pastrami-gorging customers and bawling kids, and at Krum's, just down the east side of the Grand Concourse, hungry shoppers plagued with sweet-tooth ogle Ronnie Krum and Shelley Eichen's delectable displays of hand-dipped chocolates, candies, and roasted nuts. "Yeah, yeah, who's next," growls the plump lady with a bouffant thatch behind the counter. The oglers remain mute, a safe distance from the counter, gazing at the glittering array. "More browsers," she mutters. Then, "Don't anyone want to buy anything?" at

——————— DIRECTIONS ———————

Subway: IRT 4 to Fordham Road/Jerome Avenue
Bus: Bx1, Bx2, Bx15, Bx17, Bx20, Bx25 to Jerome Avenue

higher volume. Finally, "Hey, you're blocking the aisle. You wanna buy or what?" She tries to look exasperated but eventually gives up and smiles at a tiny girl with pigtails. "Hey, you, come here." The girl waddles shyly to the counter, where she receives a large soft-centered chocolate. It works. The customers relax and smile and three step up to the counter to buy.

Across the road the great glazed edifice, Loew's Paradise, stands like a baroque palace on the Grand Concourse. Once, when the clock worked, the green copper horses in the tower above the main entrance pranced around to the ringing of bells. Today they're mute and motionless. Only the architecture itself is noisy.

Back near Fordham Road there are elegant expressions of Art Deco. Sachs and the RKO Fordham theater are notable examples. Most shoppers never notice them. Some saunter by, swaggering to a disco beat; others, hunched and heads down, scurry from shoe store to snack bar to clothes shop in an endless search for the ultimate bargain. A few pause at Sutter's on the east side of the Grand Concourse just north of Fordham Avenue to nibble the delicate French confectionery ("only real creamery butter used").

It's busy, brash, and bustling. But the break is sudden. The strip ends at Webster Avenue, across from the Fordham University campus. Strolling through the gate just past Fordham Station, we enter a quiet world of green lawns, elm-shaded walks, and Oxbridge-style quadrangles. (Visitors are allowed in to see the administration building or attend activities at the campus center.) Students lie spread-eagled in the sun. Baseballs snap off bats near Collins Hall, but no one runs very fast. Three sophomores huddle over textbooks and notes and smile in unison at a stubby-bearded tutor strolling purposefully toward the administration building, originally an 1836 Greek Revival mansion known as Rose Hill (the white extensions on either side detract from its original grace and character).

There's a sense of longevity and tradition to the place, one of the largest Catholic institutions in the country, with an enrollment of 7,500 students. It was founded as St. John's College in 1841 by the Right Reverend John Hughes, who was later appointed New York's first Catholic archbishop. Later it came under the control of the Jesuits and was renamed a university. At that time the Bronx consisted of a straggle of tiny towns along the Boston Post Road—

Mott Haven, Morrisania, West Farms, Eastchester, and Pelham. Significant development came later in the forties after the opening of the New York and New Haven rail service, although most of the area maintained its bucolic quality well into the latter years of the century. Even today, long after the hill-leveling, the highways, and the interminable tracts of tenement development in the southern portion of the borough, the Bronx possesses the finest system of parks in the metropolitan region. Not surprisingly, it was Frederick Law Olmsted, New York's master park planner, who conceived and helped implement this remarkable network of great open spaces tied together by tree-lined "parkways." Henry Hope Reed called his work "one of the rare visions in New York's city planning." The Fordham campus abuts the Botanical Garden and forms an integral part of his concept.

We continue to stroll eastward past the 1845 St. John's Church (University Chapel). Note the elaborate copper tower over the nave and the elegant stained-glass windows bequeathed by Louis Philippe, king of France. Nearby is the somber bust of Orestes A. Brownson, a close friend of Emerson and Thoreau. The memorial is a classic understatement of societal ethics in the late 1800s—"He loved God, Country, and Truth."

Passing the contemporary-style campus center (it's worth making a detour here to check on public events at the university), we emerge on the green swath of Edwards Parade dominated at the far end by the tower-topped Keating Hall. Built in 1936 as the graduate school, it's a splendid hybrid in the "Collegiate Gothic" style. Students bask in the sun beneath the turrets and crenelations, and frisbees glide gracefully over the velvet lawns.

Leaving the campus by the parking-lot exit to the north of Keating Hall we cross Southern Boulevard and enter the New York Botanical Garden (daily 10 A.M. to sunset. Museum and conservatories close at 4:30 P.M. Free). Here you're on your own. Pick up a map at the gate and select whichever features appeal most. Incorporated in 1891, the design was patterned after Kew Gardens in England and contains a glorious array of specialized gardens, a forty-acre hemlock forest, the Bronx River in a craggy gorge, an 1840 snuff mill once used by the Lorillard family, a museum and, of course, the popular conservatory, which only recently was completely refurbished and has become one of the main attractions in

The Bronx River Gorge

the Bronx. Yet ironically, although the garden is a favorite haunt of local residents, it's unexplored territory for many inhabitants of the other four boroughs. "I never knew it'd be like this," gasped John Travis, a Manhattanite who rarely leaves his cozy niche on the Upper West Side. "She made me come," he told me, pointing to a grinning girl friend. "She read something about the green-houses being open again with the palm trees an' all, so she said we had to come." I asked if he was enjoying himself. "It's really fantastic. Over there"—he pointed to the verdant hemlock forest in the northern portion of the park—"you can get lost it's so quiet. We walked down by the river, by the waterfall, and it was just like being in the country. Could have been a hundred miles away. Vermont or some place like that."

I agree. I've had some of my best New York park walks here, especially in the early spring and late fall when there are few people in the more remote parts. If you don't mind sharing the attractions with other avid admirers, though, be sure to visit Lord and Burnham's conservatory building with its ninety-foot-high double-glass dome supported on slender cast-iron columns, and the elegantly columned Watson building, which houses the museum and botanical library. (Pick up a copy of the seasonal educational program here listing scores of courses and lectures in botany, gardening, landscape design, crafts, and even winemaking and local history. It's an incredibly active place.)

If it's quiet you're after, follow the paths through the forest and the river gorge and across the delicately arched footbridge to the unpretentious snuff mill near the rose gardens. Built around 1840 to replace an older mill, it was operated by Pierre Lorillard's sons Peter and George who, according to a personal epitaph in ex-mayor Philip Hone's diary, "led people by the nose for the best part of a century and made an enormous fortune by giving them to chew that which they could not swallow." For the weary there's a snack bar at the lower level of the mill with a riverside terrace, but don't eat anything here unless you really have to, as we'll soon be visiting one of the prime, though little-known, gastronomic centers of the Bronx.

Follow signs for the Bronx Zoo (daily 10–5 P.M. Admission $2 except on "free days"—Tuesdays, Wednesdays, and Thursdays) and cross the hectic Bronx and Pelham Parkway, heading for the towering Rainey Memorial Gates. This exotic fantasy of bears, deer, and lions was the work of architect Charles Platt and sculptor Paul Manship. "Some call it the Commodore Perry Gate," an elderly gentleman informed me as I stood admiring its exuberance. "He brought his animals through this way into the zoo. He traveled all over the world finding them." The man explained he was a lover of Bronx history and went on to regale me with tales of Bronxdale, a little village that used to exist alongside the river not far from the gate. He also told me stories of the Indian moccasin paths that followed the valley northward to Connecticut and, pointing to the parkway bridge over the river, explained it was named after Carl Linnaeus, the eighteenth-century Swedish botanist responsible for developing a system of botanical terminology in Latin. Our conversation continued to touch on almost every aspect of Bronx history—dates, events, and personalities far too numerous to discuss here. Then suddenly he burst into song. I remember one line: "I will look upon thy face again, my own romantic Bronx . . ." He explained after what can only be described as a heartily confident rendition that he'd taken Joseph Rodman Drake's famous poem and set it to music. "It came to me one night, all of a sudden. Sometimes I can't always remember the tune so I make it up a bit." Reluctantly I left the kind man, so in love with his native Bronx. Look out for him. He usually takes a stroll most afternoons around the lower end of the Botanical Garden. Be prepared for a lengthy diversion.

Admittedly, the zoo is no nook or cranny, but for most it's just too tempting a place to miss (if you are adamant, however, follow the parkway west to Southern Boulevard and walk south to 187th Street. We'll meet you there.). Beyond the Rainey gates we're greeted by a frolicking group of mermaids and cupidlike children riding seahorses in the sprays of the Rockefeller Fountain. William Rockefeller was the donor. In 1902 he had this boisterous creation shipped piece by piece from Como, Italy, and in 1910 it was placed in its present location. In conjunction with the gates, it forms a most imposing entrance to this, the largest zoo in America. Living within the 252-acre woodland sanctuary are more than 3,000 animals, including such rare species as Siberian tigers, Mongolian wild horses, European bisons, snow leopards, and the Pere David deer. Many exhibits are open-air re-creations of natural habitats—the African plains, South American pampas, the North American buffalo plains, elk forest, and wolf wood—others are splendidly imaginative indoor exhibits replicating rain-forest environments, "The World of Darkness," the habitats of reptiles, crocodiles, and monkeys. It's a wonderland of experiences, particularly for children. There's a special touch-and-pet zoo for youngsters, safari trains, and a cable-car skyfari crossing the central portion of the zoo from the Southern Boulevard entrance to the African plains exhibit in the southeastern corner. Pick up a guide map at the entrance and select the exhibits for yourself. Then after you've had your fill, leave by the Southern Boulevard exit at 185th Street (past the Buffet Terrace).

At 187th Street we enter another special little world, unknown to most non-Bronx residents. Walk slowly westward. Prepare your palate for a gastronomic romp and your pocketbook for merciless forays. Smell the air. The aroma of fresh-baked bread hangs thick above the street and wafts between the lines of washing dangling out of tiny windows. A fishmonger's display spills out on crates and tables—huge cream slabs of baccala (dried salted codfish), boxes of turquoise-blue soft-shell crabs, scungilli, oysters, clams, sea urchins, mussels, squid, butterfish, and evil-looking black eels. Porgies lie glistening and plump, salted whitefish fill a yellow plastic bucket, and hundreds of tiny whitebait, slivers of silver, are piled in moist mounds. After the silence of the Botanical Garden the racket here seems overwhelming. Everybody shouts at everybody. Greetings fly across the street like bullets. Motorbikes and mopeds crackle. Romantic love songs blare from tinny radios in the social clubs and kids tear down the sidewalks on skateboards bawling eloquent epithets at one another. It's Italy! It can't be anywhere else. It's the back streets of Naples, the eastern neighborhoods of Rome, the tenements behind Milan Cathedral.

Actually, it's the Arthur Avenue district, New York's most authentic Italian neighborhood and one of the most colorful places I've found for Saturday shopping. If you've never been here before, spend a while just getting to know the place. Continue the stroll west along 187th Street to Arthur Avenue, then turn south as far as Crescent Avenue before reversing direction and returning along the opposite side of the avenue to 187th Street. Complete the reconnaissance with a brief detour to the left on 187th Street and then back again to the Arthur Avenue junction. By this time you'll have a reasonably clear idea of neighborhood structure, so repeat the process more slowly, pausing to sip, nibble, and sample whatever and whenever the urge takes you. Indulge a little.

Buy a fresh warm loaf of lard bread packed with bits of prosciutto, a few ounces of thin sliced Calabrian soppressata salami, a bag full of green and black olives fresh from the barrel, a slab of fontina cheese, and a straw-covered flask of chianti (a Ruffino or Frescobaldi). Adjourn to the little park at Arthur and Crescent avenues and *mange, mange, mange!* Alternatively, if you'd prefer to do your eating indoors, select one of the neighborhood Italian restaurants and enjoy a plateful of pasta with a choice of a dozen or more sauces—pesto, oil and garlic, sausage, calamari, anchovy, mushroom, marinara, lobster, à la Caruso, à la Mario, etc., etc. Some of the restaurants are obviously designed to appeal more to the outsider, with paintings of Venetian canals and the sounds of soft guitar music. Dominick's, however, a tiny sweaty bar and eating room in the middle of Arthur Avenue, has no frills, no panderings to elite tastes. What it does have is some of the best (and most authentic) dishes in the district, and a devoted clientele who attack the vast platters of pasta and sauces and meats and more sauces with an elbow-to-elbow gusto usually associated with a baseball game. Of course, if you weakened and ate during your exploration of the gardens or the zoo, you'll perhaps be more interested in browsing through the bakeries, the salumerias, and the noodle factories. So—browse. Peep in at the sacks of dried fagioli beans at Le Tre Corosse Importing Company, the bunches of army-green oregano, the clusters of chili peppers, and the carefully constructed pyramids of half-gallon olive-oil cans. Stroll through the poultry market, a richly redolent environment filled with guinea hens, rabbits, turkeys, ducks, and huge white cockerels. Admire the windows of pork stores filled with bright pepperonis, mold-flecked salamis, and fennel sausages. Best of all, spend time in the noisy retail market with its wonderful mounds of fresh vegetables, more sacks of beans than you've ever seen in your life, barrels of olives—all sizes and colors—and in the delicatessen-style outlets smothered in wizened sausages and whole prosciutto hams. Mike Greco calls over from behind his pepperonis and provolones—"Hey, you wanna try some of this salami?" Alfio Gentile rattles off the names of all his dried beans, discusses the individual merits of his twenty-five different kinds of imported Italian pasta, and gives me an excellent recipe for preparing fava beans. Another man at a vegetable stall offers me an apple—"Try it. They just came in." I leave weighed down with shopping bags.

Look out for the pasta stores, especially Mario Borgatti's, where it's almost impossible to leave without a box of his plump cheese, meat, or spinach ravioli, or his richly golden fettucini noodles. Worst of all, of course, are the pastry shops. Unless you have a will of iron, pass them by; once inside, it's too late. The aroma of crisp brown cream-filled cannoli, Italian cheese cakes, puff-pastry sfogliatelle, sweet panetone breads, and babas au rhum has sealed the doom of many a diet-bound customer.

The walk north on Arthur Avenue to Fordham Road enables first-timers to regain their equilibrium and seal their depleted pocketbooks. If you ate at Dominick's, maybe a brief jog would help restore the circulation and alleviate the guilt.

Passing the entrance to Fordham University again we proceed back up the hill and veer off Fordham Road to the right, at Kingsbridge Road. Poe Park is in front of us, a delightfully shaded summer oasis complete with bandstand and, unexpectedly, a diminutive clapboard cottage where Edgar Allan Poe lived from 1846 to 1849 (Tuesday–Saturday 10 A.M.–1 P.M. and 2–4 P.M., Sunday 1–4 P.M. Free). The park is invariably full of noise, full of life, but inside the simply furnished house the mood is very different. Poe's beloved wife, Virginia, died here in 1847 from tuberculosis. Poe could do little to save her. Ironically, the success of such major works as "The Raven" and "The Murders in the Rue Morgue" had in no way alleviated the poverty in which he and his wife had lived for years. His mother-in-law, Mrs. Maria Clemm, tried desperately to help by peddling some of Poe's more obscure manuscripts and even scavenging vegetables and herbs to feed the destitute family. But nothing could save Virginia, and she shivered to death under Poe's West Point coat, the only substantial blanket they owned. Afterward he began frequenting the boisterous taverns on Fordham Road until rescued from alcoholic oblivion by a friend, a Jesuit priest who took him into St. John's College, and spent long hours helping him to reconcile himself to his loss.

Poe Cottage

But Poe could not accept solace. He almost seemed to welcome grief and sorrow as a birthright and entered his final period of decline, dying a "stranger" in a Baltimore hospital two years later. Somehow during this final period he managed to produce one of his finest poems, "Annabel Lee," a memorial to his beloved wife:

> For the moon never beams, without bringing me dreams
> Of the beautiful Annabel Lee;
> And the stars never rise, but I feel the bright eyes
> Of the beautiful Annabel Lee;—
> And so, all the night-tide, I lie down by the side
> Of my darling—my darling—my life and my bride,
> In her sepulchre there by the sea—
> In her tomb by the sounding sea.

This tiny cottage reflects the spirit of this sad, brilliant man.

We're off again, west along Kingsbridge Road, past a series of

Hebrew-signed kosher butchers and delicatessens, to visit the monolithic 258th Field Artillery Armory (designed by Pilcher and Tachall in 1917). Originally home of the Washington Grays, formed as a guard of honor at President Washington's first inauguration, this towered and turreted structure is said to be one of the largest armories in the country and occupies an entire block. It is 106 feet high at its tallest point and boasts a drill floor measuring 300 by 600 feet. Unfortunately, visitors are not allowed inside.

We end by wandering through the pleasantly shaded (if somewhat noisy) St. James Park, back to Fordham Road. The rush and tumble of the street still continues, the crowds churn along the sidewalk, and the exasperated lady at Krum's is still trying to cajole her customers into buying her glistening candies.

Remember the silence of the hemlock forest.

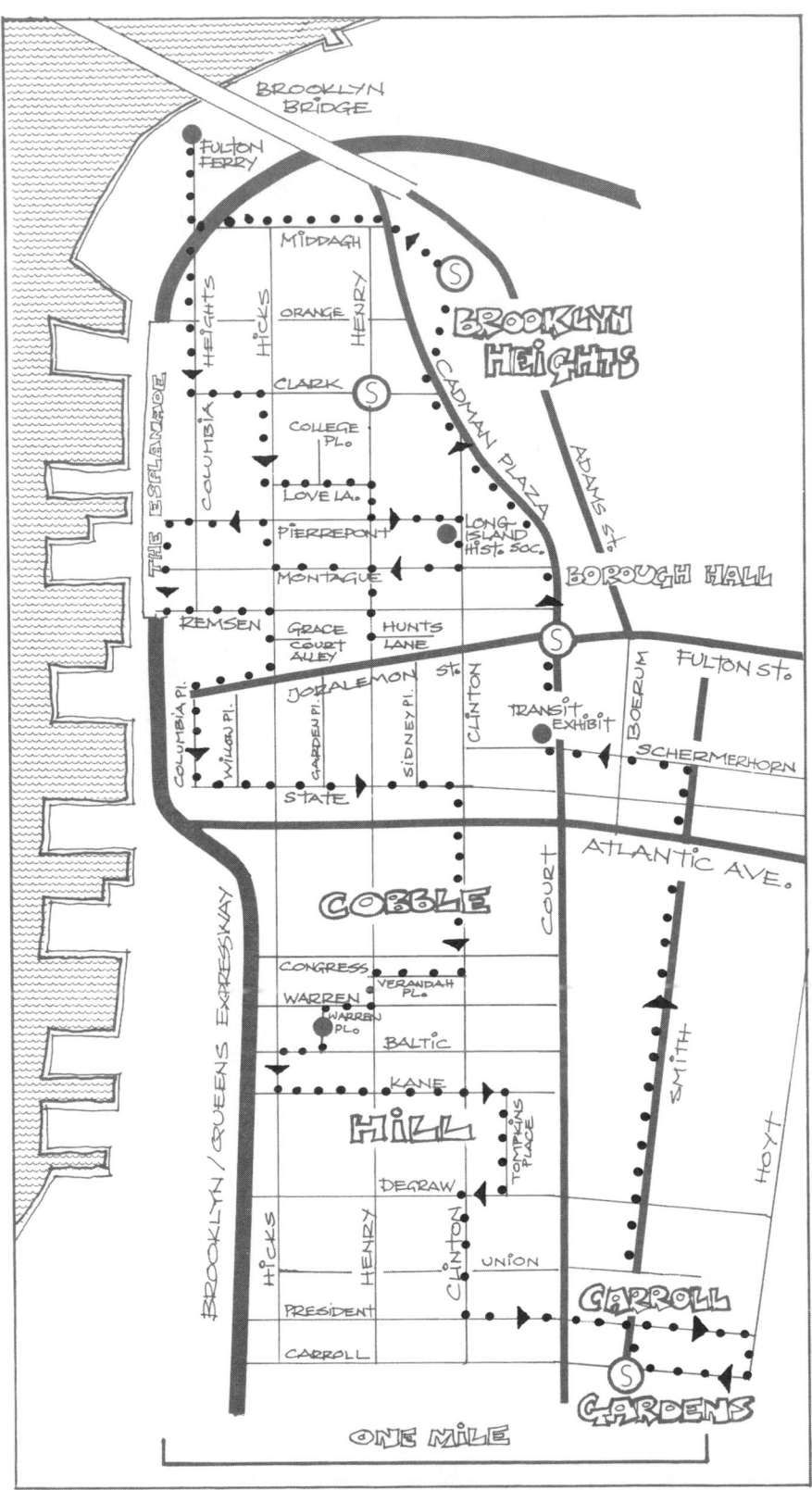

13
THE BROOKLYN
WATERFRONT

Forget the subway. Why not come the hard way and the best way—across the Brooklyn Bridge? (BMT N or RR to City Hall/Broadway; follow signs for Brooklyn Promenade.) There are few walking experiences in New York to match an early-morning stroll between the silver cables, between the great gray piers, above the traffic, looking out across the East River, the harbor, and Governor's Island. If you start early enough, you'll feel the city coming to life, the stirrings of Colossus (if you start too late you may find the noise and fumes on the bridge a bit overbearing).

As you approach the Brooklyn side, down a long descent, the yellow and green mini-city of the Jehovah's Witnesses organization dominates the waterfront. Farther down there's the Brooklyn Heights esplanade cantilevered over two levels of centipedelike traffic. In the foreground are the docks and the masts of sea-battered ships just in from Russia, New Zealand, and Latin America. Finally there are steps, an underpass, and you're out in the sunshine of Cadman Plaza, Brooklyn.

In all fairness I should warn participants in this walk that we cover quite a distance and that you might prefer to save the stroll across the bridge to the end of the journey.

Leave Cadman Plaza and cross over to Middagh Street. The for-

--------- **DIRECTIONS** ---------

Subway: IND A or F to High Street/Brooklyn Bridge
Bus: B15 from Canal Street, Manhattan, B25, B41

Old Fireboat House Museum

mal sweep of lawns, statues, and the great white façades of the
Civic Center give way to a narrow thoroughfare lined with nineteenth-century homes, a few clapboard cottages, and refreshing
shade from garden trees. There has been considerable restoration
of the block, not all of it successful, but at the top of the street, at
Columbia Heights, is the gray and prune Eugene Boisselet House,
"The Queen of Brooklyn Heights," built around 1830, complete
with rear stables and carriage house. The whole structure is a little
worn and slightly lopsided. The main entrance with its tiny windows and miniature columns tilts to the right, yet somehow this
only serves to emphasize the dignity of this lovely place.

At Columbia Heights, there's an interesting detour down the
hill, between the Watchtower warehouses (once the Squibb Pharmaceutical Factory) into the Fulton Ferry Historic district. As early
as 1659 there was a "fferry" across to Manhattan in the form of a
rowboat. Demand was spasmodic and the boatman, Cornelis
Dircksen, spent most of his time farming nearby. A customer
would signal a need for his services by blowing on an old coach
horn that dangled from a tree on the riverbank. Later the opera-
tion was taken over by Robert Fulton, who provided a steamboat
link in 1814. From that time, the Heights developed rapidly as a
fashionable residential area.

Today, when the Ferry Plaza is devoid of trucks, it's a delightful
corner of Brooklyn. At the top end there's Front Street Tavern
(quite a lively place in the evening, even though there's not much
other activity in the area yet). The charming yellow fireboat house
on the waterfront is now a museum of the National Maritime Historical Society (daily noon–6 P.M. Free) and the huge Empire
Warehouse Company building (next to the Eagle warehouse with
its sturdy brick arches) might be transformed into a commercial
complex similar to San Francisco's Ghirardeli Square. So far not
too much in the way of restoration and reuse has been undertaken, but the potential is obvious to anyone with a smattering of
imagination. A view of the area, looking northward from the Furman Inn on Furman Street toward the old fireboat house, is just
one example of the striking character of this historic district.

Back on Columbia Heights again, there's the world headquarters of the Watchtower Bible and Tract Society (Jehovah's Witnesses) located in one of the most successful examples of "infill"

architecture on the Brooklyn waterfront. Across the road is the residence where daily tours of the factory begin. These tours are open to anyone. The best time to arrive is before 1 P.M. They take at least an hour and a half and give a fascinating glimpse of this highly structured organization. Not everyone, though, welcomes the presence of this complex in the Heights. I remember one day I happened to be passing the residence just after midday when, without warning, and from every direction, came scores of eager-faced young men, all heading for the main entrance. They apparently were the factory workers, all Jehovah's Witnesses, on their way to lunch. However, hardly had the front end of this stream of bodies reached the residence when a little man, obviously irate, came up Pineapple Street waving a handful of printed sheets. He stood immediately outside the door and began a long fire-and-brimstone diatribe urging the young men, whose minds were obviously focused on lunch, to mend their ways and join some other religious organization. He was greeted with tolerant smiles until the last worker had disappeared into the building. Briefly he spoke to the door and then, tying his pamphlets up with string, he marched back down Pineapple Street, still looking irate. "He's here most days," one of the young men told me. "He's really quite a nice guy, but I don't think he likes us very much."

As Brooklyn Heights is the most popular and best known of all New York neighborhoods outside Manhattan, we'll avoid some of its more famous landmarks and explore instead its nooks and crannies unknown to most outsiders—even to many of its residents. Of course, you may prefer just to stroll along the esplanade starting at Orange Street and rejoin the walk on Atlantic Avenue, in which case enjoy yourself. Together with the Brooklyn Bridge, it's one of the finest walks in the city.

What I find most fascinating in the Heights are those hidden cul-de-sacs where old carriage houses and stables have been converted into charming cottages. Walking south down Hicks Street from Clark Street turn left into Love Lane and look out for the secluded College Place, a narrow alley of cottages marred somewhat by the parking garage at the bottom end. More attractive examples can be found a little farther to the south at Grace Court Alley and Hunts Lane, both of which we visit later in the walk.

At Pierrepont Street we enter the elite heart of the neighborhood. Occasionally in the middle of a sedate line of townhouses will appear some highly adorned mansion, like a bejeweled dowager duchess among her servants. The Herman Behr house, at Henry and Pierrepont, is a red sandstone creation full of massive arches, bays, odd chimneys, ornate steps, and a profusion of carved dragons, showing their fangs to the street. Farther to the east, the imposing structure at Pierrepont and Clinton streets is the Long Island Historical Society building. The façade is decorated with terra-cotta busts of important historical figures (including token representations of a Viking and an American Indian over the door). A magnificent collection of material on Long Island, New York City, and New York State is available to nonmembers for a $1 fee, and there are exhibitions open to the public (Tuesday–Saturday 9 A.M.–5 P.M. Free). A visit here is highly recommended.

Everyone who knows the Heights knows Montague Street, the hub, the nexus. The spirit is effervescent and gay (in both senses of the word). It's less somber than some Greenwich Village streets, although the same kinds of shops are found here—some in basements, some up flights of steps overlooking the street. Restaurants and sidewalk cafés abound. There's music. Groups gather at corners or on the stoops. There are bulletin boards everywhere filled with wanted, for sale, for rent, lost kitten, and cheap-typing notices, all handwritten on grubby index cards. There's a sense of community. One feels that the people who live here really care for and love their neighborhood.

A short detour south along Henry Street leads us to Hunts Lane, another of Brooklyn Heights's hidden mews. I chatted with one of the residents, an elderly lady, who had spent much of her life in London. "I lived just off Kensington High Street and d'you know, I could still be there, this place is so much like my old home. I was in a mews, just like this, and all the stables were converted into flats with pretty flower boxes on the window ledges. There's something very comfortable about living in a little hidden street like this. We all know one another. It's like sharing a secret with friends."

If you have left a visit to the esplanade until now, then stroll west along Pierrepont Street past what many consider to be the

Hunts Lane

most refined structures in the Heights: numbers 2 and 3 Pierrepont Place. There's some disagreement as to whether the architect was Frederick Peterson or Richard Upjohn, who was responsible for a number of churches in the area and who lived nearby in Cobble Hill. However, there's no disagreement that the view westward past the mansions, out over the East River, is one of the finest in New York. There's a remarkable sense of "hereness" and "thereness." In the foreground are delicate iron railings, an ornate gas lamp, the shade of small garden trees, a bench or two. Then beyond the esplanade is the panorama of the Manhattan towers, the East River bridges, Governors Island, Staten Island, and way in the distance, past the Statue of Liberty, the rolling landscape of New Jersey. Whatever the time of day, whatever season, whatever kind of weather, this view cannot fail to touch the observer. Even if you've been here a dozen times before, come again and enjoy the sudden contrast with the intimate, human-scaled streets of the Heights.

Leave at the Remsen Street end and notice, to your left, the lovely Montague Terrace possessing all the grace and relaxed dignity of a London street. Thomas Wolfe lived here while writing *Of Time and the River*, as did Jules Feiffer and W. H. Auden. In fact, this was just one of Wolfe's many apartments in the Heights during the thirties. At one point he lived at 101 Columbia Heights and, in a letter, remarked that he had a "nice view of New York harbor and of the skyscrapers"—an unusual piece of understatement. Impressive premiums are paid for such views today.

The Heights of course has long enjoyed a literary reputation, and the list of its writer-residents reads like a Who's Who of twentieth-century American literature: Truman Capote, Hart Crane, John Dos Passos, Norman Mailer, Arthur Miller, and Henry Miller, to name but a few.

Strolling south down Hicks Street, pause at Grace Court Alley, a third secluded mews, before moving on to explore the tranquil "places" south of Joralemon Street. Each is a mere one block in length and terminates at both ends in cross streets, Joralemon to the north and State to the south. There's virtually no through traffic, and large London planes provide a canopy of shade over the streets. Most of the townhouses were built in the mid-1800s and reflect the fashionable revivals of that era. Although Sidney and Garden places are the more refined, Willow Place boasts a most unusual terrace of simple row houses, whose modest appearance has been transformed by the addition of a long, columned portico. The whole odd affair has been painted white and looks like some hybrid from the Deep South. Ironically, though, the naïveté of the concept creates a charm that the more self-conscious designs on adjoining streets could never possess.

Columbia Place has an even odder collection of clapboard cottages with fragile porches, left over from a longer row built in the mid-1800s. On the opposite side are the Riverside Houses, one of Alfred Tredway White's projects in this area and partially emasculated by subsequent construction of the Brooklyn–Queens Expressway. White was impressed by attempts in London to provide inexpensive yet sanitary and pleasant apartments for low-income families. He saw no reason why the idea could not be adapted to meet New York needs and yet still provide reasonable profit to the developer. So with his motto, "Philanthropy plus 5 percent," he financed the construction of a number of these projects (we'll explore two more in Cobble Hill) and not only provided a much-needed housing resource but also never failed to make his profit.

The charm of this southern corner of Brooklyn Heights has been noticed even by the power companies. Near the corner of Joralemon and Hicks there's a small plant disguised as a house, and along Willow Place a larger structure blends well with the street. The fire companies went one better. Way over on Jay Street near the Civic Center is the Old Brooklyn Fire Department Headquarters (see "Mini-Tours"), one of Frank Freeman's creations, which, both in scale and style, reflects the sonorous character of adjoining governmental buildings. In contrast, the delicate firehouse of Engine Co. 224 on Hicks Street between State and Joralemon is sensitive to the character of the street, although the architects, Adams and Warren, overindulged a little in ornate trimmings. But of course, as we've seen, that kind of superfluous extravagance was hardly unique in this neighborhood.

Immediately to the south of State Street, the Heights ends abruptly in a rash of galleries, health food shops, Syrian bakeries, and Middle Eastern restaurants. Atlantic Avenue, though, has none of the warm intimacy of Montague Street. Architecturally, it's a messy street without spatial character, unity, or style. Yet it has its devotees, Heights residents who think it's the best street around, less self-conscious than Montague, less brash than Fulton. The restaurants—the Adnan, Lebanon, Tripoli, Sinbad—are all reasonably priced and serve authentic Middle Eastern cuisine, but it's the honeyed confectionery, the homemade ice cream (try the pistachio), and the fresh-baked breads that are most tempting. The windows of the import-export stores brim with water pipes, caftans, trays, samovars, Turkish coffee contraptions in gleaming copper—even ornate camel saddles. Then there are the olives in vats, dried beans, sacks of almonds, grains, cooked figs, couscous, and bottles of thick flavored syrups. Some of the stores seem to have remained unaffected by all this exotic merchandising. Look at the barbers near Hicks Street. Can you remember a more traditional enclave of neighborhood masculinity, with its tiled floor, ancient swivel chairs, large mirrors, and the line of ivory-handled cut-throat razors over the wash basin? I chatted with one of the portly regulars who has lived most of his life on Atlantic Avenue. "I've seen 'em come 'n' go. I remember when this was all them Scandinavians, we usta call 'em Vikings. They owned most every place. Then there were some Indians, but they din' last long. Then these Arabs came and they've been here a while, but they'll go like all the others. The Spanish are movin' in now and we got them arty people and all that natural stuff—organic this 'n' that. Hell, I've seen 'em all. It's a crazy street."

Go south from Atlantic Avenue, down Clinton, into the second historic district along this walk, Cobble Hill. Actually, the name is a bit misleading. The British are said to have lopped off a good portion of the hill after Washington used it as a vantage point during the Battle of Long Island. Nonetheless, it's a most attractive area of brownstone terraces with Romanesque-Revival and Queen Anne detailing. It lacks the sparkle and the visual surprises of the Heights, but has a far more harmonious appearance—a sedate spirit made additionally attractive by fine rows of shade trees.

Don't mind the first couple of blocks south of Atlantic Avenue on Clinton. The neighborhood improves rapidly as you stroll down toward the tiny Cobble Hill Park, at Congress Street. Here's a delightful place to pause awhile if you resisted the restaurants along Montague Street and Atlantic Avenue. On the north side is an imposing terrace, spoiled somewhat by insensitive modifications. On the south side there's a line of smaller row houses, obviously not designed to face directly onto the park. They were once part of a mews when the park was occupied by more elegant townhouses. Yet, like those tiny carriage cottages in the Heights, they possess, through their very simplicity, an integrity unmatched by the ornate "Revival-style" terraces.

The same might be said of Alfred Tredway White's Warren Place Workingmen's Cottages, which can be reached by a short detour west along Verandah Place to Henry Street and a right turn on Warren Street. Here, facing each other across a narrow garden full of rhododendron bushes and replanted Christmas trees are two rows of cottages reminiscent of some of the homes built by industrialist-philanthropist Sir Titus Salt in his famous model factory town at Saltaire, Yorkshire, England. It's a charming concept and a fashionable place to live at the moment, although anyone

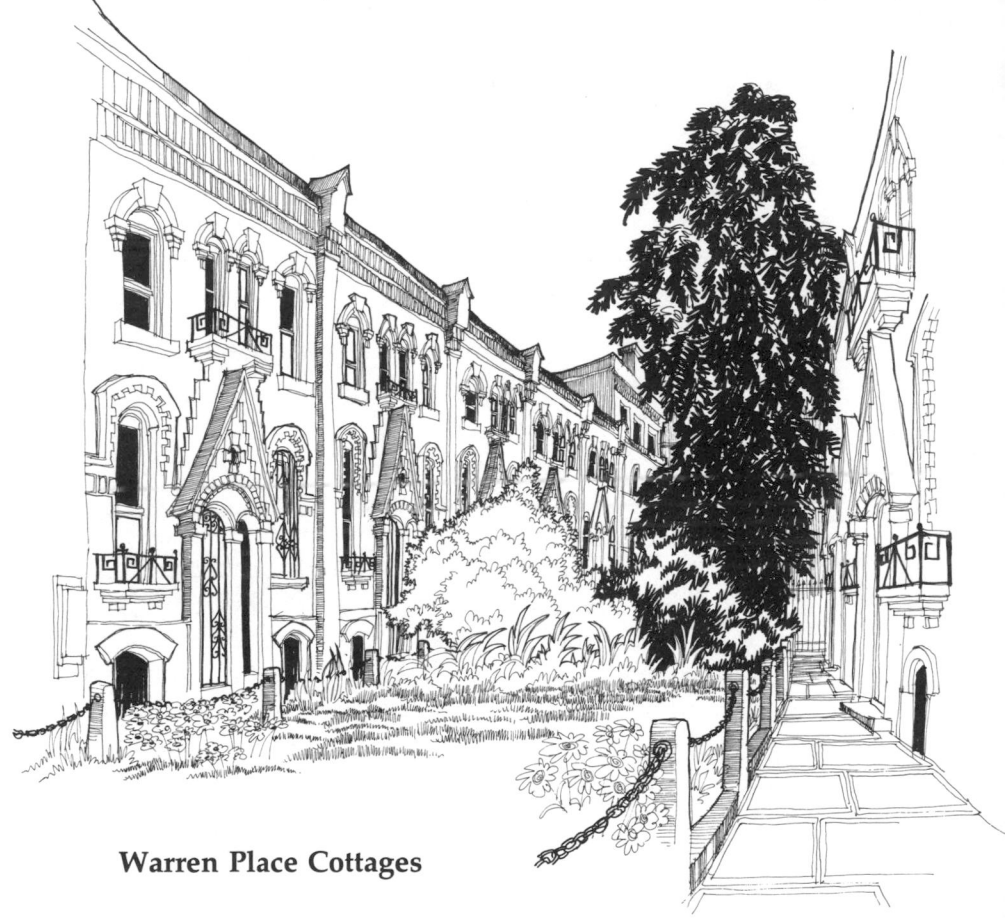

Warren Place Cottages

overweight would have problems squeezing through the narrow doorways. A little farther up the street is the third of White's developments along the Brooklyn waterfront, the Tower Buildings, similar to the Riverside Houses on Columbia Place in the Heights except that in this case the central recreational courtyards are still in existence and apparently well-used. A block farther south, between Baltic and Kane streets, there's a final complex, the Home Buildings.

Back on Clinton Street take a look at the Christ Episcopal Church on the corner of Kane Street. This was one of Richard Upjohn's works prior to Trinity Church in Manhattan, and it contains furnishings designed by Louis Comfort Tiffany, son of the famous glass craftsman. Note in particular the beautiful pulpit and lectern. Continue south on Clinton to Degraw Street, then stand and look back. This is one of the best sections of streetscape in Cobble Hill with the finely detailed Upjohn tower rising above the tree-shaded street and the refined row houses. Also take a look at Tompkins Place, one block east of Clinton, between Kane and Degraw streets. It would have taken very little to spoil the harmony of this scene—a poor piece of modernization, a break or two in the terrace, the intrusion of a gas station. Note some of the other streets in this area and you'll recognize how very delicate this kind of environment is and how it needs to be protected. The creation of a historic district is obviously a partial answer but far more important is the care and concern of the residents. Where this is lacking, no amount of publicity and moaning from outsiders will make any difference. The spirit must come from within. We'll see more evidence of both kinds of environment on the last part of this walking tour.

Three blocks south of Degraw Street, take President Street eastward (turn left) and follow it past Carroll Park to the Carroll Gardens historic district. In what is obviously a marginal neighborhood, President Street and Carroll Street east of the park have maintained their totally unique charm. Although built at different periods by different developers during the mid- and late-1800s, both streets possess a remarkable unity of design. Carroll Street is the more dignified space, characterized by the even height of the terraces, the regularity of the front garden walls, the lines of street trees, and the rhythm of steps and stoops. President Street is less even in character and has a more informal feel. The view north is particularly appealing as the street frontage continues along the north side of the park and up to the austere United Church of Christ at Court Street. Alas, the district is too small and nearby streets are declining. To the north, Union, Sackett, and Degraw streets all retain their essential character, particularly east of Smith Street, but without the protection of a historic district they may soon fade rapidly.

How are the feet? If you've had enough walking there's a subway at Carroll and Smith streets to whisk you home. If, however, you feel like trundling on, go north on Smith Street through a rather poor but colorful Spanish neighborhood full of Puerto Rican bakeries, noisy record stores, fish markets, butchers' shops with rows of smiling pigs' heads in the window, and the inevitable stores selling garish plaster madonnas, lions, parrots, and buddhas so popular with the Latin population. To the right, down Union Street are the remnants of the Gowanus Canal once described by McCandlish Phillips as "a richly aromatic avenue of steadily declining commerce." (And he wasn't referring to the aroma of spices!) There's not much to see except a stretch of murky water and a lock gate but, when this whole section of Brooklyn was a flourishing port, the canal was one of the busiest stretches of water in the harbor, and teams of bargemen supplied the factories and warehouses along its length.

Follow Smith Street past Willie's Fruit Market (a masterpiece of "folk architecture") up into the Brooklyn Civic Center. The first edifice you meet is the House of Detention on the north side of Atlantic Avenue. A line of people wait outside on the street at the inmate-visitors entrance. They all seem to know one another and greet wives, daughters, and mothers (the line is almost all female) arriving to visit incarcerated family members. Around the corner, adjoining the Quaker Meeting House at Schermerhorn Street and Boerum Place, there's a handwritten sign on a door: "Newgate. Free child care for visitors to the Brooklyn House of Detention." At least someone is trying to reduce the indignity and callousness of making children wait in line on the street. For that matter, why should anyone have to wait in the street?

Across the road, in what was once an entrance to the Court Street Subway, there's the New York Transit Exhibition (daily 10

A.M.–4 P.M. 50¢ token), a splendid panorama of transportation history in the five boroughs. Down on the lower level, the platforms are lined with old and new subway cars—the BMT Triplex 1927 through to the BMT-IND R 46 1976 cars, capable of 80 mph. Upstairs there's a slide show (it ends with a convincing plea for subsidized transport), bus engines, models of trams and trolley cars, early subway maps, fly-blown architects' renderings of subway-station designs à la 1930s, and a particularly archaic restroom which, it turns out, is not part of the exhibition but intended for current use! The whole presentation is excellent even if you're not a subway buff.

On the return leg of the journey stroll up past Borough Hall, past the Federal Building and Court House and the splendidly ornate General Post Office, back into Cadman Plaza. Note the statue of Henry Ward Beecher, considered by many to be the finest work of John Quincy Adams Ward, and one of the most impressive civic sculptures in New York. A short distance to the west, down Orange Street, is the plain Plymouth Church of the Pilgrims, where Beecher delivered his dramatic sermons for many years during the mid-1800s. He, along with his sister Harriet Beecher Stowe (author of *Uncle Tom's Cabin*), were ardent abolitionists, and this modest church became a mecca for the noted liberals of his day. Appropriately, there's also a bust of Robert Kennedy in the plaza, a modern-day "abolitionist" of those injustices that still plague minorities today. Maybe that's a good place to end the walk (unless of course you skipped the Brooklyn Bridge section, in which case, enjoy the rest of your stroll). Relax at Cadman Plaza, or better still, take your shoes off and massage your feet.

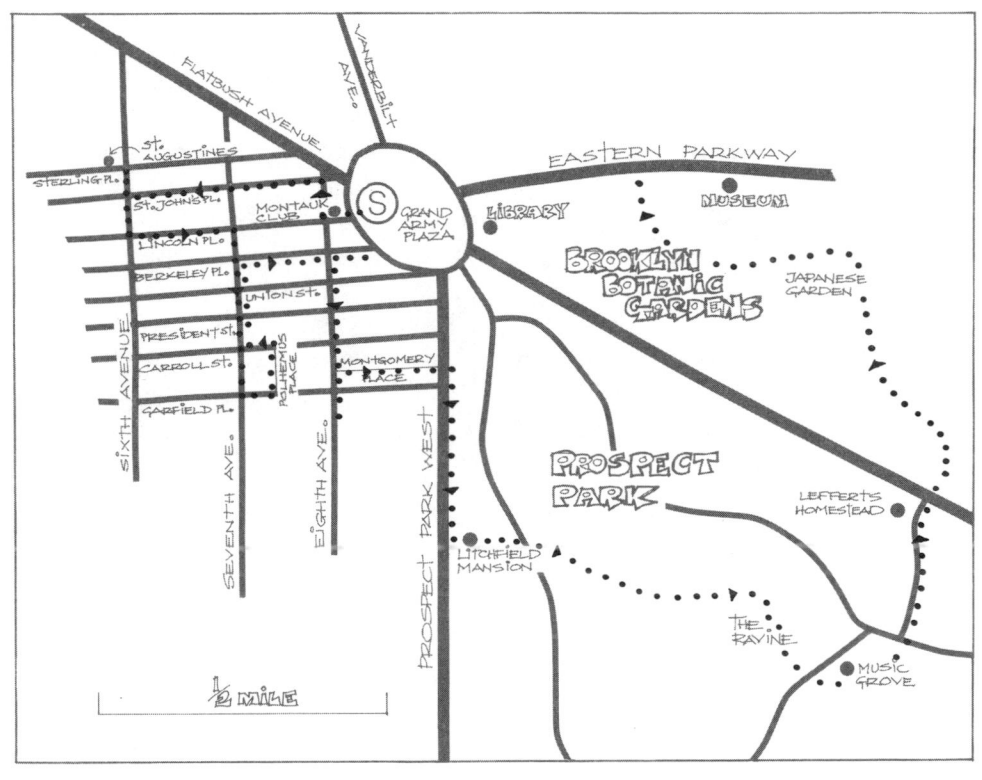

14
PARK SLOPE

In 1891 the first president of Brooklyn's newly opened Montauk Club declared: "A club should be an integral part of daily life. A man has his own church, and he should have his own club. It fills a need that cannot be met in any other way." At that time the great mansion and apartment residents around Grand Army Plaza and also Prospect Park West overlooking the park itself were collectively known as the "Gold Coast." Wealthy lawyers, merchants, and men of professional distinction lived in the elegant rows of townhouses that sloped downhill from the park. Most were built after the 1883 opening of the Brooklyn Bridge and reflected the abundance of architectural influences in those affluent days—Italianate, French Second Empire, Victorian Gothic, Queen Anne, Romanesque Revival, and a frivolity of "neo" styles. "Wealth," said one millionaire physician of the times, "should be apparent but not obvious. One's city house should be possessed of dignity and refinement. In one's country house, idiosyncrasies may be allowed to show. It is expected in fact." So, appropriately, Park Slope was developed with dignity and taste. Lower down the hill, however, toward the Gowanus Canal, far less care was taken and fragmented rows of brownstones mingled with noxious industrial plants and warehouses. Below Sixth Avenue was considered "blue nose" territory, named after a colony of Newfoundland fishermen who lived here and fished from Sheepshead Bay to the

─────────── **DIRECTIONS** ───────────

Subway: IRT 2, 3 to Grand Army Plaza
Bus: B41, B69, B71 to Grand Army Plaza

south. A local lady diarist wrote in 1903: "We do not journey below 7th [Avenue] and we instruct the servants to go about their shopping in other places. Here on the hilltop the breezes are fresh. We look over the farms and orchards and take our walks in the park. On Sundays a group of us visit the [Brooklyn] museum and rest by the fountain in the plaza. There can surely be no finer place of residence in the whole city."

In that respect at least, Park Slope has changed little since those idyllic days. Contemporary residents are as proud of their property as were their counterparts almost a century ago. "For Sale" signs in the windows of local real estate agents emphasize not so much the space and internal characteristics of available townhouses as the quality of external detailing, the name of the original architect, and any little bits of history that give the place distinction. For example—"Superb four story neo-Grec 1907 townhouse with four-columned doorway, Corinthian capitals, and copper-finished mansard extension. Work of a Stanford White student. Hart Crane lived here and it was originally home of the founder of the Gage and Tollner restaurant [a famous Brooklyn landmark]." Obviously, such details as the number of bedrooms and condition of fixtures are regarded by purchasers as mundane irrelevancies.

In the last ten years Park Slope has bounded back from the doldrums that afflicted it after the Depression. The "Buy a Brooklyn Brownstone" slogan worked its magic on the imaginations of scores of Manhattan residents, and the renaissance began bringing the new people up Flatbush Avenue to begin a fresh life on these airy slopes. "We still got problems, though," one elderly resident told me. "Some streets below Seventh Avenue and down round Ninth Street are real bad—junkies, muggings, the lot. I'd never go down there, even in daylight. But the new people are helping. We get lots of those block-party things in the summer. That's real nice, 'specially for us that have been here a long time. Reminds me of how things were when I was a kid. There was the rich folks right on top of the hill. They kept to themselves mostly but the others lower down were really nice. It was like a village then. You knew everybody in your street. It's getting to be like that again."

Writers, architects, artists, musicians, and editors at Manhattan's prestigious publishing houses live happily alongside large Italian and Irish families, the neighborhood's more traditional residents. Places like Ryan's Bar at Garfield and Seventh Avenue are the stout and whiskey headquarters for the older Irishmen; not far away, on Union Street, the Camperdown Elm attracts mainly new people. The Hopper-like Purity Café and the Economy Restaurant appeal to a cross-section of residents with conversation stretching the gamut from dogs (the racing kind) to Degas. Garden shrines of pastel madonnas contrast with diminutive art galleries, grand pianos in parlor windows, and carriage lamps on the stoops. But the most important ingredient—harmony—is here. You can feel it in the spirit of the clean streets, the polished door-knockers, the proud new owners of old brownstones carefully patching heavily detailed cornices, and in the hearty bon-vivant atmosphere of the Seventh Avenue strip.

Let's begin our walk at the Montauk Club (Lincoln Place and Eighth Avenue), focal point of the old and new in Park Slope. The architect, Francis H. Kimball, based his design on a Venetian palazzo with motifs strongly reminiscent of the Doge's Palace on St. Marks Square in Venice. The ornate and imposing structure contains a wonderful array of terra-cotta bas-reliefs on three of its four façades. Note the frieze depicting the history of the Montauk Indians, after whom the club was named. Various other panels contain carved Indian heads, a picture of the founders of the club laying the cornerstone, and, on the Lincoln Place façade, elaborate gargoyles supporting the balcony. Inside it's all a club should be—finely paneled walls, creaking floors, hazy light filtering through subdued stained-glass windows, ocean navigation charts browned in their frames, etchings of Park Slope in the 1890s, and an almost tangible sense of decorum and propriety. Although the club has had to liberalize its membership policy, welcoming women and families, the flavor remains masculine and "leathery."

Down St. Johns Place toward Seventh Avenue we experience the architectural unity of these sloping streets, the evenness of the stoops, the regularity of the roofline with only occasional eccentric extensions to add a touch of variety. The flavor is slightly formal, yet lively music drifts from open doors, a girl sits half out of a window combing her hair, and, farther down, kids chase one

St. Johns Place

another with Starsky-and-Hutch determination, bawling and bellowing. The street, like most in Park Slope, is an essay in subtle browns, beiges, and creams. Very mellow.

Around the junction of St. Johns Place and Seventh Avenue we find a cluster of churches. (Park Slope has long been noted for its crenelated skyline of church towers and spires.) On the northeast corner is the Grace United Methodist Church, a chunky red stone creation built in 1882. Note the stubby flying buttresses and the thick tower, which once supported an elegant spire. Occasional theatrical productions are offered here and most Saturdays there's a flea market (11 A.M.–4 P.M.) in the adjoining building. Across the road, still with its stone steeple intact, is the Memorial Presbyterian Church (1882) with an adjoining chapel added in 1888. Its most notable features are the Tiffany stained-glass windows and the delightful sculpture of an angel and three young children, softening influences on an otherwise rather stern structure.

A little farther west on St. Johns Place is the English country-style St. John's Protestant Episcopal Church. Set back behind a small lawn, its flavor is delightfully rural in this intensely urban setting. "I got married in there." A broad middle-aged lady in a wide-brimmed hat stopped to watch me sketching the two magnificent 1888 townhouses opposite the church. "I was only twenty-three then." She sighed. "He was thirty-one—or -two—I forget which. But it was a lovely wedding. Lost him last year. Heart attack. Very sudden. He was such a lovely man too." We both paused. It seemed the right thing to do in the circumstances.

I don't know what it is that attracts people about a person sketching, but I invariably find myself a captive audience listening to long life stories or opinions on every imaginable subject. My function, it appears, is to be silent. Once the initial interchange is completed ("Oh, you're drawing, are you?" "Yes." "Ah.") the monologue invariably begins. I've listened to some wonderful tales. (I've also had some rather unusual propositions.) Normally I continue sketching and just enjoy the anecdotes and experiences of my storytellers. They might make an interesting book one day.

The most elegant church in Park Slope and, from my experience, one of the finest in the five boroughs, is St. Augustine's Roman Catholic Church at Sterling Place and Sixth Avenue. This 1892 essay in Victorian Gothic extravagance was the work of the Parfitt Brothers, prodigious designers of churches in the area. Rarely has such harmony of design been achieved with such a wealth of materials and detailings—brownstone, brick, copper, marble, turrets, towers, gargoyles, statues, full columns, semicolumns, and windows of all shapes and sizes. Inside, the flavor is equally exuberant. The richly carved altar wall in white stone stands at the end of a cathedrallike nave. The colored rays of light through the elaborate stained-glass windows bounce off the delicate supporting columns and reflect on the ornate hand-painted ceilings and walls. A mosaic of a pelican feeding the young from her own blood dominates the open floor area in front of the altar and finely detailed angels, madonnas, and prophets provide an almost baroque setting for Sunday observances. Unfortunately, the church is closed during the week except for masses at 9 A.M. and 4 P.M., but if you're really anxious to see inside, someone at the adjoining rectory will normally try to oblige.

Walking back up the slope along Lincoln Place, we arrive at Seventh Avenue, hub of the district. From the windows of the rather aloof brick building on the northwest corner trickle the elegant sounds of pianos, violins, and voices that have made the Brooklyn Conservatory of Music so famous and well-loved. Stroll down the avenue and enjoy its flavor. There's a neighborhood feel here, a sense of camaraderie among the shoppers and the browsers. The art galleries, the "One Smart Cookie" store, the "Leaf and Bean" (a wonderful array of teas and coffees and all the paraphernalia for making the brews), and a scattering of other outlets reflecting the tastes of the "new people" sit comfortably alongside the more traditional grocery stores, the older restaurants, and the staunchly Irish taverns. Streetcar tracks are still visible in places. A large Italian lady surrounded by a bunch of tugging kids waddles along the sidewalk carrying two enormous bags of groceries with loaves of crisp bread sticking out of the top. Following are a denim-adorned couple in fine-cut leather boots and sloppy flat caps making their way to Ann and Richard Hayton's popular Village Green plant store (Union Street and Seventh Avenue). On walls and windows are the posters and flyers that tell the nook-and-cranny explorer so much about a community—a craft fair, flea markets, meditation sessions, weekend encounter groups, pedigree dogs for sale, folk music in one of the nearby taverns, an experimental theater group beginning its first season, a new health-food restaurant opening soon. Other signs for bingo evenings at a nearby Catholic church and a Guinness stout flyer on a store window reflect the interests of the more indigenous residents.

Seventh Avenue lacks the architectural unity and the decorous flavor that characterize many of Park Slope's east–west streets. A brief loop up Garfield Place and along Polhemus Place is a reminder of the utter tranquillity of the side streets. Note the interesting groups of townhouses designed to appear as large individual mansions. But the life and the vibrancy of the avenue is more than adequate compensation for its physical deficiencies. Spend time here browsing before returning to Eighth Avenue via Berkeley Place.

Stroll up toward the Grand Army Plaza and look out for the elaborate mansion (274–76) dwarfed by the thirteen-story block of apartments facing the park. Architects are often entranced by its unusual combination of Romanesque Revival and neoclassic influences—an "inspired idiosyncrasy." Others find the bold detailing combined with its ponderous granite bulk of huge rough-cut blocks the perfect reflection of many early "Gold Coast" residents—strong-willed businessmen and merchants who had wrenched their way to the top of the money pile and didn't mind showing it. The more sedate residents, those blessed with inherited wealth, normally chose less demonstrative expressions of their status, but not George P. Tangeman, owner of the Royal and Cleveland Baking Powder Companies. He had the firm of Lamb and Rich design a house befitting his concept of himself, and 274–76 was the result.

He was not alone. Note the splendor of the mansions along Eighth Avenue as we head south toward Montgomery Place. Each is a totally individual expression of architectural style, yet there is harmony here. Magnificent detailing characterizes each one even down to the intricate door-knockers and elaborate terra-cotta ornamentation. The array of capitals, crenelations, stained glass, towers, bays, wrought iron, fanlights, brick-laying techniques, and stonework is virtually encyclopedic. Just down Union Street, though, the houses at 905–13 almost carry their joyous Queen Anne and Romanesque-Revival frivolities to an extreme. As an architect friend of mine remarked, "One more bull's-eye window and you'd have a fairground."

Residents in this part of the Slope have included such notables as Thomas Adams, Jr., owner of one of the largest chewing-gum factories in the country, Charles L. Feltman, who supposedly introduced the hot dog to America, and members of the F. W. Woolworth family. The term "Gold Coast" was certainly appropriate to this particular part of the neighborhood, and the massive bulk of the pentagonal Temple Beth Elohim seems completely in keeping with the flavor of the street.

Montgomery Place has a totally different character and is the result of a rather interesting experiment in townhouse design. Known as the "block beautiful," it was developed in the late 1880s by Harvey Murdoch and reflects his attempt to introduce a wide variety of styles to alleviate the repetitive nature of typical Park Slope streets. Unlike adjoining Carroll Street, where a similar effort undertaken by at least ten of New York's leading architects resulted in a somewhat disjointed whole, Montgomery Place relied heavily upon C. P. H. Gilbert's unifying influence. He designed almost half of the individual structures with his typical flair for large unadorned areas contrasted with exquisitely rich detailing. The other designs were also doubtless supervised by him, as there's hardly a discordant element in the whole creation. More recent development, however, in the form of apartment structures facing Prospect Park West, has destroyed some of the street's spatial charm. The houses at the top end appear a little dumpy against the towering brick walls of the high-rises. The view west, looking downhill, is far more satisfying.

On Prospect Park West we find another splendid selection of individually designed mansions. At the corner of Montgomery Place is an elegant residence of exquisitely laid Indiana limestone. In comparison to other houses in the vicinity, the structure is rather small, but what it lacks in bulk it makes up in the richness of its decorative trimmings. Note the copper-topped tower above the dormer window—just the right touch of refinement.

A little farther south is the Henry Carlton Hulbert Mansion, built in 1892 and again reflective of the power and wealth of many of the "Gold Coast's" residents. The Ethical Culture Society purchased the property in 1928 along with the adjoining, and equally interesting, William H. Childs Mansion, and uses the two as a school and meeting house for its members. The City Landmarks Commission waxed eloquent over both structures in their descriptive reports, so before we finally leave the historic district, spend time examining these turn-of-the-century creations. The Childs Mansion particularly contains an unusual range of gargoyles, Flemish-bond brickwork, a distinguished finial, bay windows, and two prominent chimneys. Guarding the door are twin lions, an idea repeated on the other side of the road at the entrance to Prospect Park, except that these are panthers proudly standing on vast granite pedestals. At least some people think they're panthers. The artist, Alexander Phimister Proctor, always referred to them as pumas, and Stanford White, who designed the pedestals, called them "those magnificent cats." Whatever they are, they rank alongside Edward Clark Potter's twin lions at the New York Public Library for force of personality.

The Litchfield Mansion sits in Tuscan splendor on a knoll just inside the park. It was built in 1855 from designs by Alexander J. Davis, one of the leading American architects of his time, and was the first mansion to be erected in the Park Slope area. The railroad entrepreneur Edwin C. Litchfield lived here until 1882, although for many years he rented the property from the City of Brooklyn, which had purchased it for eventual use as headquarters for the Brooklyn Parks Commission. Regrettably, its continued use as offices of the Parks Department has diminished its internal interest, although one can still sense the grandeur of the place in the entrance rotunda and main staircase. Visitors are also bemused by the ornate corn-stalk capitals on the columns at the side of the mansion.

If you intend to take the rest of the walk across Prospect Park and up through the Botanic Garden, then pick up the free map here, which lists the prime points of interest. There's also usually a photographic display of the park's delights in the foyer.

Olmsted and Vaux's Prospect Park is undoubtedly one of the most beautifully landscaped creations in the five boroughs, with a wonderful array of meadows, streams, lagoons, pools, and playgrounds. The architects McKim, Mead and White and Frank J. Helmle are well represented here, and the park contains a wealth of revival-style creations—the Grecian Shelter, the Boathouse, the Tennis House, the Picnic House, and the Shelter Pavilion, all finely articulated structures completely in harmony with the roll-

The Ravine—Prospect Park

ing estatelike setting. The problem here is to find a relatively quiet walk through the park that avoids the more popular sections. On summer weekends, of course, it's almost impossible. Even the most inaccessible recesses contain their share of a snuggling, romping, ball-playing populace. However, during the week or out of season I find that a stroll directly through the heart of the park from the Litchfield Mansion to the Willink Entrance on Flatbush Avenue, by way of the Picnic House, Ravine, Music Grove, and the Eastwood Arch, is a delightfully tranquil experience. The ravine with its tumbling stream and waterfalls is an especially lovely place to find a woody spot off the path and rest awhile.

The Lefferts Homestead (Wednesday, Friday, Saturday, and Sunday 1–5 P.M. Free), just by the zoo at the eastern entrance, is a recreation of a late-eighteenth-century Dutch-style farmhouse with the exception of the huge Federal doorway, which obviously has little relationship to the rest of the diminutive structure. Again one needs to pick a quieter time to enjoy its charm. Like the Dyckman House in upper Manhattan, it possesses a steeply pitched roof supported by delicate columns. Inside are typical room settings of the seventeenth and eighteenth centuries featuring a Gilbert Stuart portrait of George Washington, a Hepplewhite sofa, a Chippendale highboy, and several ancient Dutch Bibles. For those unfamiliar with the house, it's a fascinating diversion.

Across the road is the Brooklyn Botanic Garden (daily 8 A.M.– sunset, Saturday and Sunday from 10 A.M. on. Free), one of my favorite niches in the borough, and a totally delightful way to complete our loop walk back to Grand Army Plaza. The lower gardens and the conservatory tend to attract the majority of visitors, which leaves the Japanese Garden and the various tree-lined walks in the upper section relatively quiet. Pick up a pamphlet at the entrance and select your own route through here. One's pace tends to slow immediately after passing through the gates and reading the sign in the children's garden:

> He is happiest who hath power
> To gather wisdom from a flower.

In addition to beds of carefully nurtured plants and flowers there are the quiet niches like the Herb Garden, the far side of the lake in the Japanese Garden, and the beautiful Fragrance Garden specially designed for sensory exploration. "Rub, touch and smell" urges the sign. Braille notations throughout make it a particularly rewarding experience for visually impaired people. Then there's the remarkable Ryoanji Temple Stone Garden, a replica of a 500-year-old garden in Kyoto, Japan. Referred to as the "meditation garden," this skillful blending of raked sand and large rocks standing independently in an enclosed courtyard has a quality of total peace and harmony. As the leaflet explains, harmony is the prime expression—"that Harmony which underlies the universe, the world, and man; the Harmony of force, of nature and of spirit; the Harmony that makes man to know himself a brother of the rocks and the wind and the sun." Rarely in this sprawling bustle of a city does one discover a place like this, a place where people sit quietly without talking, without the restless shuffle that characterizes so much of life in New York. They sit, sometimes for an hour or more, absorbing the "knowingness" of this utterly peaceful place. As a prominent American architect said: "It is deceptively simple in design, but this is what gives it power." And there is power here—an almost tangible sensation of silent, infinite energy.

Just outside the courtyard is the Roji Garden, based on a traditional network of Japanese teahouse paths. The subtle interplay of textures underfoot, ferns and shrubs, water, and lanterns provide a constant sense of change and yet, once again, the overriding sense of harmony and completeness prevails.

Here in the garden people tend to walk slowly, enjoying the surprises that await even the regular visitor. An elderly lady beckoned me over as I ambled toward the crabapple arbors. "Look, do you see him?" She pointed excitedly to a beautiful red-feathered bird singing deep in the bushes. "It's a red cardinal!" she gushed. "It's the first time I've seen one here—ever. I've been coming every week for fifteen years and I've never seen one here before. Isn't he absolutely wonderful!" The cardinal must have known he was being admired and sang even louder. The lady and I smiled at each other and at the bird. I realized that if I had smiled at her in the street she probably would have ignored me completely, suspecting some motive of a most ulterior nature. But here in the garden, it's neutral ground. People can feel safe to smile, to talk to strangers, to sit quietly looking at rocks and sand, to watch streams cascade in tiny waterfalls. Try to end your walk here, in the shadow of the Brooklyn Museum. It's one more reminder that the city is still a lovely place to live in.

Queens

15
FLUSHING

After emerging from the subway at Roosevelt Avenue and Main Street, I usually have my shoes shined. It's a ritual. It gets the day, and the walk, off to a good start, especially when my shoes are shined by none other than Tony Avena himself. His stand is located under the Long Island Railroad bridge, just up Main Street from the subway. Small, wiry, and always sparkling, Tony can detect the mood of his customers in an instant and carefully molds the conversation to the moment. Grumpy individuals full of the woes of the world leave with polished shoes and shining spirits. "Where else can a fellow have such a good time meeting interesting people," Tony told me. "I can listen all day to stories about other people's lives. Everyone's different, everyone's got something to say." Tony's enthusiasm is shared by his brothers, Charlie and Jimmy, who work in the stand with him. Between the three of them, they offer a remarkable range of services, including the sale of flower arrangements, key duplicating, hat blocking and cleaning (note the custom blocks on the shelves to the right of the shoeshine "thrones"), and an inexhaustible supply of information on local history, neighborhood characters, and the changing features of "lovely Flushin'." Tony and his brothers were all brought up in the Hell's Kitchen district of Manhattan, learning street wis-

────────── **DIRECTIONS** ──────────

Subway: *Start:* IRT 7 to Main Street, Flushing
  Return: IRT 7 at Shea Stadium
Bus: Q13, Q14, Q15, Q16, Q28, Q44

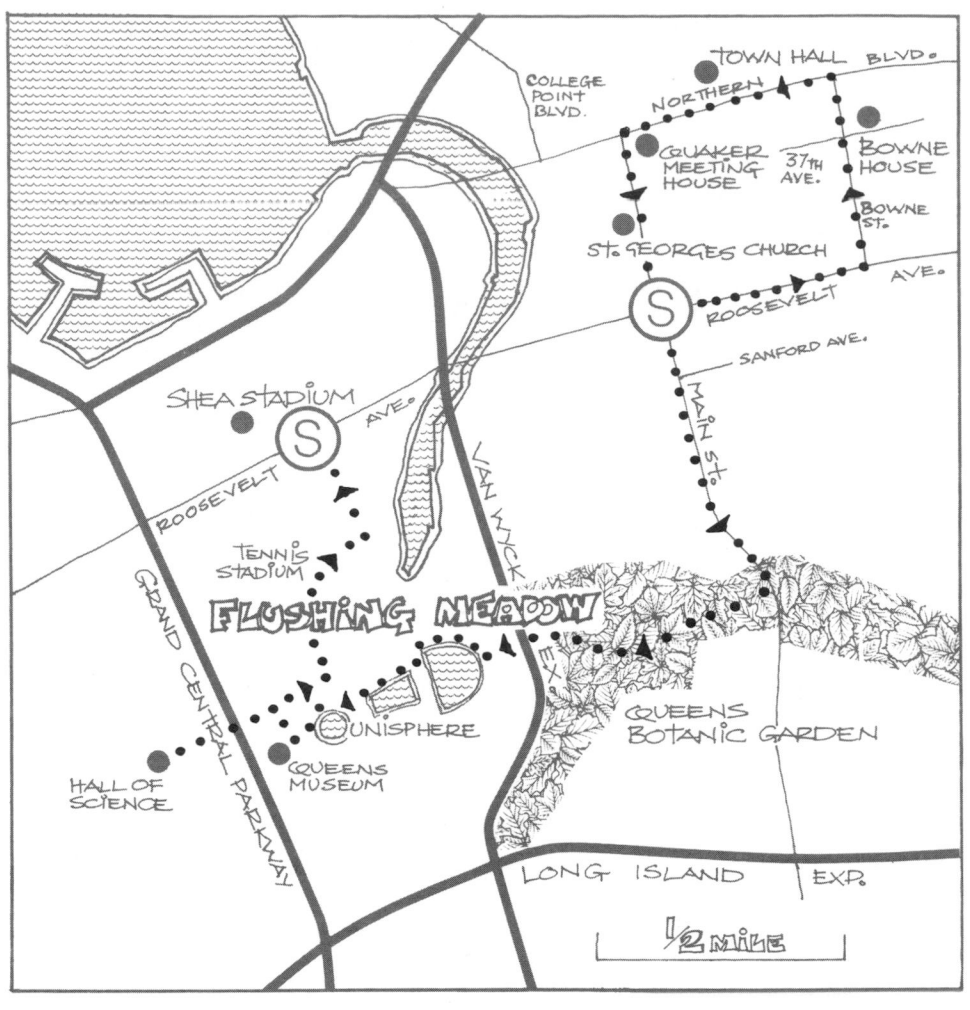

dom at an early age. Their father was also a notable "bootblacker." ("Forget 'shoe-shiner,' " Tony told me, "that's not the right word.") When he died in 1937, Tony had become a master of the art. He moved out to Flushing originally at the time of the 1935 World's Fair in Flushing Meadow and stayed on. "It was a lot different then," he told me. "There were all apple orchards and farmlands round here. Not much housing and stuff in those days 'cept for fancy mansions with captains' walks and suchlike. Nowadays"— he gestured with his arm—"well, just look at it. Busy as hell. Gets busier all the time, too." I asked if he planned to retire. "Retire! I'll retire when they carry me out. What should I do, stay home and vegetate? I couldn't do without people."

Stroll eastward along Roosevelt Avenue, past the Lippman Arcade. Note the store full of comic books at 136–79, "More than 50,000 in Stock." Buyers come from all over the five boroughs to browse through the racks here of Thor, Marvel Man, and monster comics, many of which are more than ten years old. Most are in the $1–$5 range, but according to the sales assistant at the desk, "We've got some in the back worth fifty dollars and more—real collectors' items." He showed me a comic-book catalog and there they all were— *The Mummy's Tomb, Superman and the Venus Spider, The Creature That Dripped Blood, The Mad Thing,* and thousands more, many with sample illustrations bounding off the pages. "It's a real hobby for a lot of people—collecting these things," he told me. "Some of these are real rare—worth hundreds of dollars."

At the corner of Roosevelt Avenue and Bowne Street is the elaborately detailed Community Church with its prominent brick tower. Built in 1892 in confident Romanesque-Revival style, the church is now a meeting place for various local religious groups including the Korean Church of Queens, which holds services here every Sunday at 2 P.M.

Tree-shaded Bowne Street has a tranquil spirit and is a perfect setting for the diminutive Bowne House at the corner of 37th Avenue (Tuesday, Saturday, Sunday 2:30–4:30 P.M. Free). Inside one begins to appreciate the long and fascinating history of Flushing and its once-staunch Quaker community. The town was actually named after Vlissingen in Holland. Many of England's persecuted Quakers had found refuge there before sailing to the New

World in the 1640s and 1650s. But even in America they discovered religious freedom to be somewhat less abundant than they had expected. Peter Stuyvesant regarded the Quakers as "an abominable sect" and in his edict of 1657 declared that the only permitted religion in the New Netherlands was the Dutch Reformed Church. He forbade the assembly of other groups and threatened imprisonment of anyone found entertaining a Quaker or holding a Quaker meeting. But the people of Flushing objected strongly. Selected lines from their famous "Remonstrance" to the Governor on December 27, 1657, possess the same firmness of tone and intent as the Declaration of Independence itself:

> You have been pleased to send up unto us a certain prohibition or command that we should not receive any of those people called Quakers because they are supposed to be by some, seducers of the people. For our part we cannot condemn them in this case, neither can we stretch out our hands against them, to punish, banish or persecute them . . .
>
> Therefore if any of these said persons come in love unto us, we cannot in conscience lay violent hands upon them, but give them free egresse and regresse unto our Town, and houses, as God shall persuade our consciences. And in this we are true subjects both of Church and State, for we are bounde by the law of God and man to doe good unto all men and evil to noe man.

(The complete text of the Remonstrance is contained in the "Freedom Mile" brochure available at the Bowne House, and also on a plaque in the garden.)

John Bowne arrived here in 1651 and later, after joining the Society of Friends, he openly invited Quakers to meet in the kitchen of his pleasant English-styled country cottage. As a result he was subsequently deported to Holland in December 1662. Stuyvesant thought he had rid himself of "a troublesome menace" but failed to recognize Bowne's resilience and sense of outrage. Within a short time he was back, having argued his case before the Dutch West India Company, who sent a disciplinary note to Stuyvesant instructing him to insure that "the people's conscience should not be forced by anyone, but remain free in itself." From then onward the Quakers, and many other budding religious sects, experienced increased freedom of worship. The founder of the Quaker faith, George Fox, preached under the shade of two oak trees outside the Bowne house in June 1672, and praised the residents of Flushing for their faith and fortitude. A large gray rock marks the site today.

Spend time inside the Bowne House. The simplicity of its structure and its fittings reflects the austere life of many early Quaker families, although the kitchen suggests that, while unimpressed by material abundance, they were well aware of the importance of ample sustenance. The fireplace is large enough to roast an ox (and obviously was used regularly for this purpose, hence the unusual width of the kitchen door), and the oven with its domed rear section could bake as many as forty pies or loaves simultaneously. My charming female guide explained, almost defensively, "They had to work ever so hard in those days, so I suppose they needed a lot of food." She then went on to point out the hidden entrance to a tunnel that linked the Bowne house to the Aspinwall House (originally located on Northern Boulevard near the present YMCA). This was part of the underground railroad system in the years preceding the Civil War which provided runaway slaves with a safe, if occasionally circuitous, route from the South to New England and Canada. "The Quakers were very active in that movement," she explained. "That's why they call this part of Flushing the 'Freedom Mile.' So many things happened here that helped establish our basic freedoms—freedom of worship, freedom of slaves, freedom of education (the nearby Flushing High School is the oldest free public high school in Greater New York), and freedom of public assembly. It's quite amazing, really. People don't normally think of Flushing as being a hotbed of freedom movements!"

Passing through the herb garden at the rear of the house we come to the magnificent Weeping Beech Tree, a rare mutation brought by the farmer-horticulturist Samuel Parsons as a cutting from Belgium in 1847. Today, with a circumference of fourteen feet, a spread of almost ninety feet, and a height of more than sixty feet, this unique creature is now an official landmark designated as such by the New York City Landmarks Preservation Commission. In summer when the leaves are full, it becomes a gentle cascade of greens, moving in the breezes blowing off Flushing Bay—without doubt one of the most beautiful trees in the city.

Farther east on 37th Avenue, shaded by the beech, is the colonial-style Kingsland House (Tuesday, Saturday, Sunday

2:30–4:30 P.M. Free), originally built as a farmhouse in 1774 almost two miles east of its present location. The name *Kingsland* was derived from Captain Joseph King, an English sea captain who inherited the house in the early 1800s. His daughter subsequently married Lindley Murray, after whose family Murray Hill is named. Various generations of the Murrays lived in this sturdy structure. Most of the permanent collection is maintained upstairs in the Victorian Room. The other rooms are used for regularly changing exhibitions and displays. On my last visit the building was being extensively restored, both inside and outside, but the guide assured me that all would be back to normal quite shortly.

In the adjoining park there's another tree worthy of note, a splendid cedar of Lebanon. Once again we are indebted to Samuel Parsons, after whom nearby Parsons Boulevard is named. He and an equally renowned horticulturist, William Prince, both selected these fertile hills above the bay as suitable locations for their famous nurseries. George Washington recorded a visit in 1789 to "Mr. Prince's fruit gardens and shrubberies" and was entertained royally by the citizens of Flushing on that occasion except for a slight mishap with a cannon, which blasted off harmlessly while Washington was delivering his address—sending the father of our country scurrying for cover. The official title of the nursery was the Linnaean Botanic Garden, and following its inauguration in 1737 Prince developed one of the largest arrays of tree specimens in the country. A century later, in 1838, Samuel Parson's nursery began to flourish on the site of the present playground adjoining the Kingsland house. Like Prince he specialized in unusual species of trees, and the results of his labor can still be enjoyed throughout the town.

Passing the Collegiate-Gothic crenelations of Flushing High School we stroll west on Northern Boulevard to the odd cluster of historic buildings around the Civil War monument. Most notable is the cream-and-chocolate-brown Town Hall, officially a Romanesque-Revival creation, but with all the idiosyncrasies of late Victoriana. Its history is equally eccentric. Built originally in 1862 as the Flushing Town Hall, the building has functioned as a municipal courthouse, theater, bank, ballroom, Supreme Court chamber, and headquarters of a local artillery company. Guests within its halls have included Tom Thumb, Jenny Lind, Samuel Clemens

Flushing Town Hall

(Mark Twain), President Ulysses S. Grant, Theodore Roosevelt, P. T. Barnum the impresario and circus king, and scores of other prominent persons in politics, the theater, and the arts.

Recently, after long years of nonoccupancy, Steve Phillips and a number of other dedicated citizens assured its preservation by opening it as a nineteenth-century-flavored restaurant and theater. "God, we thought we'd never get the place going," Steve told me as we strolled through the Town Hall's paneled corridors. "Eighteen months of paperwork—eighteen months! And that was just to get it to public auction. We could have lost it even then if someone had bid higher. As it was, we were the only nuts who wanted it." It took a lot more work before the place could be opened. "You should've seen the pigeons, hundreds of them, great mounds of droppings . . . the place was a real mess. But then, that first night when we turned the lights on the stage and the audience watched our first play, hell, I could have wept. Just to hear laughter in the building after so many years . . . it was beautiful. It made everything worthwhile."

Steve is still changing and adding to the original concept of a theater-restaurant. He showed me the stately bar in the old courtroom, an English inn-styled restaurant (once the judges' quarters), and the larger main restaurant, adorned with hand-screened wallpaper. He told me of plans for experimental theater productions and supper-club entertainment. "We've got to have music and laughter in the place, 'else we get in trouble with the ghost!" It appears that Jonathan Anderson Parker, a young orchestra conductor with a promising future, used to perform at the Town Hall until he lost his life in the Civil War battle of Simpson's Creek. Occasionally since then the building has resounded to the strains of ghostly music, rainbows, and displays of light. A number of times a wraithlike figure of a Union soldier has been reported moving slowly downstairs from the theater itself. "It seems to have stopped now," Steve told me. "The place is full of noise and fun again, so maybe old Jonathan's content."

Past the Masonic Hall and the "fairy-castle" brick armory on the other side of the road is an austere, gray-shingle structure rich with the patina of age. This Friends Meeting House, built in 1694, with subsequent additions in 1717, is one of the oldest houses of worship in the nation. Except for a period between 1776 and 1783 when it was used by the British as a prison and a hospital, it has been an active meetinghouse and is open to the public on the first and third Sunday of each month 2–4 P.M. If you've never seen a meetinghouse before, try to arrange a Sunday visit here. The restful serenity of the cemetery shaded by the elm tree planted to commemorate Washington's visit to Flushing in 1789, and the utter simplicity of its interior, provides a sense of peace rarely found in the more ornate churches. The doors from the front porch are moved by weighted ropes and pulleys and open directly into the main room. Open-back wooden benches face the center of the room. The second floor is supported by forty-foot oak beams, hand-hewn from individual trees. Ships "knees" taken from an early sailing ship secure them to the wall timbers. The typical Quaker meeting is characterized by silence and absolute integrity.

Friends Meeting House

These qualities above all others are predominant in this memorable place.

Nearby various statues and memorials commemorate the Spanish-American War, the Civil War, and World War I. The landscaped oasis in the center of Northern Boulevard is named in honor of another notable Flushing resident, Daniel Beard, naturalist and illustrator and one of the founders of the Boy Scouts of America. Beyond is the ponderous bulk of the RKO Keith's theater, once a famous home of vaudeville and a showcase for rising stars of the time.

We turn abruptly south back onto Main Street, which, as we climb slowly uphill, seems to possess some of the flavor of typical small-town main streets all over the country. Flickers of Art Deco mingle with ceramic-tiled single-story stores, clapboard façades, and pudgy, pompous banks. There's an elegant street clock, fifteen feet of baroque cast iron, occupying part of the sidewalk. Nearby is the prominent spire of St. George's Episcopal Church. This is the third church on the same site, the first having received a charter from King George II in 1761. Francis Lewis, one of the signers of the Declaration of Independence, was vestryman here from 1765 to 1790.

A brief detour eastward down Roosevelt Avenue takes us past an unusual store selling bonsai plants, two Sneakers' Choice outlets (literally—tens of thousands of sneakers) and one of the most fully stocked martial-arts centers I've found outside Manhattan. If you've ever wondered what empty hand conditioners, Pan K'uei strikers, makiwaras, nunchakus, ko-budo sais, bokkens, naginatas, shurikens, and suburitos are (no, none of them are edible), this is the place to learn. There are some grisly implements here, the kind that convince me never to upset a martial-arts expert.

Back on Main Street, those already feeling weary from our walk around the Freedom Mile might wish to return to the city. We shall continue, however, on the second leg south on Main Street past Tony Avena's shoeshine stand and a tempting array of restaurants toward the Queens Botanical Garden (Wednesday–Sunday 9 A.M.–dusk. Free. TU. 6–3800). Note the groups of civic-style buildings at Sanford Avenue—the proud-columned post office, the colonial mansion now used as a private high school, and the magnificent domed synagogue built in 1926.

This particular botanical garden is the most recently developed in New York City but offers a wide variety of exhibits and an interesting range of lectures, demonstrations, and workshop courses in home gardening, tree-care, flower arrangement, and even how to attract different species of birds into your own garden. At regular intervals throughout the year there are shows and festivals—the Tulip Show in April, the Spring Plant Sale, the Rose Festival in early June, and the chrysanthemum and yuletide plant sales in fall and winter, respectively. If you're interested in small-scale gardens, pick up the descriptive pamphlet at the entrance. This provides details on the more than twenty individual exhibits in the garden from the fifty thousand roses in the Jackson and Perkins memorial garden to the subtle fragrances of the Herb Garden and the more exotic species displayed in the Exhibition Greenhouse. Press-button taped commentaries are effective introductions to the different displays.

From the smaller gardens we pass out into open parkland beyond. In the late spring the flowering Japanese cherry grove frames the view westward into Flushing Meadow and the prominent remnants of the 1964–65 World's Fair. The path continues under the Van Wyck Expressway and into the vast panoramas of the fairground. Except for hot summer weekends it's usually pleasantly quiet here. The highway traffic provides a distant background hum—nothing more. Breezes ripple the broad ponds, and dogs romp across the short-mown lawns. The tree-lined boulevards and great spaces were, of course, designed for tens of thousands of visitors and were originally lined with exotic architectural displays from more than fifty nations. Now all that remains open to the public today is the Queens Museum in the Skating Rink, the diminutive Queens zoo and farm, the Hall of Science, and the Queens Theatre. Events and times keep changing, so call 360-8196 for the latest information.

Also look out for the notable pieces of sculpture including Donald De Lue's *Rocket Thrower*, the vast *Unisphere* (a hollow steel globe built and donated by the United States Steel Corporation), and Paul Manship's elegant fountain sculpture depicting the zodiac signs, hidden in a little wooden dell in front of the New York Pavilion. My favorite, José de Rivera's *Free Form*, is a thin, curved construction in polished metal which seems about to float off its marble plinth. Not far away and in complete contrast is the single unpolished "Column of Jerash" from the "Whispering Columns" of the Jerash Temple, built by the Romans in Jordan in A.D. 120. It was given as a gift to the fair by Jordan's King Hussein.

When you're ready to leave the park, head north toward Shea Stadium and the adjoining subway station (IRT 7 train), following the footpath past the Singer Bowl (now the U.S. Tennis Association Courts). Look back at the towering rockets of the Hall of Science exhibit. If you stand in the right place you'll see the outline of the Empire State building immediately between them. Half-close your eyes and it's hard to distinguish the skyscraper from the rockets—an appropriate reflection on twentieth-century life.

16
JAMAICA BAY AND
THE ROCKAWAYS

In the middle of Jamaica Bay the subway train stops. It's strangely quiet and the handful of passengers look a little disconcerted. They're accustomed to the clanking, rumbling, screeching of the train as it lumbers under the East River and across Brooklyn, and this sudden silence is unexpected. One little man with a green felt hat pulled down over his ears looks around, sniggers briefly, and studies the wrinkles on his fingers with intense concentration.

You can hear the gulls. That's something—sitting in a subway train with all the windows closed and you can still hear the gulls. Across the bay the planes at JFK are huddled like somnolent swans and the wavy haze makes their bright white fuselages ruffle like feathers.

It's all too brief. A moment of stillness. The train jerks and slowly rolls on across the bay. The passengers look up and the

--- **DIRECTIONS** ---

Subway: IND A or E to Broad Channel and Rockaway Park (double fare)
Bus: Q21 to Broad Channel and Rockaway Park
    Q22 (east/west) to Jacob Riis Park/Playground and Far Rockaway
Auto: Cross the North Channel Bridge via the Jamaica Bay Wildlife Refuge to Rockaway Park and return via the Marine Parkway Bridge and Sheepshead Bay
NOTE: On weekends the Nostalgia Special Train, made up of old restored vintage subway cars, runs from the 57th Street/Sixth Avenue station (1 P.M.) or from the New York Public Transit Exhibit in Brooklyn (3 P.M.) to Rockaway Park and back. Call 330-3060 for details.

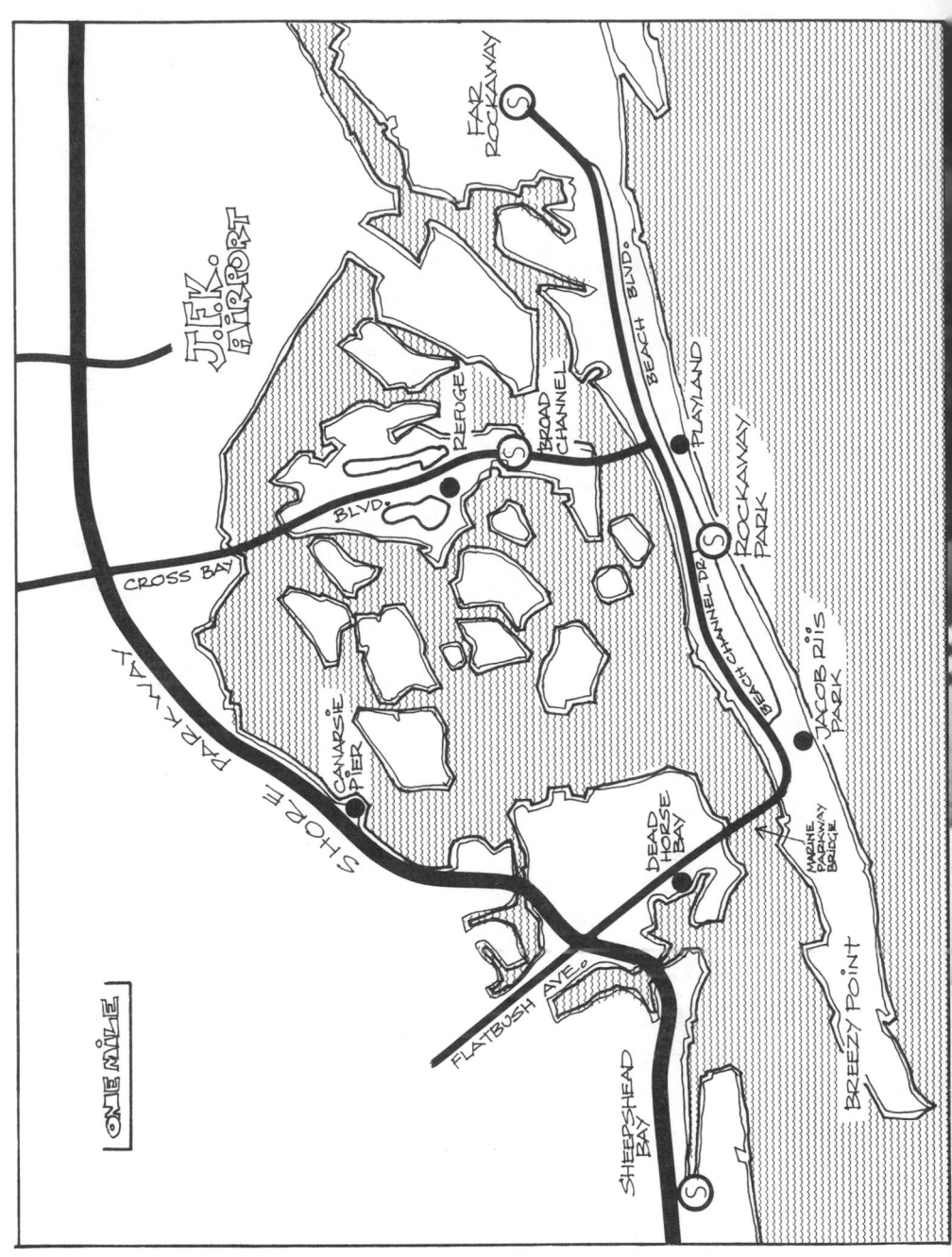

little man in the hat stops peering at his fingers and stares officiously at a guard walking through the car.

I leave the train at Broad Channel and walk into what looks like a Maine fishing village. Lines of tiny shacks are perched on shaky wooden piers. A few are lopsided. Small boats bob in the waves rolling under the piers. Nets and floats lie discarded in piles and the smell of seaweed wafts down the narrow streets of this unusual little community. To the west and rising in shimmering silhouette behind the ticky-tacky shacks and the bobbing boats and the piles of shells and strands of seaweed are the towers of the World Trade Center.

One wonders how these architectural forms can possibly exist in such close proximity to one another. But of course—this is New York and anything can happen, anywhere, anytime.

There are some, though, who do find the anomaly intolerable. They would like to see Broad Channel eradicated forever and replaced by some more regionally oriented facility, reflecting the future scale of Jamaica Bay's proposed Gateway National Recreation area. The inhabitants, a determined bunch of Irish Catholics, react to such proposals with deep-felt derision. One elderly lady, her weathered face wrapped in a black shawl, said heatedly: "The city'll never get us out of here. We call this place our 'island kingdom' and we'll fight with everything we've got to keep it."

A store owner explained the problem to me: "Y'see, the city owns all this land, has done since 1915, and we lease it from them. So I suppose they could close us all down in a flash if they wanted. They keep talking about it. They say it's too expensive to bring us up to standard. Who needs it? Things are okay just as they are. This is one of the safest places in the city. Why the hell won't they just sell us the land and have done with it?"

The residents live under constant threat of eviction, and they resent it. Many are reluctant to carry out needed improvements to their homes because next year—well, they may not have a home. So the place has a rather worn look, but there's a charm that's unique in the metropolitan area. The twelve hundred families who live here more or less permanently are a breed apart, a tiny tribe of Jamaica Bay natives with their own customs and social norms and a very direct view of the world: "As I see it, this is

Broad Channel

America, an' the reason I'm here is because I can do my own thing in peace as long as I don't disturb no one else and well, I ain't disturbin' nobody—so let me get on and do what I'm doin'. Heck, all I want is my house and the sea and some quiet—an' I got all that right here.''

Take a stroll around Broad Channel, along narrow paths with names like Fifth Avenue, the Bowery, and Broadway. Dogs run loose among the marsh grasses and chase minnows in the shallows. An old gentleman with white whiskers sits in a creaking rocking chair overlooking a neat garden with a statue of the virgin Mary in the middle surrounded by thick bushes of red roses. Three fishing smacks sit on wood blocks above a barnacle-encrusted wharf. Nearby there's a battered old armchair with a ripped vinyl cover. "That's the captain's chair," I was told. "He comes most every day and sits awhile. Never talks to anyone. Just sits and looks at the bay." There are piles of lumber everywhere. People are always patching up their homes. Improvement loans are unavailable because of the lease situation, so everyone helps everyone keep the place livable.

Their real fear is the ambitiousness of the federal government with its grandiose plans for the Gateway Recreation area. "Hell, they've told us they want our village for a bird sanctuary," remarked an old man who'd lived in Broad Channel since it was a quiet fishing island prior to the First World War. Plans are indeed ambitious. Voluminous tomes, filled with colorful architectural renderings, propose massive new beach and picnic areas on the Rockaway peninsula, along the northern marshy fringe of the bay, and down the eastern coast of Staten Island. "Gateway Villages" are envisaged providing year-round educational, recreational, and cultural programs at Fort Hancock on Sandy Hook, Fort Wadsworth on Staten Island, and Floyd Bennett Field just across the Marine Parkway bridge in Brooklyn. Expanded and improved wildlife reserves in the central portion of the bay are planned. Other projects include hostels and camping facilities, new marinas, new fishing piers, new wetland areas, and even the provision of extensive water-transport facilities linking all parts of the recreation area. No wonder the residents of Broad Channel are worried: "Lord knows what it'll do to the traffic through here. They've widened the road once and split our community right down the middle. They may try and do it again, and that could just about kill us off!"

Just a mile or so up the road from the village is the entrance to the Jamaica Bay Wildlife Refuge located on the famed Atlantic flyway. Here is a different world, a place of silence and beauty where one can sit by marsh paths and enjoy the slow curve of a flight of geese over the feather-topped reeds, the rustlings and scurryings in the undergrowth, blue herons lifting themselves languidly from still pools, the wild cry of sea gulls cavorting in a stiff breeze, the calls and chirrups of scores of different birds, some of them rare species on the American continent. It's almost a two-mile walk around the main lagoon (pick up the map given out by the refuge guides that pinpoints places of interest).

Many disinterested visitors have returned from the walk as budding ornithologists. There are also the confirmed devotees such as Cheyenne Bode, an Indian painter of birds and one of the most familiar figures in the refuge. Like other regulars he uses the dial-a-bird service (832-6523) to check on the latest arrivals at the refuge.

Enthusiasts scamper over Cross Bay Boulevard and visit the fresh-water pond on the other side of the island. Here the trails are less developed and one can easily find a niche in the reeds to watch life on the lake, undisturbed except for the occasional passing subway train at the far edge of the marsh.

It's hard to see why Broad Channel residents are so upset about

Barbadoes Basin Cottages

Gateway proposals in this area. To date most of the park staff has been involved in developing programs and courses for schoolchildren and residents of the five boroughs. Even longer-range plans for a major expansion of public beach on the Rockaway peninsula, linking Jacob Riis Park with the tip of Breezy Point, should not directly affect the small community. Yet the lingering fear of ultimate doom persists. "They'll get us somehow," said an old fisherman living in one of the shacks at the end of a shaky pier.

I catch the subway again and take it to Rockaway Park, the final destination on the western leg of the peninsula. Just before we reach Beach Channel Drive I quickly sketch another strange little community of shacks stuck out in the water near Barbadoes Basin—remnants of the old summer cottages once so popular on the peninsula. At Rockaway Park it's warm outside and a breeze filled with the freshness of the sea wafts across the platform. Although still early in the day the sign for Gallagher's Seafood and Steak Restaurant, half stripped of its neon trimmings, flickers on and off erratically, and fat sparrows guzzle the garbage outside the kitchen.

The beach is empty. Just me and the clams. Thousands of them. Sitting on the sand and looking toward Breezy Point at the tip of the peninsula and there's this great long line of clams, half clam shells, broken clam shells, crabs, starfish, and seasnails. It looks like the remains of some vast midnight luau attended by all the residents of the Rockaways. Some of the clams are still alive. I tap one and the shell snaps together in a flurry of clam juice and bubbles.

I love strolling on deserted beaches. This one's pretty clean, too. Better than Coney Island. I take my sandals off and walk in the oozy part where my feet sink into the wet sand and it squelches and gurgles between my toes. I stop and sit on one of the break-waters and feel the waves. The wood is worn and the grain reads like contour lines. It's very deep brown with rusty bolts sticking out like old worn limpets. A dog lolls up, sniffs the wood, and lolls off lazily to the next breakwater.

I keep looking at the waves. The other way is the boardwalk, which won't last out the decade, and a score of those dull brick apartment buildings, all about the same height, looking as if they were designed by some hack engineer, bored to tears with himself and life in general.

Farther down it gets better. Some of the old pre-World War II summer cottages have been converted into year-round houses. Anywhere else they'd look like slums, but here they're fine, especially the ones which seem to be slowly rolling into the sand. An elderly couple sitting on the porch smile and wave. I smile back and remember, I've hardly seen anyone younger than sixty since I got off the train. No wonder I've got all this beach—and all these clams—to myself. The Rockaways are full of old people. Someone once told me, "It's like Coney Island—except here the dogs have got crutches."

It was a wild place back in the 1880s when the Irish made this their own weekend resort. Extravagant hotels, with names like "The

Tack-a-Pou-Sha," and dripping with gingerbread trimmings, rose up behind the elaborate bathing pavilions which graced the beaches.

The resort was popular with politicians of all guises. President Taylor and his daughters spent a summer at the magnificent Marine Pavilion, described by one enthusiast as "a large and splendid edifice in a style not excelled by any hotel in the Union." Longfellow and Washington Irving were also devotees of the place until it burned down in the hot summer of 1864. But it was the Tammany politicians who gave the Rockaways real flavor and a reputation for indulgence in the grandest of manners. Lillian Russell, long accustomed to extravagant living as companion to Diamond Jim Brady, loved the place and often arrived there on the Long Island Railroad, which crawled to the beach at a mule's pace, whistle screaming, the engineer bawling at the bemused spectators, "She's here—she's back!"

Hotels were built, burned, and built again—larger and more grandiose with such fashionable English names as the Bayswater and the Windsor. In 1881 a group of wealthy investors, using more than one million dollars of Tammany funds, erected a vast self-contained "hotel-city," five blocks long from First to Fifth avenues in Rockaway Park. This enormous structure boasted numerous ballrooms, restaurants, arcades, enclosed gardens, suites large enough for a sheik and his harem, a rooftop observatory, and even its own private gas and water plants.

Just off the Far Rockaway coast, linked by five-cent ferries, was Hog Island, otherwise known as "The Irish Saratoga." This narrow sandbar only a few feet above sea level was the favorite haunt of the Tammany boys. They covered every buildable inch of the islet with bathing pavilions, bathhouses, bars, and restaurants. Thousands flocked across to lie on its white beaches or to concoct avaricious schemes for city-swindling in the cool confines of Patrick Craig's Dining Emporium. Then suddenly, as if by direct command from on high, the island was Sodom-and-Gomorrahed, suddenly and completely, in a tumultuous storm on September 10, 1896. Residents on the mainland couldn't believe their eyes. The *Brooklyn Daily Eagle* reported: "What was formerly the islet is now one mass of floating debris, composed of bath houses, chairs, tables and other fixings and furniture of the pavilions and restaurants on the outer beach!" But not only were all the buildings gone—the island itself had totally disappeared. The current was so strong that the sandbar had been washed away—nothing was left.

It was a blow, but the Rockaways recovered and expanded. Piers were built, hundreds of summer bungalows were constructed, the six-mile boardwalk was erected in 1924 (at that time it was the largest in the country), and in 1937 the huge Jacob Riis Park was opened, named after the famed Danish photographer and author of *How the Other Half Lives.*

But gradually fashions changed. Other resorts on Long Island and to the north along the Connecticut coast began to attract the crowds. The Rockaways became slightly old-fashioned, a little seedy. The flimsy summer cottages started to be used as year-round homes by low-income families, the boardwalk began to deteriorate, the beach was not cleaned as regularly as before.

Today, Jacob Riis Park (Q22 westbound) still attracts the summer crowds. Bathing here is strangely but voluntarily segregated. Each breakwater section is occupied by a distinct group. Go take a look on a hot summer afternoon—it contradicts the old melting-pot myth. The boardwalk is still usable, if a bit shaky in places, and the beach is usually far quieter than Coney Island or Jones Beach. The Irish are still around in force, too. Liz Mahoney's Pub, Hickney's Blarney Stone, and the Leprechaun Bar remain with their draft Guinness signs and occasional smatterings of the old brogue. Plaster madonnas, painted in heavenly pastel shades, sit in front yards around Rockaway Park. A local newspaper carries invitations for:

"The Shannonaires" sponsored by St. Brendan's Gaelic Society of Rockaway Park at St. Francis de Sales Auditorium

Another reads:

St. Patrick dance and bon voyage party by the American Irish Society at the clubhouse. 1, Shamrock Lane . . .

Begorrah! And the Guinness is good.

I catch a bus (Q22 eastbound). A sign reads "Come to Playland," so I get off and wander into this little bubble of fun. It's lively, but too small. Surrounded on three sides by oppressive streets lined with flaky shacks, it's not the kind of place I'd come to regularly for a wild weekend. The walls are high, though, and you can't see too much on the outside, and the music pounds from a hundred squeaky speakers. Have a hot dog, take a ride, lose a buck, win a prize, sing a song, smile a smile, drink a beer, and then go and stretch out on the beach before the sun goes down.

I catch another bus, this time to Far Rockaway (Q22 again). It's full of old people beaming, shouting, whispering, coughing. The driver's reaching the limits of exasperation.

"Lady, get away from my wheel . . ."

"I'm not getting off in the middle of the bus."

"Lady, do me a favor . . ."

"You always jerk when I'm on the steps . . ."

"Mrs. Stein, come and sit here. Excuse me, I'm saving that seat for Mrs. Stein . . ."

". . . and I said, 'Look, son, I don't want to be any trouble,' and he says, 'Momma, you're no trouble, no trouble at all' . . ."

"I know. My son Samuel . . ."

"He's a lovely boy. I've always liked . . ."

"I know. My son Samuel . . ."

"Lady, will you sit down, or get off the bus . . ."

"Have we passed the post office yet?"

"That's two more stops . . ."

"My son Samuel says . . ."

The bus stops. The chatter stops. Everybody's staring at the door. A little gray hand grasps the rail. Then comes a hat. Then a little wrinkled face. The bus driver looks at his watch. The new passenger is very old, very pale, and puffing. She makes it to the top step—just. The door slams, there's a quick lunge, and off we go. The chatter starts again. The old lady clutches for a rail and misses. Her bag bangs the driver on the shoulder. He doesn't seem to notice—just keeps on blasting down the road hitting every pothole in sight. The old lady looks like she won't make it, so a man stands up and offers her his seat. The passengers give him a funny stare.

Out of the windows it's all housing-authority apartments and occasional flickers of sea between the monoliths. At least the slums have life—with the corner bar and its greasy glasses and cigarette burns and the madonnas in the front yard and the chalk marks in the street and the busted-up Chevy with no wheels in the gutter and the little old lady with no teeth who shouts at nobody in the street . . . ah, memories of Jane Jacobs.

I get off the bus in Far Rockaway. The driver folds over his wheel in an instant coma. It's a busy little place. Across from the new shopping plaza there are two Chinese restaurants, a McDonald's, and a theater showing mildly pornographic films. The best building, an elaborate little wedding cake which once contained the Rockaway Bank, is slowly being submerged by angular redevelopment. There's talk of preserving it as a landmark.

If you've come by subway or bus, Far Rockaway is a good place to end the journey and return home (IND A from Mott Avenue). If you're traveling by car or bicycle, however, there are a few other places around the bay well worth visiting. Just over the Marine Parkway bridge, for example, opposite the Floyd Bennett Field, is Dead Horse Bay, a wild area of dunes and sea unknown to most visitors. If you can find a place to leave the car (possibly near the marina) stroll westward over the sand hills crusted with brittle marren grass and wander around the bay at will. It's one of those places ideal for an afternoon's quiet contemplation. Away to the west are Manhattan Beach and Coney Island, but farther to the south, beyond the sandy tip of Breezy Point, is the great gray-blue Atlantic, stretching over a thousand horizons to Europe and Africa. It's one of my favorite places.

If you fancy a spot of fishing, continue north along Flatbush Avenue and take the Shore Parkway as far as Rockaway Parkway and the Canarsie Pier. Here's a small parking lot and a regular contingent of fishermen religiously casting into the murky waters below the pier rail, with the familiar furtive exchange of informative tidbits, the boasting and braggadocio, the sense of kinship and the studied calm on the face of a man who knows he's got a big one at the end of his line. Fish are more plentiful in the bay and pollution levels are slowly being reduced. Fluke, "schoolie" bass, whiting, bluefish, sand porgies, hackleheads, and cod are common. There are even reports of American lobsters as large as three pounds in the shallows, although I've yet to see one.

Those unfamiliar with this part of New York should follow the Shore Parkway to the Sheepshead Bay waterfront. If you can, come very early, around 6 A.M., and watch the fishing boats leaving their wharves along Neptune Avenue. Better still, take an ocean-fishing trip. It's a competitive business. There are signs galore all along the sidewalk: "Whiting Tonight," "Whiting and Cod—Guaranteed," "Short and Long Cruises," "Captain Jones—

leaves 5:30 A.M.—the Earliest," "Captain Simpson Departs 6:30 A.M.," "The Longest Cruise—Leaves 7 A.M."

If that sounds a dauntingly early time to be up and about, visit Sheepshead Bay in the evening and dine at one of the waterfront restaurants. The famous Lundy's has an excellent shore dinner served in dining rooms as big as Munich beer halls.

To the west, at the far end of Neptune Avenue, is an entrance to Plum Beach, another one of the lesser-known beaches in the area. Before or after a stroll on the sand, pop into Shatzkin's, and try

Sheepshead Bay

one of their marvelous knishes—there's a choice of twenty-five unusual flavors, including boodumm (potato knish with salami slices), beef frankfurter knish, pizza knish, chow mein knish, kasha knish, fish knish, and cheese knish.

Alternatively, take some of their frozen delicacies (potato blintzes, blueberry blintzes, potato pirogen, and mini-knishes) home for dinner, a splendid way to round off an exploration of Jamaica Bay.

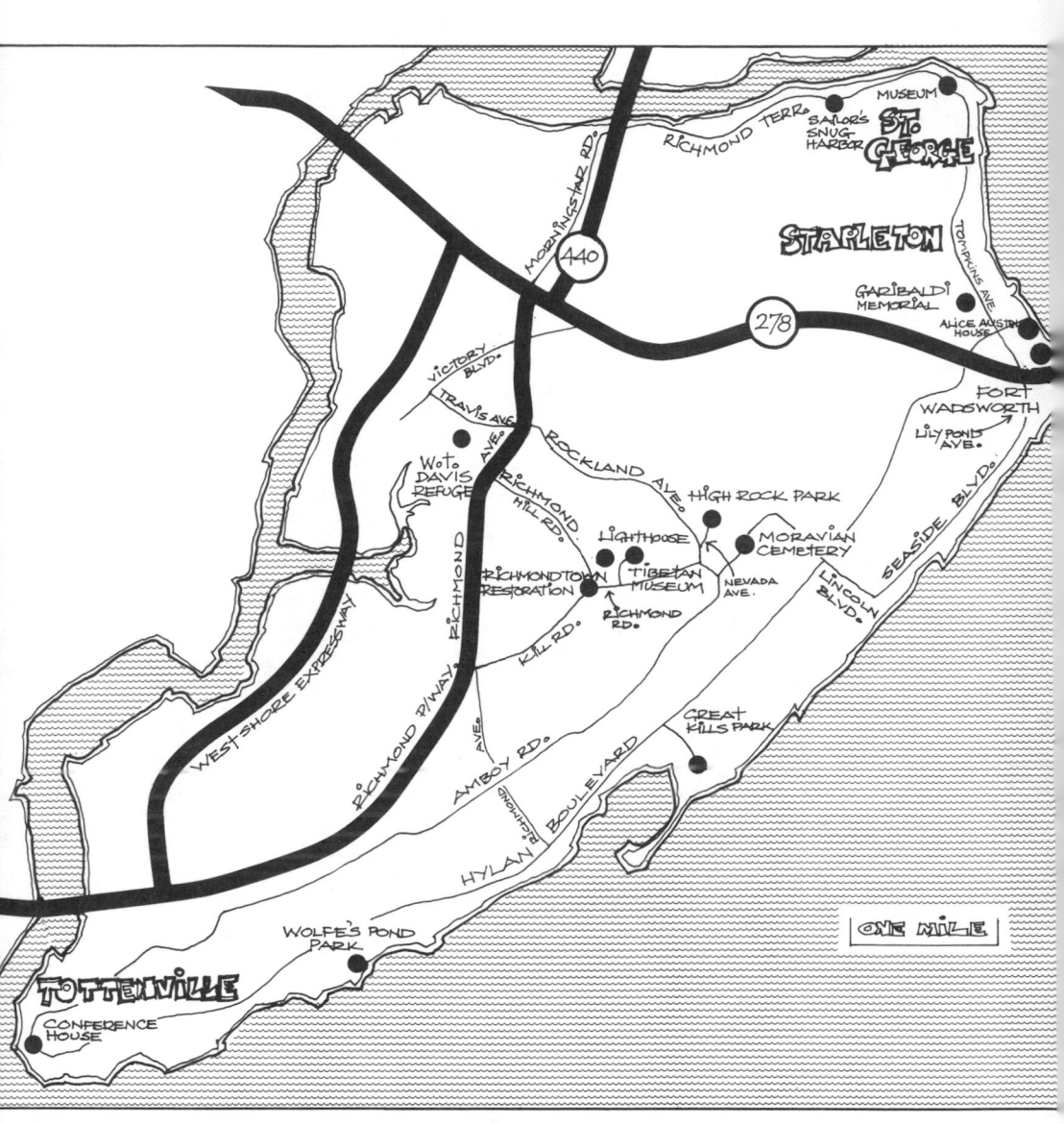

17
STATEN ISLAND

"It's that damned bridge. That's been the trouble." I was on a steep rise at the far end of the old Moravian cemetery in Dongan Hills, Staten Island, chatting with one of the groundskeepers. Why, I remember less 'n ten years back when all this was jus' fields 'n' woods—all the way down to the beach there. Look at it now. It's rubbish, all rubbish. Wouldn't give you a dollar for those frilly things they call houses. There's not a bit of green left."

It's alarming to study maps of the island and see how fast the land has been used up. At the turn of the century there was almost nothing here—just a few farming communities nestling in the folds of a rolling landscape. The only real town of any size was New Brighton, to the west of today's ferry terminal at St. George. This was a fashionable seaside bathing resort for the wealthy families of New York and many of the southern states, until pollution wrecked the beaches and industrial development marred the New

---
DIRECTIONS

Ferry: From Staten Island Ferry Terminal on Manhattan to St. George (25¢ return/$1.50 auto)

Bus: From St. George Ferry Terminal buses leave for all parts of the island. Trains also stop at most communities along the eastern side of the island as far as Tottenville

Auto: Brooklyn-Queens Expressway to Verrazano Bridge

NOTE: This tour is best undertaken by car. If that's not possible, I suggest you select those places that appeal most and work out a public transport itinerary at the St. George bus-terminal information office.

223

Jersey shore. The rest of the island was woods, marshes, and fine stretches of white sand, the haunt of gulls and horseshoe crabs.

The Verrazano Narrows Bridge was opened to traffic in 1964, and since that time the population of the island has doubled. Planners have not had a chance to keep up with the island's growth. Highway engineers have scrambled to provide more and more miles of expressway to cope with the glut of automobiles. If Robert Moses and his like-minded disciples had been given their way the island would even have lost its few remaining open spaces and sections of its fragile shoreline. Then there was a great outcry. The citizens demanded a stop to the ticky-tacky suburban sprawl, the highways that inevitably bring more sprawl, the filling-in of the marshes and the kills (streams), the destruction of historic buildings—the mindless pursuit of growth in the name of "progress."

It was almost too late. Another decade and the island would have become just another few square miles of homogenized suburbia. As it is, there's been a slowing down, a rethinking of priorities, a redefinition of the concept of community, a new concern about the quality of environment. So, fortunately, there's still much to see and do on the island, and this circular tour includes most of the highlights—an old fort, five museums, nature reserves, woodland walks, a restored early American village, an old stone house where an attempt was made to end the Revolutionary War, a cottage where Garibaldi rested briefly and made candles for a living, and meanderings among the marshes, along the reed-lined kills. Take your time. Pause occasionally to stroll the uncrowded beaches or explore park trails. Enjoy this island and be thankful that at least a portion has been saved.

Let's begin at the most obvious place—the Staten Island Ferry Terminal at St. George. Pigeons and sparrows chirp and swoop across the vast waiting hall. The smell of fresh pizza and browning frankfurters wafts over the benches, and groups of people wait impatiently for the ferry gates to open. In the corner past the newspaper stand is a small sign denoting the ferry museum (Monday–Thursday 8 A.M.–3 P.M. Free)—a recent creation and an excellent place to spend a few minutes before or after the ride to Manhattan. Outside there are displays of ferryboat history and descriptions of their individual fates. The E. G. *Diefenbach*, for example, originally used on the Brooklyn–St. George run, was purchased by the government of Nicaragua and now provides a four-hour trip across the Bay of Fonseca to El Salvador. The *Hamilton* is owned by Costa Rica and makes regular runs out of Punta Arenas. The *Cranford* has now become "the Ferry Boat Restaurant" at Brielle, New Jersey, and the *Miss New York*, decommissioned in 1975, has been sold to the Venezuelan government. There's one of the old ferries, though, that until recently nobody seemed to want. I saw the *Mary Murray* sitting in one of the docks south of the terminal. Her once bright yellow hull was browning and some of her windows were smashed. There's talk of turning her into a nautical museum, but funds are scarce and interest seems marginal at best.

Inside the museum, a small white-tiled room, there are models of old ferryboats, ship's bells and wheels, wind-worn and sea-sprayed logbooks, paintings and odd bits of ferry-related flotsam and jetsam. It's worth a visit, but one hopes that one day it may grow into a more significant collection—perhaps on the decks of the old *Mary Murray*.

Up the hill, along the street behind the Borough Hall, is the Staten Island Institute of Arts and Sciences (75 Stuyvesant Place; Tuesday–Saturday 10 A.M.–5 P.M., Sunday 2–5 P.M. Free. 727-1135). If you come by car, watch the parking meter carefully. The local traffic vultures swoop in quickly and silently. My trip to this free museum cost $10!

Again, like the ferry museum, this has a rather limited display, but the people who run the place, members of the Staten Island Institute of Arts and Sciences, always seem enthusiastic and determined to see the place grow. Downstairs is a rather odd assortment of fossils, seashells, paintings, Indian artifacts, an old piano, some beautiful examples of eighteenth-century wood carving, and a series of satirical prints reflecting that long and bitter struggle between Horace Greeley and "Boss" Tweed. Along one wall is the museum shop, an even more unusual collection of donated bric-a-brac from Victorian earrings to miniature telescopes and clay pipes. If you know what to look for you might find a few remarkable bargains.

Upstairs is a more spacious display of Staten Island history. Old maps and etchings of the once pastoral landscape indicate the extent of development during the last few decades. Across the landing, in the art gallery, I once enjoyed an exhibition of Barbury

Brown's illustrations for the book *High Rock* by John G. Mitchell. This excellent publication describes the creation of the High Rock Park conservation area in the wooded hills east of Richmondtown, which we visit later in the journey.

Leave the museum and travel west along Richmond Terrace following the waterfront. It's all a little run-down today, but try to imagine the scene (described in *Light and Shadows of New York*) as it was around 150 years ago.

> No factories marred its shoreline, graceful trees bordered its sides and from New Brighton to St. George the elms arched overhead, completely shading the road. On this drive the rich and great disported themselves of an afternoon and pretty carriages, shiny harness and prancing horses paired to and fro . . . handsome houses with lawns and gardens were on the landward side of the terrace and toward the water green banks sloped to the kills, whose waves lapped up on pebbly beaches. . . . The New Jersey shore was a vast expanse of green salt meadow, shimmering in the sunshine.

Little wonder this became an early seaside resort for the wealthy and later a literary colony—attracting such notables as the humorist Bill Nye, Charles Mackay, George William Curtis, Ralph Waldo Emerson, and Henry David Thoreau. It was here also that Commodore Cornelius Vanderbilt began to amass his great fortune. Encouraged by his wily mother, he ran a small ferry linking the island with Manhattan. Gradually, using profits and financial leverage in an unusually gifted manner, he acquired more boats, obtained valuable government contracts during the 1812 war, and ultimately had his armada of ships plying transatlantic routes before turning to railroads and building a second transportation empire. When he died he was said to be worth more than a hundred million dollars. His son William took control of his interests and doubled the estate. Both of them lie together in a vast eleven-acre plot in the Moravian cemetery, close to Richmondtown. The great gray basilica-size mausoleum sits on a terrace overlooking the eastern half of the island. It's an awesome structure. One can't help ponder the ironies of life and death here. But there's a great spirit of peace in the untouched woods that surround the structure—an interesting contrast too between the wilderness of nature and the conscious creations of man. Vanderbilt spent over a million dollars on his memorial, but he, like all the other occupants of more humble graves lower down the hill, was eventually reduced to a few ounces of gray dust.

Little remains today of the old Richmond Terrace environment. The New Jersey shore is lined with old wharves, petroleum storage tanks, and factory buildings. Large ships move slowly along the narrow channel under the Bayonne Bridge. Up the slope from the shore the old resort mansions are dilapidated, jostled by undignified clapboard structures. The once prominent New Brighton village hall with its classically austere façade and mansard roof is now an abandoned wreck. It may soon be lost. Yet there is one glimmering gem here—a remarkable complex set in eighty acres of lawns, gardens, and ponds, known as the Sailors' Snug Harbor (Sunday 1–4 P.M. Free. 448-2500). The main buildings, lined like a series of Grecian temples along the waterfront, were until recently a home for retired seamen. The central building, approached from Richmond Terrace through a most unusual pedestrian gatehouse, was opened in August 1833, funded by Robert Richard Randall, the son of a wealthy New York shipping merchant and occasional privateer. Many subsequent additions were made until by the early 1900s there were almost a thousand "aged, decrepit, and worn-out sailors" living here in a self-contained complex complete with church (a miniature version of St. Paul's in London), theater, recreation hall, two chapels, a fishpond, a gazebo, and a greenhouse. By all accounts the sailors, who always addressed one another as "captain," were not as decrepit as the philanthropic Mr. Randall had supposed. Regular drinking sorties were made by ferry to the pubs and taverns in lower Manhattan, and a nearby watering hole known as the Old Stone Jug (today the Neville House, at 806 Richmond Terrace) became such a popular rendezvous for the old salts that it was purchased and closed down by the governor of Snug Harbor.

New York is fortunate not to have lost Sailors' Snug Harbor, considered by many architectural historians to be the finest grouping of Greek-Revival buildings in the country. A few years ago, over Landmarks Preservation Commission protests, local courts ruled in favor of replacing the present structure with a more efficiently designed establishment better suited to geriatric care. Fortunately, the city was able to negotiate an amicable settlement.

The sailors moved to a new institution in North Carolina (taking with them their collection of hand-crafted model ships, made at Snug Harbor) and the city purchased the buildings and grounds for use as the Staten Island Cultural Center.

But the problems of preservation have only just begun. Maintenance costs are estimated today at over one-half million dollars a year and grants are still pending. Desperate efforts are being made by local groups, most notably the Staten Island Institute of Arts and Sciences, to raise funds. The Botanical Society also initiated efforts to maintain the beautifully landscaped grounds of the harbor. Public tours are offered by local residents, art shows are organized here, and there's talk of opening the large barn as a crafts center. But the great establishment is slowly deteriorating.

Sailors' Snug Harbor

The theater is a mess and the recreation hall, as big as a railway station, needs urgent attention. The enthusiasm of the local people is admirable but, unless regular funds are forthcoming, their efforts will be in vain and the islanders will be in danger of losing one of their most notable historic landmarks.

Continue west along Richmond Terrace. This whole northern shoreline of the island has seen far better days, but if old ships, chubby tugboats, and abandoned ferries are to your liking you'll find much of interest behind the ramshackle buildings along the street. Past the Bayonne Bridge turn left onto Morningstar Road and continue south along Richmond Avenue. At the junction with Victory Boulevard turn right and then left at Travis Avenue. Here's a glimpse of Staten Island as it once was—views along a

Richmondtown Restoration

winding kill, acres of tall reeds waving in a breeze full of the smell of sea, herons standing single-legged in marsh pools, and invisible creatures making rustling sounds in the shallows. It's all too brief, though. Determined individuals can make arrangements for specially organized field trips through the William T. Davis Wildlife Refuge (727-1135), but for most visitors it's a fleeting experience. Soon one is back among the new houses with their plastic-stone façades and plaster gnomes prancing across Astroturf lawns.

Go south on Richmond Avenue and almost immediately east at Richmond Hill Road. At the top of the hill the highway crosses Latourette Golf Course and then without warning drops sharply down the slope into the Richmondtown restoration, Staten Island's most ambitious preservation project.

Much has been written about Richmondtown. There have been controversies over the use of funds, furious debates over the architectural relevance of some of the properties relocated to the site, lawsuits, claims of fiscal corruption, and most frustrating of all, long periods of inaction. But even in a state of incompletion it's a charming place to spend a warm afternoon, and will be even better when the traffic is routed around the restoration. Originally known as Cocklestown because of the abundance of shellfish in the nearby kills, the community was established in the late 1600s and later prospered as the county seat. In 1898, however, Staten Island became part of greater New York and the town was largely abandoned as growth centered around the docks and ferries at St. George and New Brighton.

Even as far back as 1939, the Staten Island Historical Society recognized the potential value of preserving the village as a show-place of regional architecture and country life during the seventeenth, eighteenth, and nineteenth centuries. Members began by buying and restoring the 1695 Voorlezer's House, the oldest elementary school building in the country. Then, slowly, more properties were acquired and examples of early island dwellings such as the Lake-Tysen House (1740) and the Britton Cottage (1640) were moved to Richmondtown and restored. Today there's almost a complete village here. Up on the hill, with its sturdy white pediment resting on four fat Doric columns, is the County Courthouse (1837). Across the street is the museum located in the Surrogate's Office, and down the slope of Court Place there's the Stephens House and general store, and the Victorian Edwards-Barton

House. Between Richmond Road and Mill Pond (complete with ducks, geese, and turkeys) are the restored homes, a basket-maker's shop, a cooper's shop, and a saw mill—and there's more to come in the future. Visit the museum (Tuesday–Saturday 10 A.M.–4 P.M., Sunday 2–5 P.M.) and pick up brochures on the resto-ration—they provide details on each of the buildings, and members of the Historical Society occasionally act as guides. Visi-tors (call 351-1611 for details), particularly those who live in New York, are always surprised by the scale of the restoration and sometimes even its existence. "Why, I just had no idea all this was here," an elderly lady told me as she walked along the paths be-tween the old clapboard buildings. "I live just on the other side of the bridge, I've been there all my life, and this is the first time I've ever come. I wish I'd known about this before. It's a lovely, lovely spot."

There are a few other places you should visit while you're in the area—places not well known to outsiders. On the hill overlooking the restoration, for example, is a huge stone lighthouse built in 1912 which still operates in conjunction with the Ambrose Light. It's unusual to find a lighthouse so far inland, but this one is situ-ated on some of the highest land between Maine and Key West. Nearby Todt Hill (409.8 feet) is in fact the highest point.

A little farther down the hill, at 340 Lighthouse Avenue, is one of the most unusual museums in the greater New York area, the Jacques Marchais Center of Tibetan Art (call 987-3478 for times and special events). Once you enter its silent garden, New York and its trappings are left behind. Bright goldfish move slowly through pools, life-size Buddhas beam from leaf-shrouded glades, carved rabbits, monkeys, and snakes occupy niches in the walls, sacred mantras are carved on garden stones. The place is a minia-ture facsimile of a Tibetan lamasery. There's a library here, a small gift shop, and a magnificent Tibetan altar with a central sculpture of Tsong-Kha-Pa, a religious reformer and founder of the Yellow Hat sect of Buddhism. He is surrounded by religious objects—prayer wheels, butter lamps, offering cups, masks, horns, altar tablets, and incense burners. Wall banners (tankas) made in Tibet present teachings of the various deities. The place is a treasure house of Buddhist art and is said to be the largest private collec-tion in the world.

Leaving the museum, it's hard to return to the hustle-bustle outside—so don't. Instead take Richmond Road east to Rockland Avenue, turn left, and then after a short distance, turn right along Nevada Avenue. Follow this to a small parking area just inside the lovely High Rock Park Conservation Center (daily 9 A.M.–5 P.M. Free. 987-6233). Here you can continue your reveries and contemplation in a seventy-acre woodland complete with ponds, swamps, a visitors' center, a tactile garden of plants for the blind, and four distinct exploratory trails. Watch the toads and turtles around Loosestrife Swamp. Listen for woodpeckers or the rustle of rabbits in the undergrowth. Find your own quiet here in the heart of the island, and listen to life around you. One person I talked to traveled regularly all the way from the Bronx just to sit in this silent place.

When the weather is good a thorough exploration of Richmondtown and other nearby places of interest can take a good part of a day, but if you still have some time left, drive to Tottenville at the southern tip of the island. Here you'll find the ambience of an old country town full of Victorian villas, narrow lanes, and views of the ocean between clusters of large trees. It's a different world, as yet undamaged by the commercialism to the north. At the end of Hylan Boulevard is the Conference (Billopp) House (Tuesday–Sunday 1–4 P.M. Adults 50¢. 984-2086), dating back to 1680, where Lord Howe entertained John Adams, Benjamin Franklin, and Edward Rutledge on September 11, 1776, and endeavored to persuade them to accept British peace terms. The occasion was marked by decorous civility on both sides. Adams was particularly impressed with the setting and noted that Howe "had prepared a large handsome room by spreading a carpet of moss and green sprigs, from bushes and shrubs in the neighborhood . . . and he entertained us with good claret, good bread, cold ham, tongues and mutton!" The conference was, however, a failure and the long Revolutionary War began in earnest shortly thereafter.

On the return journey up Hylan Boulevard to the Verrazano Bridge or the ferry, there are plenty of delightful parks and beaches to while away a warm afternoon. Wolfe's Pond Park has excellent bathing and boating facilities, and farther to the north Great Kills Park and the adjoining Miller Field reflect another attempt to preserve a segment of island marshlands while at the same time providing valuable recreational facilities and a fine stretch of bathing beach. Frustrated New York fishermen fed up with grimy catches from the Hudson or East rivers should be relieved to hear that the park authority claims there's an abundance of flounder, bass, porgie, bluefish, and even crabs here.

At Miller Field is the start of the Franklin D. Roosevelt boardwalk, a 7,500-foot-long oceanfront stroll that eventually leads to Fort Wadsworth, under the Narrows Bridge. Here is the last of the island's five museums, this time a military display (call 447-5100, ext. 731, for hours. Free), and a chance to explore the intricacies of the Battery Weed, a trapezoidal structure on the water's edge with four levels of gun turrets. The original fort, a diminutive timber blockhouse, was built by the Dutch in 1663 as a defense against local Indians. It was erected, however, somewhat after the fact. During the early skirmishes between settlers and natives variously known as the Pig War, the Peach War, and the Whiskey War, the settlers had been driven off the island on each occasion and eventually ended up buying the land back from the Indians at least five times before peace was finally made. Cornelius Meyer, one of the early settlers, complained: "They [the Indians] supposed that ye island by reason of ye war, by killing, burning and driving us off, was become theirs again." It was also at Fort Wadsworth that the last shot of the Revolutionary War was fired. The British, who captured the island almost as soon as the conflict began, left ignominiously on evacuation day in 1783, jeered by crowds of Americans. The infuriated commander of a British warship fired a cannon shot at the fort. The shot missed—but the jeering echoed halfway across the Atlantic.

A short distance north of the fort, at the end of Hylan Avenue, is the Alice Austen House, one of Staten Island's most delightful architectural anomalies. What originally began as a diminutive Dutch farmhouse (1691–1710) was later transformed into a rambling villa trimmed with delicate Gothic-Revival details by John Austen, a prominent New Yorker and grandfather of Alice Austen. In 1868, Alice came to live here and used the house as a base during her remarkable life as a photographer and promoter of the women's liberation movement. For decades her work was unrecognized. Her photographs and glass negatives, more than 7,000, were stored away in shabby boxes. A tendency to injudicious spending dissipated her fortune and in 1945 she had to sell the house and live in a charitable institution for the poor. Then in 1951 an article in *Life* Magazine featuring her photographic work brought her belated fame and comfort for the remaining months of her life. The house stands today as a fitting memorial to this remarkable woman.

Before leaving the island, make one final stop. Take Tompkins Avenue from its junction with Wadsworth Avenue north as far as Chestnut Avenue. In a garden raised above the street is the Garibaldi Memorial, a simple clapboard house with a restrained Victorian-Gothic character (Tuesday–Friday, 10 A.M.–5 P.M., Saturday and Sunday 1–5 P.M. Free). Here the great Italian liberator lived following the fall of the Roman Republic in 1849. In the back garden there's a furnace where he made candles for a living. It was a penurious existence for a man who later went on to lead the legendary One Thousand in the liberation of Sicily and Naples, and saw the unification of all Italy—his life's ambition.

Staten Island must have once had the power to inspire great men. Poets and writers collected here, the Vanderbilt empire began here—even sailors ensconced at Snug Harbor became young salts again, full of tales of prowess and daring on the high seas. The island still has some of that invigorating quality left. Try to ignore the blight—come and enjoy its history, its open spaces, and the feeling that Manhattan must be at least a hundred miles away.

MINI-TOURS
The Make-Your-Own-Walk Kit

INTRODUCTION

We've covered a lot of ground on the walking tours—we've discovered dozens of little-known museums, hidden parks, odd stores and pubs, secluded courts, forgotten architectural gems, quiet riverside paths, neighborhood markets, and even an old farmhouse in the middle of the city. And yet, after all that walking we've only just begun to explore New York's nooks and crannies. In the pages that follow are more than 150 additional discoveries in all parts of the metropolitan area. The general location of each is shown on a map, so select those that interest you and devise your own walking tours. Enjoy.

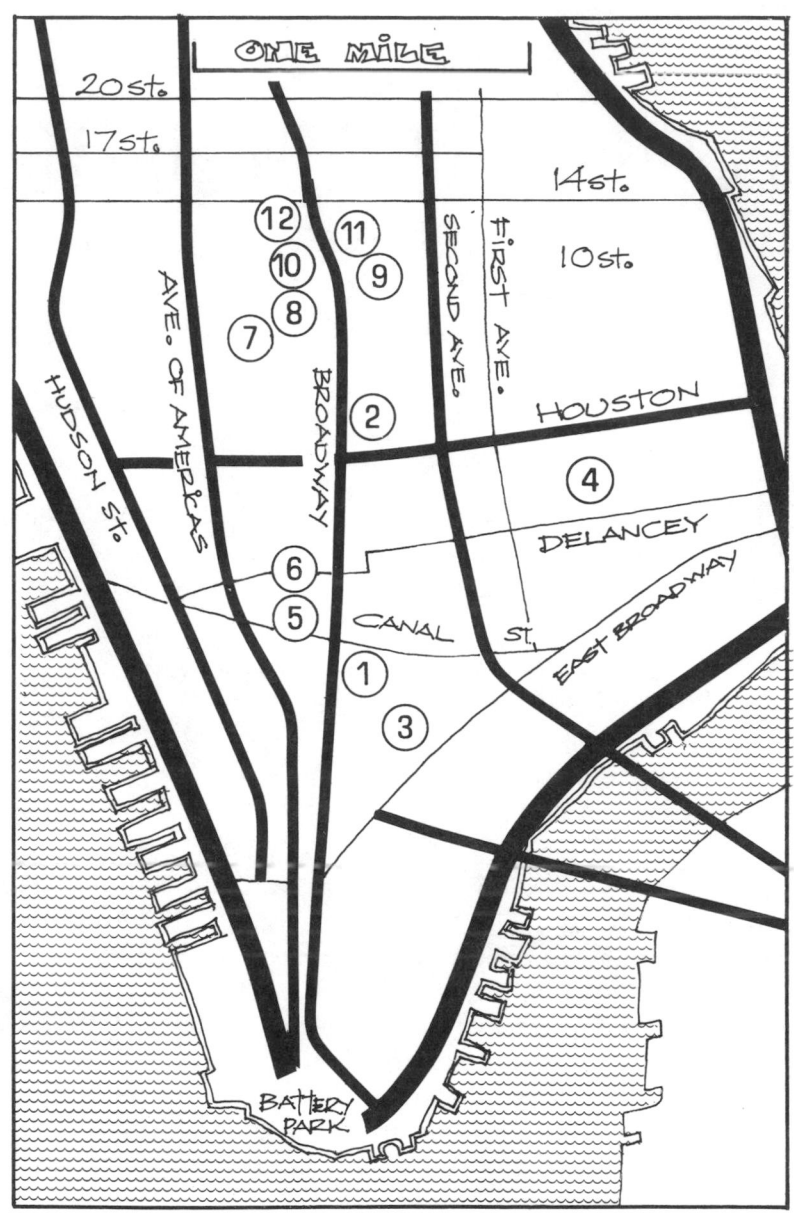

1

THE BATTERY TO
14th STREET

FABULOUS FIREHOUSES

Some of the most spectacular civic architecture can be found in the old firehouses scattered around the five boroughs. In Manhattan my two favorites are:

1. Engine Company #31 Firehouse (1895), 87 Lafayette Street (at White Street). A wonderful French château by (who other than) Napoleon Le Brun!

Subway: IND E or BMT RR, N, QB to Canal Street and Broadway
Bus: M1, M6

2. Engine Company #33 Firehouse (1898), 44 Great Jones Street (at Lafayette Street). In an otherwise somber neighborhood, this Beaux-Arts creation brings sparkle and charm (also visit the Old Merchants House nearby).

Subway: IRT 6 to Astor Place
Bus: M1, M2, M3, M5, M6

3. NIGHT COURT

100 Centre Street, Room 218
566-6342
Subway: IRT 2, 3 to Park Row; IRT 4, 5, 6 to Brooklyn Bridge/Worth
    Street
Bus: M1, M6, M15, M102

If you're looking for real courtroom dramas with Perry Mason-like cross-examinations and emotional confessions of hidden guilt, it's best to visit the Supreme Court and other courts around the

Engine Company No. 31 Firehouse

square during the day. The night court usually peaks around 10 P.M. and is a more sober reflection of the city's subpopulation, its prostitutes, drugged-out youths, bail-jumpers, and petty muggers. There's an air of lethargy here, a tedium of legal jargon, and paper processing. Occasionally, though, the reality breaks through even to the gray-faced judge who listens patiently to a mother's "he's really a good boy" plea (the hundredth of the week) and admonishes a whimpering youth with a stern warning instead of the ritual sentencing.

4. A MANHATTAN WINERY

Shapiro's House of Kosher Wines, 126 Rivington Street (at Norfolk
  Street)
475-7383
Sunday Tours: 10 A.M.–5 P.M.
Subway: BMT J, M and IND F to Delancey Street/Essex Street
Bus: M9, M14, M15

The third generation of Shapiro's is now running this smallish establishment deep in the heart of the Lower East Side. The Sunday tours include a full description of the kosher wine-making process and tastings (ask for their Cream White Concord or the unusual Honey Wine). Even if you don't particularly like the thick, sweet, labrusca-flavored kosher wines, it's an interesting place to visit when Orchard Street gets overcrowded.

5. THE CANAL STREET BAZAAR

Between West Broadway and Lafayette Street
Subway: BMT N, QB, RR to Canal Street and Broadway
Bus: M1, M6, M10

Marvelous! Everyone knows about Canal Street and its hodge-podge of surplus stores and flea markets, but few have actually explored it. How many, for example, have visited the City Dump with its oscilloscopes, sweep generators, sound analyzers, and programable regatrons, or the four plastic/plexiglass stores with their transparent skylights, plastic rods, tubes, and cubes of all sizes and colors, Styrofoam planks, and loads of free advice. Then there are the used office-equipment outlets, stores selling bits and pieces of transistor radios and tape recorders, the fabric and brass lofts (just up Greene Street), Abco's wonderful array of burglar alarms, Canal Rubber Supply's hoses, stripping, tubes, and three discount stationers. Best of all is the Soho-Canal Street Flea Market at Canal and Greene streets with belt buckles, jewelry, prints, old clothes, records, books, hand-painted cards, teapots, lampshades, and glasses of cold lemonade.

Farther up, east of Lafayette, is a mini-diamond district—less raucous but equally diverting.

6. MUSEUM OF HOLOGRAPHY

11 Mercer Street (near Canal Street)
925-0526
Wednesday–Sunday noon–6 P.M. (Thursday until 9 P.M.)
Adults $1.50, children under 12 and senior citizens 75¢
Subway: IRT 6 or BMT N, RR to Canal Street
Bus: M1, M6

If you're not one of the fifteen million visitors to Disney World's "Haunted House," then you've perhaps never experienced the magical illusions of laser photography, otherwise known as holography. Let this delightful museum be your introduction to a fascinating art, full of future possibilities. You can even buy your own three-dimensional masterpiece to take home. "The Kiss" is a beauty.

7. GREY ART GALLERY AND STUDY CENTER (NYU)

33 Washington Place (Washington Square East)
598-7603
Tuesday, Thursday, Friday 10 A.M.–5 P.M., Wednesday 10 A.M.–8:30 P.M.,
    Saturday 1–5 P.M.
Free
Subway: IND A, B, CC, D, E, F to West 4th Street
Bus: M1, M2, M3, M5, M6

The largest collection of contemporary Asian and Middle Eastern art in the city (thanks to Ben and Abby Grey) plus an excellent array of nineteenth- and twentieth-century paintings, drawings, and sculptures from Europe and America. Exhibits change every six weeks and the gallery normally closes down for two weeks between each one, so call for details and also ask for the dates of special lectures and films.

8. WASHINGTON MEWS

Subway: Any train to Union Square
Bus: M2, M3, M5

Nestling behind gates between University Place and Fifth Avenue is what looks like a perfect example of thirty converted stable cottages. Actually, only five of them have ever seen a horse and carriage. The rest were added in 1916, but their delicately painted stucco exteriors give the alley all the ambience of a Mediterranean scene complete with wisteria vines and cobblestones.

One lesser-known attraction here is La Maison Française (16 Washington Mews, 598-2161) where lectures, forums, and movies, all in French, are open to the public during the academic year.

While you're in the neighborhood, stroll along the north side of Washington Square and turn up MacDougal Street to 8th Street. On your right, next door to William Shakespeare's Restaurant, is the diminutive MacDougal Alley, an elegant collection of mews cottages that once housed such notables as the sculptor Jo Davidson and the original action painter Jackson Pollack.

9. GRACE CHURCH—the Rectory

804 Broadway (at East 11th Street)
Subway: Any train to Union Square
Bus: M1, M2, M3

A lovely little Gothic-Revival masterpiece by James Renwick, Jr., next to his famous 1843–45 church with its lacelike tower. The adjoining Grace Church School, organized in 1894, was the first such establishment in New York for training choir boys.

Grace Church Rectory

10. GALLERY OF PREHISTORIC PAINTINGS

20 East 12th Street (between Fifth Avenue and University Place)
674-5389
Monday–Friday 10 A.M.–5 P.M., Saturday 9 A.M.–noon
By appointment only. Free
Subway: Any train to Union Square
Bus: M2, M3, M5

A relatively recent newcomer, this unusual loft gallery contains over sixty full-size silk-screen recreations of cave paintings from Europe, Africa, and America, and features guided tours, lectures, and workshop demonstrations. Director Douglas Mazonowicz gives a convincing background description of these splendid artworks.

11. ANTIQUES AND AUCTIONS

All around East 12th Street and University Place as far as Fourth Avenue are a score of antique stores (with a heavy preponderance of furniture) and auction rooms. Check the Saturday *New York Times* for details on auction hours and the sale of special items. Combine your exploration of these cavernous establishments with a visit to the Strand bookstore (828 Broadway at East 12th Street).
Subway: Any train to Union Square
Bus: M1, M2, M3, M9, M15, M101, M102

12. THE NEW MUSEUM

65 Fifth Avenue (at 14th Street)
741-8962
Call for hours
Free
Subway: Any train to Union Square
Bus: M2, M3

Another newcomer to this part of town is this small gallery of contemporary artists in the New School building on the corner of 14th Street. A welcome diversion.

2
14th STREET
TO 59th STREET

1. "GREENMARKET"

Union Square at 17th Street
Subway: Any train to Union Square
Bus: M1, M2, M3, M5, M6, M7

This impromptu Saturday farmers' market on the north side of the
square is a project sponsored by the Council on the Environment
of New York City. Others are planned, or possibly already
flourishing, so call 566-0990 for details.

2. WITCHCRAFTING

The Warlock Shop, 35 West 19th Street
242-7182
Occult Lecture, Sunday 3 P.M. (Store hours Monday–Saturday
  noon–8 P.M., Sunday noon–6 P.M.)
$1
Subway: Any train to Union Square
Bus: M2, M3, M5, M6, M7

This is the "largest complete occult shop in the world," according
to Herman Slater, its owner, and contains the only "above-
ground" pagan temple in New York State, meeting place of the
Ordo Templi Orietis Society. For the uninitiated there are Sunday
lectures and other classes leading to active participation in the
rituals. Even if you're not anxious to be "involved," come and
admire Mr. Slater's remarkable array of bits and pieces of dead
creatures, human skulls (yes, real ones), and all the tools for budding neophytes. Bring a crucifix just in case.

245

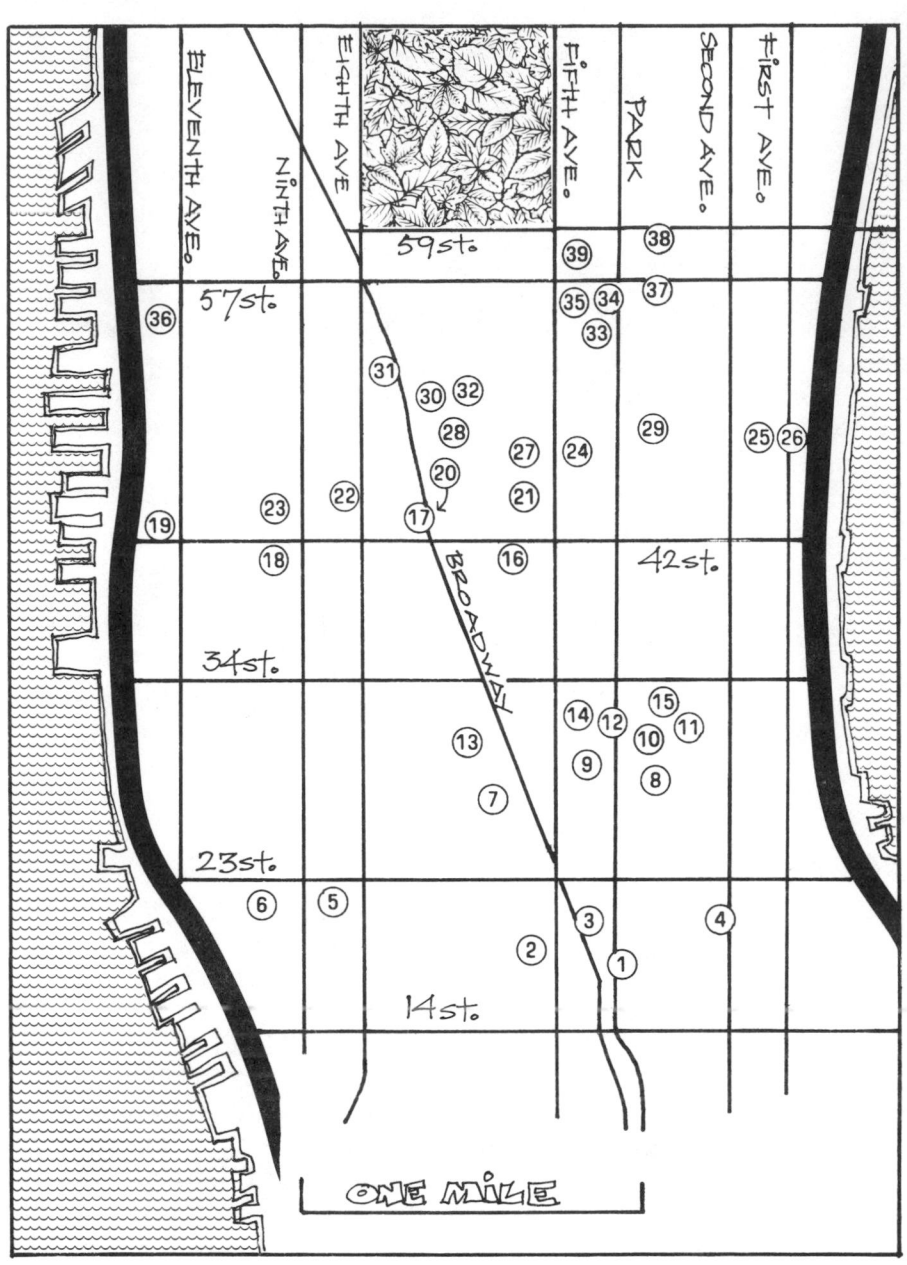

ELEVENTH AVE.

NINTH AVE.

EIGHTH AVE.

FIFTH AVE.

PARK

SECOND AVE.

FIRST AVE.

59 st.

57 st.

42 st.

34 st.

23 st.

14 st.

BROADWAY

ONE MILE

36

39

38

35 34

37

33

31

30 32

28

29

27

24

25 26

20

23

22

17

21

19

18

16

14

15

13

12

10 11

9

8

7

6

5

3

4

2

1

3. THEODORE ROOSEVELT BIRTHPLACE

28 East 20th Street
260-1616
Daily: 9 A.M.–4:30 P.M. (closed Monday and Tuesday from October-mid-
  May)
Adults 50¢; others free
Subway: IRT 6 to 23rd Street and Park Avenue South
Bus: M1, M2, M3, M5, M6, M7

Located in an architecturally fragmented section of town, this imposing Greek-Revival townhouse, birthplace of the nation's twenty-sixth president, reflects the spirit of the times in which Theodore Roosevelt lived. There's a massiveness to the structure restrained only by the discipline of the design—an apt description of Roosevelt himself.

The lower-floor museum presents a chronology of his life with a remarkable array of valuable memorabilia. The remaining five rooms recreate the ambience of a Victorian townhouse and are furnished exclusively in the style of that era. It's the kind of place you come to for an hour and stay half a day.

4. POLICE ACADEMY MUSEUM

235 East 20th Street (between Second and Third avenues)
477-9753
Monday–Friday 9 A.M.–4 P.M.
Free
Subway: IRT 6 to 23rd Street and Park Avenue South
Bus: M15, M101, M102

The world's largest collection of police artifacts and memorabilia, historic items, emergency-service displays, and odd weapons. (Yes, there really was a gun in a violin case, and some pretty gruesome alternatives too.) Visitors can also tour the academy itself.

5. GENERAL THEOLOGICAL SEMINARY AND HISTORIC DISTRICT—CHELSEA

Daily 9 A.M.–6 P.M.
Subway: IND AA, CC, E to 23rd Street and Eighth Avenue
Bus: M10

Much of Chelsea's Greek-Revival– and Italianate–flavored historic district along 20th and 21st streets between Ninth and Tenth avenues was part of Clement Clarke Moore's ("'Twas the night before Christmas . . .") pastoral estate and it's thanks to his foresight as an amateur architect and planner that we can enjoy its delightful ambience today.

The General Theological Seminary (Chelsea Square) occupies the central portion of the district. Visitors are encouraged to stroll

Chelsea

through its shady grounds, to the accompaniment of bird song or of psalms from behind the ornate doors of the Chapel of the Good Shepherd. Alternatively, browse through the ecclesiastical tomes in St. Mark's Library here.

Although relatively small, the historic district contains a number of notable features, including Paul Frieberg's children's park at Tenth Avenue and West 22nd Street, and the 1831 L and S Dairy building (183 Ninth Avenue at 21st Street). This Federal-style charmer with its three adjoining wooden houses brings a little of the flavor of Williamsburg to this corner of the city.

Spend time exploring the area. Admittedly, the streets outside the historic district lack much of its charm, but there's evidence of enthusiastic renewal, and the stores along Eighth and Ninth avenues reflect the whims of an increasingly cosmopolitan population.

6. THE EMPIRE DINER

210 Tenth Avenue (near 23rd Street)
243-2736
Open all the time
Subway: IND AA, CC, E to 23rd Street and Eighth Avenue
Bus: M10, M26

Just down from the popular Pottery Barn and Workbench stores on Tenth Avenue (between 23rd and 24th streets) is this little chrome-plated diner, beloved by Chelsea's celebrities for its unique character and unusually ambitious menu (for a diner) of stuffed prawns, tortellini, shish kebab, steak and shrimp, etc.

If it's crowded here (and it invariably is during most late evenings) try Mr. Spat's across the road, which features such British delectables as Cock-a-Leekie soup, steak 'n' kidney pie, fish 'n' chips, and sherry trifle, or the Chateau Ruggero on the north side of 23rd Street. This somewhat exclusive establishment serves succulent Italian dishes in a regal atmosphere. All unexpected surprises at the tail end of Chelsea.

7. ROSES AND DAISIES AT DAWN

Wholesale Flower Market, 28th Street around Sixth Avenue
Subway: IND, B, F to 23rd Street at Sixth Avenue
Bus: M5, M6, M7 (also M2, M3 on Fifth Avenue)

A delight for insomniacs or a splendid way to end a very-early-morning trip to the Fulton Street Fish Market (see chapter 7). Most active times are between 7 and 9 A.M. The scurry and bustle is reminiscent of the opening scenes of *My Fair Lady*. One expects all the delivery boys, bawling warehousemen, demure female buyers, and bloated packers to suddenly burst into some rousing chorus. Even if you miss the wholesale antics, the street becomes a marvelous retail strip of palms, rubber plants, ferns, flowers, and dried fronds during the day. Intense and very New York.

On Sunday morning when the neighborhood is a little less frantic, there's usually a flea market during the summer at 25th Street and Sixth Avenue, in a rather worn parking lot. For 50¢, enter and browse among the Art Nouveau lamps, wartime posters, battered cameras, old magazines, suitcases, records, perfume bottles, and all the paraphernalia normally found at a country jumble sale.

8. A BIT OF BOMBAY

Subway: IRT 6 to 28th Street and Park Avenue South
Bus: M1, M101, M102

For some reason, Lexington Avenue between 26th and 33rd streets is home for half a dozen or more stores selling Indian foods of every description—lentils, dahl, a score of curry powders, ghee, bottles of brown, gold, and ochre spices, flat waferlike papadums (when quickly fried they treble in size and become wonderfully crunchy accompaniments to curry dishes), pickles, sticky desserts, and sacks of the finest long-grain Indian rice. And that's only the beginning. Come and browse.

9. "LITTLE CHURCH AROUND THE CORNER"

1 East 29th Street
Subway: BMT N or RR to 23rd Street and Broadway
Bus: M1, M2, M3, M5

This unexpected masterpiece in the "Cottage Gothic" style has been known as the Actors' Church ever since George Holland received burial rites there in 1870 (deceased actors apparently were not welcome at other nearby churches). Come through the unusual lich gate, past the Gothic-Revival rectory (with mansard roof?), and enter the intimate nave. It has all the ambience of a cozy rural church. Note the continued links with other noted actors—memorial windows to Richard Mansfield, Joseph Jefferson, Edwin Booth (portrayed as Hamlet), and John Drew, a special chapel in honor of Jose Maria Munoz, and the Actors' Memorial Window dedicated to all members of the profession.

10. PRATT-N.Y. PHOENIX SCHOOL OF DESIGN MANHATTAN CENTER

160–162 Lexington Avenue (at 30th Street)
685-2973
Monday–Friday 10 A.M.–6 P.M., Saturday 1–4 P.M. (closed August)
Subway: IRT 6 to 28th Street and Park Avenue South
Bus: M1, M101, M102

Occasionally stimulating, always diverse, exhibitions of graphic and related arts every 4 to 6 weeks at this revered institution. Call for details.

11. VICTORY GARDENS

31st Street at Third Avenue
Subway: IRT 6 to 33rd Street at Park Avenue
Bus: M101, M102

Victory indeed—over the insatiable appetites of the land developers. Here's one of the best-laid-out ("organic") allotment gardens in Manhattan, an example of how we could be using the other 1,050 acres of vacant lots around the city.

Also in the same area there's the delightful Colonial Garden at Lexington Avenue and 29th Street.

12. BELMORE CAFETERIA

470 Park Avenue (at 31st Street)
LE. 2-0510
Daily 5 A.M.–2 A. M.
Subway: IRT 6 to 33rd Street and Park Avenue
Bus: M1

Grab a ticket, stand in line, get yourself an enormous platter of breast of veal, chicken pot pie, beef stew, a free bowl of soup, a free glass of seltzer, and you're ready to join the other 350 customers in this venerable institution, one of the last great cafeterias in the city. It's a cabbie's haven. The street outside is block-to-block yellow cabs (with scattered hookers). No finesse here—just lots of food, lots of seltzer, and wall-to-wall cabbie talk.

13. THE BOXING HALL OF FAME

120 West 31st Street (between Sixth and Seventh avenues)
564-0354
Monday–Friday 10 A.M.–4 P.M.
Free
Subway: IND D or F to 34th Street or IRT 1, 2, 3 to 34th Street
Bus: M5, M6, M7, M10

This small exhibition, in the lobby of *The Ring* magazine, is for boxing buffs only. Fist casts of famous fighters (note the size of Primo Carnera's), boxing gloves, championship belts, photographs, and even round gongs make up most of the collection. For those interested in the sport, this must be something of a national shrine.

14. THE COMPLETE STRATEGIST

11 East 33rd Street
685-3880
Monday–Saturday 10:30 A.M.–6 P.M., Thursday until 9 P.M.
Subway: IRT 6 to 33rd Street and Park Avenue
Bus: M2, M3, M4, M32

If you're a war-game buff, you'll know all about this place. However, you may not know that this is also a gathering place for members of the Society for Creative Anachronism and like-minded individuals who like nothing better than to role-play their way through a fantasy-game world of elves, gnomes, ogres, knights, dragons, and fair maidens. Come see for yourself. There's no other place quite like it in the five boroughs.

15. ASTRO MINERALS

155 East 34th Street (between Lexington and Third avenues)
889-9000
Monday–Saturday 10 A.M.–6 P.M.
Free
Subway: IRT 6 to 33rd Street and Park Avenue
Bus: M101, M102

Here's the "Topkapi of 34th Street"—with radiant exhibitions of precious stones and minerals, necklaces, carved ornaments, et al. The place is primarily a store, but the displays make it a fascinating place for browsing.

16. BEAUTIFUL COMFORT

Subway: Any train to Times Square
Bus: M1, M2, M3, M4, M5, M6

There are two wonderful Beaux-Arts comfort stations on either side of Bryant Park just behind the library—alas, a most uncommon sight in Manhattan (and another alas, not usually open!). While you're in the neighborhood take a stroll across the road and through the exhibition "alley" of the CUNY Graduate Center, linking 42nd and 43rd streets. There's usually some display of interest here.

17. SONGWRITERS
HALL OF FAME MUSEUM

1 Times Square (between Broadway and 42nd Street)
221-1252
Monday–Saturday 11 A.M.–3 P.M.
Free
Subway: Any train to Times Square (also via IRT shuttle from Lexington Avenue)
Bus: M6, M7, M10, M104, M106

A bright, cheery salute to great American songwriters with Fats Waller's piano, Gene Kelly's dancing shoes, Oscars, Emmy awards, special exhibitions, all kinds of memorabilia plus daily events, a chance to chat with songwriters on Saturdays, a film, guitars, and a moog synthesizer to play—and lots of fun. You think you've got a publishable song? Well, come and talk to the experts.

18. A NEW THEATRE ROW

42nd Street (between Ninth and Tenth avenues)
Subway: IND A, AA, CC, E to 42nd Street and Eighth Avenue
Bus: M11

Who says 42nd Street is lost? Take a stroll down here to see the synergism of off-off-Broadway establishments, about seven at last count. If (when) the convention center comes there's going to be a total renaissance in this part of town. Good theater is always an excellent way to begin!

While you're in the area take a stroll up to the Landmark Tavern (46th Street at Eleventh Avenue), an excellent if rather lonely example of renewal potentials in this forgotten sector of Manhattan.

19. USED-POSTAL-TRUCKS SALE

New York Post Office Parking Lot, 42nd Street between Eleventh and Twelfth avenues
971-5244
Every Tuesday and Wednesday (except December and holidays)
(Inspection 8–10 A.M., sale 10 A.M.–4 P.M.)
Subway: IND A, AA, CC, E to 42nd Street and Eighth Avenue
Bus: M11, M16, M106

Ideal, if you happen to need a one-ton Chevrolet or Dodge truck that's spent most of its working life crashing through Manhattan potholes. Prices are posted. They're realistic anyway. (If you buy one, drive it up to Paddy's Market on Ninth Avenue and fill it. See chapter 7.)

If a truck isn't what you need, go to the Post Office auction (Room 4500, GPO, 380 West 33rd Street) and bid for anything from TV sets and artworks to crystal goblets and sofas. Call 971-7760 for dates and details.

Should this way of acquiring household and related effects appeal, there are two other similar series of auctions:

U.S. Customs auctions (620-3435 for details)
Police Department auctions (577-7291 for details).

20. NATHAN'S FAMOUS CHILDREN'S THEATRE

43rd Street and Broadway
594-7455
Sunday 1 P.M. and 3 P.M. (downstairs in the Boardwalk Room)
Subway: Any train to Times Square
Bus: M10, M104

Clowns, magicians, puppets—you name it. Delightful for kids from one to one hundred.

21. A LOCK MUSEUM

J. M. Mossman Collection of Locks, 20 West 44th Street
687-2490
Monday–Friday 9 A.M.–4 P.M.
Free
Subway: IND B, D, F to 42nd Street and Sixth Avenue or IRT 7 to Fifth Avenue and 42nd Street
Bus: M1, M2, M3, M4, M5, M6, M7

Located within the General Society of Mechanics and Tradesmen is this unique display of scores of locks, both ancient and modern. Doors will never seem the same again after a visit here.

22. McGIRR'S BILLIARD ACADEMY

709 Eighth Avenue (between 44th and 45th streets)
974-9173
Daily 11 A.M.–2 A.M.
Subway: IND A, AA, CC, E to 42nd Street and Eighth Avenue
Bus: M11, M16, M106

If the only time you've seen the inside of a pool hall is in some Cagney-style movie, pop into McGirr's place and watch the professionals (a few real ones) at play. "We're just a regular pool hall," says management modestly. For $3 or so an hour you can blaze away at the balls and maybe pick up some tips from the experts. An unusual diversion.

23. FREE THEATER

Subway: IND A, AA, CC, E to 42nd Street and Eighth Avenue
Bus: M11

Even the most off of off-off-Broadway theaters normally charge $2–$3 admittance, but the New Dramatists Theater at 424 West 44th Street (between Ninth and Tenth avenues) is absolutely free. Call PL. 7-6960 for details.

24. THE MERCANTILE LIBRARY

17 East 47th Street (between Madison and Fifth avenues)
755-6710
Monday–Friday 8:30 A.M.–6 P.M.
Membership dues: $24/year or $15 for six months
Subway: IND B, D, F to Rockefeller Center
Bus: M1, M2, M3, M4

Normally I don't feature membership establishments, but this delightful private library (established over 150 years ago) with its London-club-flavored reading room and its collection of over 250,000 books is well worth the modest fee. Special events include mail-service delivery of books, lectures, seminars with contemporary authors, and discussion groups.

25. JAPAN HOUSE GALLERY

333 East 47th Street (between First and Second avenues)
832-1155
Daily 11 A.M.–5 P.M., Friday 11 A.M.–7:30 P.M.
Contribution
Subway: IRT 4, 5, 6 to Grand Central
Bus: M15, M27

Inside this contemporary Japanese-style building is an attractive auditorium (occasional films are shown here), exhibitions on the second-floor gallery (three a year), gardens both indoors and outdoors, and a substantial reference library open to the public.

26. AFRICAN-AMERICAN INSTITUTE

833 United Nations Plaza (First Avenue and 47th Street)
949-5666
Monday–Friday 9 A.M.–5 P.M., Saturday 11 A.M.–5 P.M.
Free
Subway: IRT 4, 5, 6, 7 to Grand Central
Bus: M15, M27

To appreciate the significance of the special exhibitions here of African art and crafts it's best to take the guided tour (call for details). One leaves with a new concept of that still-mysterious continent. Rewarding.

27. THE GOTHAM BOOK MART

41 West 47th Street (between Fifth and Sixth avenues)
757-0367
Monday–Saturday 10 A.M.–6:30 P.M.
Subway: IND B, D, F to Rockefeller Center
Bus: M1, M2, M4, M5, M6, M7

In the heart of the Diamond District is a true New York book store—some say the truest—with more than half a million volumes piled, stacked, boxed, and squeezed into the narrow confines of an old townhouse. Established by Frances Steloff in 1920, it has been a home away from home for almost every notable American writer since Ezra Pound and Gertrude Stein.

Publishers reserve the upstairs gallery (exhibitions of young artists) months in advance for book-release parties, and the city litterati flock here to browse through the vast collections. A sign over the door reads "Wise Men Fish Here." It's a well-stocked stream.

28. LOOKING FOR A GUITAR?

Subway: IND B, D, F to Rockefeller Center
Bus: M5, M6, M7

Don't buy before you've explored this mini music-row on 48th Street between Sixth and Seventh avenues. Here we have Alex, Manny's, Sam Ash, We Buy Guitars Inc., and windows full of Martins, Guilds, Gibsons, Fenders, et al. Prices range from inexpensive Japanese imports to $2000 custom-made miracles. A fantasy-world for budding Segovias and Springsteens.

If the choice is too hard to make, take the weight off your head in a delightful walkway linking 48th and 50th streets at the back of the McGraw-Hill and Exxon buildings. It comes complete with waterfalls (one over a glass "tunnel") and shrub-shrouded seats.

29. ANCIENT REMEDIES

The Caswell-Massey Pharmacy (1752)
755-2254
518 Lexington Avenue (at 48th Street)
Monday–Saturday 10 A.M.–6 P.M.
Subway: IRT 6 to 51st Street and Lexington Avenue
Bus: M101

As one might expect from the oldest established pharmacy in the U.S.A., there's an Old World atmosphere here of old jars, pharmaceutical artifacts, and tales told by Philip Cohen of the special formula devised for George Washington's cologne, etc., etc. Ask questions—they love it, and pick up their catalog. A delightful surprise.

30. NIKON HOUSE

16 West 50th Street (on the Rockefeller Center Promenade)
586-3907
Gallery: Tuesday–Saturday 10 A.M.–6 P.M.; free seminars: Tuesday–
    Friday 4–5:30 P.M.
Free
Subway: IND B, D, F to Rockefeller Center
Bus: M1, M2, M3, M4, M5, M6, M7

If you find yourself in the middle of a photographic session and in dire need of technical assistance, call here between 10 A.M. and 6 P.M. and you'll get all the help you need, with maybe a few extra pointers thrown in.

In less traumatic circumstances, visit and enjoy the gallery (regular new exhibits), the free seminars, and the displays of just about every product made by Nikon.

31. ROSELAND DANCE HALL

239 West 52nd Street (at Broadway)
247-0200
Tuesday and Wednesday 6:30 P.M.–midnight, Thursday 2 P.M.–midnight,
    Friday 8:30 P.M.–1:20 A.M., Saturday 2 P.M.–1:20 A.M., Sunday 2 P.M.–
    midnight
$3

Subway: IRT 1 to 50th Street and Broadway
Bus: M10, M104

A genuine New York classic experience for those who love real ballroom dancing, those who love to watch, and others feeling just jaded or lonely. All the biggest and the best of the swing bands have fox-trotted through here since 1919. They're still doing it too for up to a thousand dancers at a time on the football-field floor. Lots of places for impromptu meetings. A kind of singles center for older adults.

32. TV SHOW TICKETS

You'll normally find free-ticket distributors on the Avenue of the Americas between 53rd and 49th Streets most days of the week. However, if you're choosy about the shows you want to see, call these numbers for information on shows and times:

ABC	581-7777
CBS	975-2476
NBC	664-4444

33. BILL'S GAY NINETIES

57 E. 54th Street (between Madison and Park avenues)
EL. 5-0243
Subway: IND E or F to Fifth Avenue and 53rd Street
Bus: M1, M2, M3, M4, M32

A genuine repository of old music hall "where nostalgia was born" complete with live acts, lots of audience participation in the chorus songs, a lantern-slide quiz, and a spirit of libatious abandonment full of cane-whirling and mustache-twirling. You can splurge here with dinner or spend your minimum on cocktails with the show. Call for details.

34. A VERY HAPPY, HAPPY HOUR

Molly Moggs, 65 E. 55th Street (near Park Avenue)
593-0535
Subway: IRT 4, 5, 6 or BMT N, RR to 59th Street and Lexington Avenue
Bus: M1, M2, M3, M4, M101, M102

Starting at 5 P.M. (till 7:15 P.M.) a magnificent complimentary buffet attracts a loyal coterie of followers to this English-styled pub. Drinks are usually priced a little over normal midtown prices, but for what can amount to a free dinner, who's complaining? The spread normally includes: Virginia ham, meat loaf, pastrami, egg/macaroni/potato salads, beets, beans, corned beef, etc. etc. Marvelous.

35. SOLID PHOTOGRAPHS

Studio for Solid Photography, 551 Madison Avenue (at 55th Street)
752-0044
Monday–Saturday 10 A.M.–6 P.M.
Subway: BMT N, RR or IRT 4, 5, 6 to 59th Street and Lexington Avenue
Bus: M1, M2, M3, M4

Using an innovative system of electronic optics and computerization, they produce convincing three-dimensional sculpture-portraits here that look almost artist-crafted, even down to the chisel marks. It's not inexpensive, but it's certainly worth pausing to admire the results.

36. VISIT AN OCEAN LINER

Subway/Bus: IND AA, CC, E to 50th Street, then transfer to the M27—the 50th Street crosstown bus

If you'd like the next best thing to a sea cruise on some of the great ocean liners of the world, Home (432-1414) and Holland-America Steamship companies (760-3800) invite you to visit their beauties for an hour or two (usually Saturdays, 2:00–3:00 P.M., between April and November. Adults $1). Call these and other companies for details of sailings (don't bother calling Cunard, though, as they don't allow nonpassengers on the *Queen*). Access is at the new pier at 55th Street and 12th Avenue (follow the signs).

   If you'd like to visit a naval vessel, call 264-7793 to see if any are in port and open to the public.

37. IRISH PAVILION

130 East 57th Street (near Lexington Avenue)
759-9041
Monday–Wednesday 10 A.M.–midnight, Thursday, Friday, and Saturday 10 A.M.–2 A.M.
Subway: IRT 4, 5, 6 or BMT RR to 59th Street and Lexington Avenue
Bus: M31, M32, M101, M102

Whether you'd like to sample one of the best arrays of Irish whiskeys in town, buy a Moynihan-style hat, try on a few Irish tweed sports jackets, or enjoy solid Irish-American fare to the music of the Clancys (sometimes live), this is your place. The clientele is usually more metropolitan than the Murphy's at the Third Avenue taverns nearby, but the flavor's most pleasant (begorrah).

Nearby at the Columbia Center (140 East 57th Street) there's free coffee at the sidewalk café during summer and a small exhibition on coffee production. Nice.

38. GENEALOGICAL AND BIOGRAPHICAL SOCIETY OF NEW YORK

122 East 58th Street (between Park and Lexington avenues)
PL. 5-8532
Monday–Friday 9:30 A.M.–5 P.M.
Free use of the research library
Subway: BMT RR or IRT 4, 5, 6 to 59th Street at Lexington Avenue
Bus: M1, M2, M3, M4, M101, M102

If you've ever wondered how to go about tracing your family tree you might consider visiting the fourth-floor library here. Alternatively, call to find out about the society's special lectures and classes.

39. GENERAL MOTORS EXHIBITION

767 Fifth Avenue (at 59th Street)
486-4518
Monday–Friday 9 A.M.–9 P.M., Saturday 10 A.M.–6 P.M.
Free
Subway: BMT N or RR to Fifth Avenue at 60th Street
Bus: M1, M2, M3, M4, M5

In addition to extensive displays of General Motors products, there are usually special exhibits here dealing with technological aspects of the company's work and research.

After these somewhat serious diversions, pause awhile in the seat of a vintage charabanc at the Autopub (immediately below in the sunken plaza), or roam the auto-flavored exhibits and dining areas. You can even enjoy a free movie classic in the theater lounge. (Your meal is your ticket.)

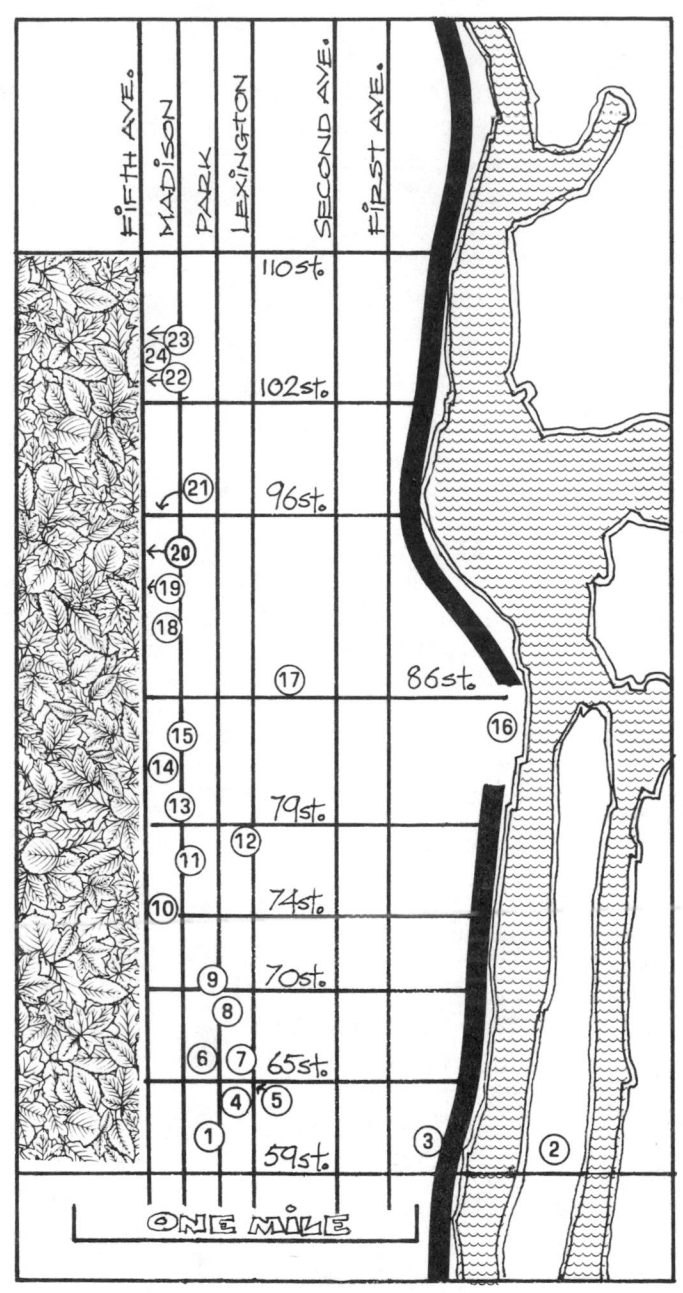

3
ABOVE 59th STREET
(EAST SIDE)

1. THE GROLIER CLUB

47 East 60th Street (between Madison and Park avenues)
838-6690
Monday–Friday 10 A.M.–5 P.M., Saturday 10 A.M.–3 P.M.
Free public exhibitions October–June
Subway: IND EE or BMT RR to Fifth Avenue
Bus: M1, M2, M3, M4, M30

There's a leathery, clublike atmosphere in this splendid stone townhouse with wonderful displays of rare books and manuscripts reflecting specific themes. Even if books don't excite you, go just for the ambience of the place.

2. ROOSEVELT ISLAND

Aerial tram from 60th Street and Second Avenue
Subway: IRT 4, 5, 6, or BMT RR to 59th Street
Bus: M15, M28, M31

A little lunge and you're off across the rooftops, up to a height of 246 feet and then down again. Electric buses provide free transport to the heart of this "little apple." The information office has a map showing the major points of interest. Visit the stone lighthouse at the northern end, the modern Main Street between the highrises, and the charming Blackwell House—one of the oldest farmhouses in the city (and that's just a start).

263

3. GARDEN IN THE SKY

Terrestris, 409 East 60 Street (between First and York avenues)
PL. 8-8181
Subway: IRT 4, 5, 6 or BMT RR to 59th Street
Bus: M15, M28, M31, M103

Come lose yourself in a rooftop greenhouse jungle of house plants and trees ("six inches to eighteen feet," claims the attractive take-away brochure). It's hot and humid, but the bird songs are sweet and occasional views over the city between the fronds are delightful.

Alternatively—be a bird for awhile. Just down the street by the river there's Island Helicopter Corporation, which offers flights over the city (start at $9 for 7 minutes). Flights also leave from 34th Street at the East River (call 889-0986 for details; reservations recommended).

4. SOCIETY OF ILLUSTRATORS

128 East 63rd Street (between Park and Lexington avenues)
RH. 4-6400
Monday–Friday 10 A.M.–5 P.M. Closed August
Free
Subway: IRT 4, 5, 6 or BMT N, RR to 59th Street
Bus: M101, M102

In addition to regular exhibitions of members' work to which the public is welcome, the society also presents its annual exhibition from mid-February to mid-March (with awards for excellence) and special displays of works by renowned illustrators. (There's also an excellent buffet lunch served upstairs, but you have to be a member or guest to enjoy that.)

5. ASIA HOUSE

112 East 64th Street (between Park and Lexington avenues)
751-4210
Monday–Saturday 10 A.M.–5 P.M., Thursday 10 A.M.–8:30 P.M., Sunday 1 P.M.–5 P.M.
Free
Subway: IRT 6 to 68th Street
Bus: M1, M2, M3, M4, M101, M102

Cofounded by John D. Rockefeller and housed in an understated glass structure designed by Philip Johnson, Asia House offers a wide range of public lectures on Asian affairs, at least three special loan exhibitions yearly, theatrical, music, and film presentations, and an extensive library. Tape-recorded tours of exhibitions are normally available. Members are entitled to (exceptionally good) group charter rates to Asia.

6. ARCHIVES OF AMERICAN ART
41 East 65th Street (at Madison Avenue)
826-5722
Monday–Friday 9:30 A.M.–5 P.M.
Free
Subway: IRT 6 to 68th Street
Bus: M1, M2, M3, M4

This is one of five regional centers across the country where the world's largest collection of sketchbooks, letters, diaries, and documents relating to the history of American visual arts is contained in microfilm form for use by scholars, researchers, and members. The actual materials are based in the Smithsonian Institution in Washington, D.C. In addition to every known art-auction catalog from 1785 to 1963, gallery records, and 150,000 photographs of artists at work, there are 2,000 taped interviews with artists, collectors, and critics.

The public is invited to visit the changing exhibits here (call in advance for details). It's a unique opportunity to glimpse the private lives of renowned artists—to sense the individuals behind the myths.

7. CHINA HOUSE
125 East 65th Street (between Park and Lexington avenues)
744-8181
Monday–Friday 10 A.M.–5 P.M., Saturday 11 A.M.–5 P.M., Sunday 2–5 P.M. (during exhibitions)
Free
Subway: IRT 6 to 68th Street
Bus: M1, M2, M3, M4, M101, M102

There are normally only two (small but usually exquisite) exhibitions here each year, so it's best to call in advance and check the program. Credit courses are also available in Chinese culture, literature, cooking, art, music, and dance and, as with most institutions of this kind in the city, members are entitled to group rates on charter flights. (The rear reading room overlooking the garden still retains all the flavor of a nineteenth-century townhouse library.)

8. CENTER FOR INTER-AMERICAN RELATIONS

680 Park Avenue (at 68th Street)
249-8950
Tuesday–Sunday noon–6 P.M.
Contribution
Subway: IRT 6 to 68th Street
Bus: M1, M2, M3, M4, M101, M102

Established in 1966 to "increase understanding among the peoples of the Western Hemisphere," the center is located in a landmark townhouse and features frequent gallery exhibitions of Latin American, Canadian, and Caribbean sculpture, musical events, lectures, and workshops. Some activities are limited to members, so it's best to call ahead.

9. THE EXPLORERS CLUB

46 East 70th Street (near Park Avenue)
628-8383
Library open to public Monday and Tuesday 10 A.M.–4 P.M.
Free
Subway: IRT 6 to 68th Street and Lexington Avenue
Bus: M1, M2, M3, M4, M101, M102, M30

If you're thinking of making an expedition to some exotic hidden corner of the world, call the club and see if any member can help you with the planning, or check on the public-lecture schedule (Mondays 8–10 P.M., September–May, $3.50). Alternatively, make an appointment to use the excellent research library here. A stimulating place.

10. CENTER FOR STUDY OF THE PRESIDENCY

926 Fifth Avenue (at 74th Street)
249-1200
Monday–Friday 9 A.M.–5 P.M.
Free
Subway: IRT 6 to 77th Street and Lexington Avenue
Bus: M1, M2, M3, M4

The primary function of this small but intriguing institution is to act as a repository of both originals and reproductions of presidential library documents from around the country. Its location in a dignified townhouse on a particularly imposing Upper East Side street is most appropriate for the scholarly types who frequent the small library here (seats only six). Occasional exhibits are planned, but it's advisable to call in advance.

11. PARKE-BERNET
980 Madison Avenue (at 77th Street)
472-3400
Tuesday–Saturday 10 A.M.–5 P.M. (call for details)
Subway: IRT 6 to 77th Street and Lexington Avenue
Bus: M101, M102

Actually, the correct title for this most revered, almost monopolistic, establishment, is Sotheby-Parke-Bernet since it was bought by the London firm of Sotheby Co. in 1964.

Although noted for its record-setting sales of Rembrandts and Medici porcelain and the like (these are the occasions for rigid enforcement of pecking-order privileges), most lots sell for far less than $500. So, if you have a few hours to spare, come and join in the fun. Just be careful not to wave your catalog around too much.

12. NELSON'S FOLLY
1129 Lexington Avenue (between 78th and 79th streets)
755-0485
Tuesday–Saturday 11 A.M.–6 P.M. (advisable to call in advance)
Subway: IRT 6 to 77th Street and Lexington Avenue
Bus: M101, M102

Marvelous—a tiny world of model ships, scrimshaw, sextants, spyglasses, ships in bottles, ships' lanterns, decoys, and old engravings (of ships of course) collected over thirty-seven years by Nelson and Virginia Cowell. It's on the second floor and you'll have to ring the bell to get in.

13. THE UKRAINIAN INSTITUTE
2 East 79th Street
288-2680
Tuesday–Friday 2 P.M.–6 P.M., Saturday and Sunday by appointment
Contribution
Subway: IRT 6 to 77th Street and Lexington Avenue
Bus: M1, M2, M3, M4

This center for Ukrainian culture, art, sculpture, folk art, and history is housed in the Van Horne Stuyvesant Mansion. In addition to the varied displays there's a well-stocked research library. Unexpected and delightful.

"Castles in the Air"—Water-Tank Disguises

ROOFSCAPES

The most neglected art forms in the city are the "castles in the air"—those wonderful disguises designed by architects to shroud roof-top water tanks. Here are a few favorites. Look up and discover your own.

Sherry-Netherland Hotel at 60th Street and Fifth Avenue
Pierre Hotel at 61st Street and Fifth Avenue
63rd Street at Lexington Avenue

Park Avenue at 72nd and 73rd streets
76th Street at Madison Avenue
80th Street at Lexington Avenue (also note the lovely garden
   across the avenue at the Unitarian Church of All Souls)
84th Street at East End Avenue

14. THE JUNIOR MET

Fifth Avenue and 81st Street
736-2211/879-5500
Tuesday–Saturday 10 A.M.–5 P.M., Sunday 11 A.M.–5 P.M.
Contribution
Subway: IRT 4, 5, 6 to 86th Street and Lexington Avenue
Bus: M1, M2, M3, M4

A lesser-known niche at the MET catering for the touch-and-try curiosity of junior visitors. Staff usually help interpret the exhibits, which appear under such titles as "The Age of Discovery" (Marco Polo et al.), "Archaeology and the World," and "The Artist's Workshop." Also a library, art classes, and special Saturday programs.

15. GOETHE HOUSE

1014 Fifth Avenue (between 82nd and 83rd streets)
744-8310
Tuesday–Thursday 11 A.M.–7 P.M., Friday and Saturday 11 A.M.–5 P.M.
Free
Subway: IRT 4, 5, 6 to 86th Street and Lexington Avenue
Bus: M1, M2, M3, M4

Unless you have a substantial appetite for books in German (15,000 volumes in the library here) you'll perhaps be more interested in the special exhibits (usually related to West German culture), lectures, and films in this delightful 1907 townhouse across from the MET. Call ahead for details.

16. THE JOHN FINLEY WALK

Between East 81st Street and Carl Shurz Park (East 84th to 90th streets)
    along the East River
Subway: IRT 6 to 77th Street and Lexington Avenue
Bus: M31

A jogger's paradise and one of the most delightful riverside walks in the city, on a broad pedestrian platform above FDR Drive. There are good views of Hell Gate, Wards Island Park, and Roosevelt Island.

Carl Shurz Park at the northern end of the walk is an exquisite swathe of lawns, shade, play areas, tunnels, and curving stairs leading to cobbled walkways. The delicate white trimmings of Gracie Mansion peer from behind dense thickets of trees, and across the road at E. 86th Street and East End Avenue is Hender-

Henderson Place

son Place, surrounded by towering apartment complexes, yet maintaining its classic repose. Lamb and Rich originally designed the thirty-two townhouses as a "single harmonic whole." Today there are only twenty-four remaining, but the subtlety of the architects' intent is still evident.

It's possible to continue walking (or jogging) alongside the river in both directions (north from 90th Street and south from 81st Street to the 59th Street Bridge), but these routes are far less pleasant than the Finley Walk itself.

17. A LUNCHTIME RECITAL

Manhattan Savings Bank
186 E. 86th Street (and Third Avenue)
688-3000
Monday–Friday noon–3 P.M.
Free
Subway: IRT 4, 5, 6 to 86th Street and Lexington Avenue
Bus: M101, M102

You'll have to come early to get a seat near the grand piano in this spacious establishment where Dorothy Denny gives her varied music recitals to a captivated audience every day. Other occasional acts and presentations are also featured here and at all the other six branches of the bank.

18. NATIONAL ACADEMY OF DESIGN

1083 Fifth Avenue (at 89th Street)
EN. 9-4880
Monday–Friday 1 P.M.–5 P.M. (closed in the summer)
50¢
Subway: IRT 4, 5, 6 to 86th Street and Lexington Avenue
Bus: M1, M2, M3, M4

The academy was originally founded in 1825 to develop and maintain "the highest standards in the arts." Many notable illustrators, architects, painters, and sculptors are current members, and regular exhibitions (eight or nine a year) include displays by the American Water Color Society, the Allied Artists of America, and work of students at the adjoining School of Fine Arts of the National Academy.

19. COOPER-HEWITT MUSEUM

2 East 91st Street (at Fifth Avenue)
860-6868
Tuesday 10 A.M.–9 P.M., Wednesday–Saturday 10 A.M.–5 P.M., Sunday
   noon–5 P.M.
Adults $1, children under 12 and senior citizens free (Tuesday is free day)
Subway: IRT 4, 5, 6 to 86th Street and Lexington Avenue
Bus: M1, M2, M3, M4

Wonderful! Inside the ponderous sixty-four-room Andrew Carnegie Mansion (1899–1903) is one of the most valuable collections of prints, wallpapers, glass, porcelain, textiles, lacework, and furniture in the country, plus a unique extravaganza of gilded bird

cages, book papers, trade cards, hatboxes, and the largest decora-
tive-arts-and-design reference collection in New York. A magnificent resource for the professional; a fascinating diversion for the
layman. Lots of special programs, exhibits, and workshops too.

20. INTERNATIONAL
CENTER OF PHOTOGRAPHY

1130 Fifth Avenue (at 94th Street)
860-1777
Wednesday–Sunday 11 A.M.–5 P.M., Tuesday 11 A.M.–8 P.M.
Adults $1, children (8–16), students, and senior citizens 50¢
Subway: IRT 6 to 96th Street and Lexington Avenue
Bus: M1, M2, M3, M4

An incredibly active institution offering community workshops in
photography, lectures, advanced weekend workshops (approved
for academic credit), film series, "dialogues," and even in-
ternships (my catalog is smothered in "must sees"). They also find
time to produce excellent photographic exhibitions often featuring leading contemporary photographers (public tours, Thursday
12:30 P.M.) and run a museum shop too. All this inside the modest
Audubon Mansion (modest at least in comparison to the other
"Gold Coast" contenders around Carnegie Hall).

21. ST. NICHOLAS RUSSIAN
ORTHODOX CATHEDRAL (1901—1902)

97th Street (between Fifth and Madison avenues)
Subway: IRT 6 to 96th Street and Lexington Avenue
Bus: M1, M2, M3, M4

A wonderful edifice with its five onion domes, ornate terra-cotta
detailings, baroque-flavored columns and trimmings, tucked away
ignominiously down 97th Street. A creature as magnificent as this
needs space. Alas, this is Manhattan, not Moscow. See it if you're
doing the museum strip along the "Gold Coast." Also take a look
at the Squadron A Armory (1895) nearby on Madison (94th to 95th
streets). Actually, there's only part of it left. The Landmarks Preservation Commission managed to save the western wall and towers
(take a stroll around "the back"—it's a park!).

St. Nicholas Cathedral

22. MUSEUM OF THE CITY OF NEW YORK

Fifth Avenue (between 103rd and 104th streets)
LE. 4-1672
Tuesday–Saturday 10 A.M.–4:50 P.M., Sundays and holidays 1–4:50 P.M.
Free
Subway: IRT 6 to 103rd Street and Lexington Avenue
Bus: M1, M2, M3, M4

Allow plenty of time here. The displays are deceptively spacious, but a tour of the four floors provides a comprehensive overview of New York's history from the pre-Dutch Indian days to contemporary issues and problems. The presentation is excellent and varied—there's "Cityrama," a seventeen-minute multimedia introduction; dioramas; a 1680 view of New York "in the round"; displays of toys, silver, costumes, ships, prints; the Rockefeller Rooms (5th floor); glimpses of life during the Dutch era; furniture from the homes of Alexander Hamilton, Duncan Phyfe, and other notables—and you've hardly begun. The collection is so varied and extensive, it's usually best to plan a number of visits. Sundays are particularly active with music concerts (3–4 P.M.) and city walking tours (pick up the program).

Also note the New York Academy of Medicine next to the museum. This unusual 1925 structure is one of the finest Romanesque buildings in the city.

23. EL MUSEO DEL BARRIO

105th Street and Fifth Avenue
831-7272
Tuesday–Friday 10:30 A.M.–4:30 P.M., Saturday and Sunday 11 A.M.– 4 P.M.
Donation
Subway: IRT 6 to 103rd Street and Lexington Avenue
Bus: M1, M2, M3, M4

A dynamic museum, always expanding, always changing but maintaining its basic themes of Puerto Rican culture, art, lifestyles, and mores in a series of exciting displays. Keep growing— please.

24. CENTRAL PARK CONSERVATORY GARDENS

105th Street and Fifth Avenue
Subway: IRT 6 to 103rd Street and Lexington Avenue
Bus: M1, M2, M3, M4

Through elaborate wrought-iron gates we enter a magic (and little-known) world of arbor walks, formal lawns, fountains, bowers of blossoms, and the sweetest-singing birds on the East Side. The Untermeyer Memorial Fountain has three frolicking nymphs ring-a-ring-a-rosing around a carved plinth—one of the most delightful creations in the park.

Many park lovers avoid the northern extremities. They shouldn't. This is wonderful territory full of woodland walks, gorges, rocky bluffs, natural streams, and waterfalls, and a peace rarely found in New York. If you're nervous, come with friends—but come. It's as good as a trip to New England (almost).

4
ABOVE 59th STREET (WEST SIDE)

1. GOOD HOUSEKEEPING INSTITUTE

959 Eighth Avenue (between 56th and 57th streets)
262-6467
Subway: IND A, AA, B, CC, D to 59th Street and Columbus Circle
Bus: M5, M7, M10, M104

Yes, there really is a Good Housekeeping Institute where experts—home economists, engineers, and chemists—test and evaluate products, recipes, and ideas before they appear in that well-loved monthly magazine. The various divisions (twenty-three in all) include the fabric-conditioning room, the needlework and sewing center, the food-department kitchens, the climatology chamber, and the toy/luggage lab.

If you'd like a tour (10:30 A.M. and 2:30 P.M. Monday–Friday) call or write ahead to the tour director.

2. BIBLE HOUSE (American Bible Society)

1865 Broadway (at 61st Street)
581-7400, Ext. 367
Monday–Friday (except holidays) 9 A.M.–4:30 P.M.
Free
Subway: IRT 1 or IND A, AA, CC, D to 59th Street and Columbus Circle
Bus: M5, M7, M104

Not just for the religious. Inside this modern yet modest midtown tower there are permanent exhibits of rare and historic Bibles, a full-scale reproduction of the 1456 Gutenberg printing press with remnants of one of the Bibles, and fragments from the Dead Sea Scrolls. Also special, often unusual, exhibitions and displays.

277

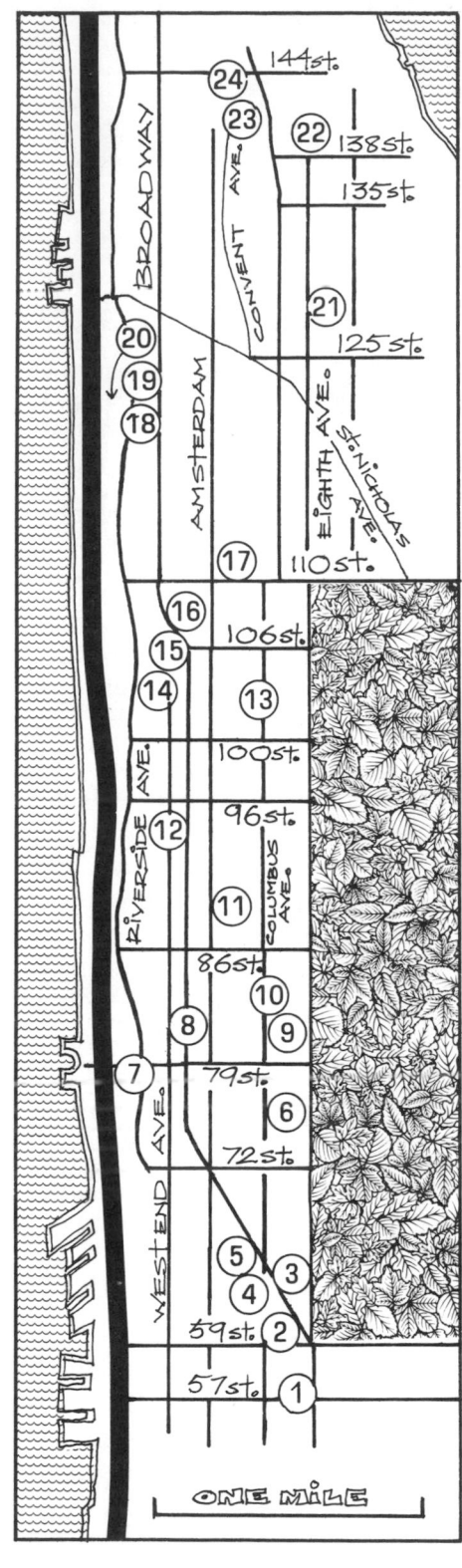

144 st.

138 st.

135 st.

BROADWAY

CONVENT AVE.

125 st.

AMSTERDAM

EIGHTH AVE.

St. NICHOLAS AVE.

110 st.

106 st.

RIVERSIDE AVE.

100 st.

96 st.

COLUMBUS AVE.

86 st.

79 st.

WEST END AVE.

72 st.

59 st.

57 st.

ONE MILE

3. MORMON VISITORS CENTER

2 Lincoln Square (between 65th Street and Broadway)
595-1825
Daily 10 A.M.–8 P.M.
Free
Subway: IRT 1 to Broadway at Lincoln Center
Bus: M5, M7, M11, M104

Not far from Bible House is this unusually imaginative introduction to the founding and nature of the Church of Jesus Christ of Latter-Day Saints. Whether or not the church's dogma interests you, the dioramas, speaking mannequins, films, select-your-own videotape service, tours, and genealogy library provide a fascinating diversion. One of the church's representatives called it "the best free show in New York." He may well be right.

4. A FREE VISIT TO AVERY FISHER HALL

Lincoln Center (65th Street at Broadway)
Sundays 11 A.M.–12:30 P.M.
Free
Subway: IRT 1 to Broadway at Lincoln Center
Bus: M5, M7, M11, M104

Eric Butterworth, minister of the Unity Center of New York City (JU 2-7128), delivers his nondenominational theological lectures here every Sunday. If you've never seen Avery Fisher Hall it's a good opportunity, and who knows, Mr. Butterworth's no-nonsense, intellectual approaches to the human condition may also prove interesting. Obviously many think so.

5. LINCOLN CENTER GARDENS

65th Street and Broadway
Subway: IRT 1 to Broadway at Lincoln Center
Bus: M5, M7, M11, M104

Just behind the white wedding-cake architecture there's Damrosch Park with free concerts in the Guggenheim Bandshell and lots of lovely shade. Also enjoy the secluded plaza west of Avery Fisher Hall with Calder's *Le Guichet* and Henry Moore's *Reclining Figure* in its reflecting pool (the pool, unfortunately, is frequently empty, much to the annoyance of the artist).

Don't miss the opportunity to visit the Library and Museum of the Performing Arts (a branch of the New York Public Library) in the Vivian Beaumont Theater building. Call 799-2200 for details on the wealth of activities here—films, concerts, special exhibits, theater, history displays, children's programs, etc. Makes you feel good to be in New York.

LOVELY STREETS—WEST SIDE
(70th–86th streets)

Try a "façade-finding" walk in this part of the West Side. Look for remnants of idiosyncratic-revival townhouses among the apartment monoliths—some of the best examples of fantasy architecture in the city.

Some favorite snippets of streets:

73rd Street between Columbus Avenue and West End Avenue
74th Street between Central Park West and Columbus Avenue
74th Street west of West End Avenue
Most of 75th Street
76th Street, west of West End Avenue (76th Street between Central Park West and Columbus is one of the most stately streets in the city and appropriately a designated Historic District)
77th Street around West End Avenue—the odd Dutch-style complex of the West End Collegiate Church and School
81st Street between Columbus Avenue and Amsterdam Avenue
83rd Street between Central Park West and Amsterdam Avenue
85th Street between Central Park West and Amsterdam Avenue

6. THE NEW-YORK HISTORICAL SOCIETY

170 Central Park West (at 77th Street)
873-3400
Tuesday–Friday 11 A.M.–5 P.M., Saturday 10 A.M.–5 P.M., Sunday 1–5 P.M.
Free
Subway: IND AA, B, CC to 81st Street
Bus: M10

This revered private institution, the oldest museum in the state, has moved seven times from its original 1804 location in City Hall to its current position near the Museum of Natural History.

The society combines its famous permanent displays—American paintings, including original paintings from Audubon's *Birds of America*, the Craft and Silver Galleries, exhibits on the Port of New York, fire-fighting equipment room, collections of cigar-store Indians and children's toys and dolls, hallways filled with early-American folk art—with an ever-changing array of special exhibitions. Some of the most popular displays include the Fahnestock Carriage collection in the basement and the Prentis Collection of colonial New England room settings. Also for the true enthusiast there's an extensive library open daily (except Sunday).

A refined and tasteful enclave of historic Americana.

7. THE BOAT BASIN
79th Street at the Hudson River
Subway: IRT 1 to Broadway at 79th Street
Bus: M5, M104

Stand by the fountain and gaze at the way the other half lives (all that brass-polishing and deck-swabbing seems like hard work to me). If you have time, spend the rest of the day meandering north through Riverside Park. The truly ambitious can make it to Inwood Hill Park right at the top of the island (with a few detours).

8. ZABAR'S
2245 Broadway (between 80th and 81st streets)
Monday–Thursday 8 A.M.–7:30 P.M., Friday 10 A.M.–7:30 P.M., Saturday
   8 A.M.–midnight, Sunday 9 A.M.–7:30 P.M.
Subway: IRT 1 to 79th Street and Broadway
Bus: M7, M11, M104

Without doubt one of the most wonderful gustatory emporiums in the city. An Aladdin's cave of culinary delights. Cramped, crowded—a cacophony of customers. An institution from the day it was founded. A place to be experienced.

If all this gets the gastric juices flowing, Broadway between 80th and 105th streets possesses the best array of Chinese restaurants in the city outside Chinatown.

9. LASERIUM

Central Park West and 81st Street (Hayden Planetarium)
873-8828
Concerts: Friday and Saturday 8:30 P.M., 10 P.M., 11:30 P.M., Sunday 8:30
   P.M. and 10 P.M.
$3.25
Subway: IND AA, B, CC to 81st Street and Central Park West
Bus: M7, M10, M11

Attend a cosmic multimedia concert. A total, as they say, mind-blowing experience in sound, shape, and color. Marvelous!

10. HAYDEN PLANETARIUM PARK

81st Street (between Columbus Avenue and Central Park West)
Subway: IND AA, B, CC to 81st Street and Central Park West
Bus: M7, M10, M11

After an invariably exhausting expedition around the Museum of Natural History, come dally awhile in this most pleasant swathe of green and shade. It's overlooked by most guidebooks.

11. CLAREMONT RIDING ACADEMY

175 West 89th Street (at Amsterdam Avenue)
SC. 4-5100
Daily 6 A.M.–dusk
$11.50 an hour ($12.00 for a half-hour lesson)
Subway: IRT 1 to 86th Street and Broadway
Bus: M7, M11, M104

"Everyone who rides in New York rides from here," says management. Since 1888 the academy has been training riders and loaning horses for use in Central Park. Lessons run for half an hour, which, if you've never ridden before, is hardly enough time to learn (although some try). If you're a proficient rider, take an hour's ride in the park. A pleasant, if not inexpensive, pastime.

12. POMANDER WALK

An alley linking 94th and 95th streets, between Broadway and West End
   Avenue
Subway: IRT 1 to 96th Street and Broadway
Bus: M7, M11, M104

It says "private" on the sign, but the gate's normally unlocked. Residents don't seem to mind visitors strolling through this unusual replica of a narrow English "walk" complete with half-timbered gables, wooden porches, flower boxes, and neatly trimmed privet hedges.

Pomander Walk

13. A JAZZ NUCLEUS

On the upper Upper West Side there's an exciting synergism of jazz bars. Call in advance to check on programs, showtimes, and cover charge/minimums.

STRYKER'S 103 W. 86th Street (at Columbus Avenue) 874-8754

THE CELLAR 70 West 95th Street (at Columbus Avenue) 866-1200

MIKELL'S 760 Columbus Avenue (at 97th Street) 864-8832

BROADY'S 798 Columbus Avenue (at 100th Street) 850-4400

And, of course, the "old faithful":

THE WEST END 2911 Broadway (between 113th and 114th streets) 666-8750

14. RIVERSIDE–WEST 105th STREET HISTORIC DISTRICT

Riverside Drive and 105 to 106th streets
Subway: IRT 1 to 103rd Street and Broadway
Bus: M5, M104

A glimpse of upper-crust life in turn-of-the-century New York. These groupings of Beaux-Arts houses with their feminine façades, full of bows and bays, were built between 1899 and 1902 under strict aesthetic covenants. If only . . .

15. STRAUS PARK

106th Street and Broadway
Subway: IRT 1 to 103rd Street and Broadway
Bus: M7, M11, M104

A balmy, shaded enclave in the heart of the Broadway commercial strip south of Columbia University. A pensive toga-clad nymph lies gazing at her own reflection in the pool beneath her plinth. This work by Augustus Lukeman, a famous Cooper Union graduate, is a memorial to Isidor (one of the owners of Macy's) and Ida Straus who were lost in the *Titanic* disaster, April 15, 1912.

16. NICHOLAS ROERICH MUSEUM

319 West 107th Street (near Broadway)
UN. 4-7752
Sunday–Friday 2–5 P.M.
Free
Subway: IRT 1 to 110th Street and Broadway
Bus: M4, M5, M104

A little-known gem.

Born in Russia in 1874, Roerich spent much of his life in America and Asia and died in a remote corner of India in 1947. His influence as an artist, mystic, and visionary was particularly notable in the twenties and thirties, and he is as well known for his attempts to promote international harmony and unity as for his unusually translucent paintings.

17. THE CATHEDRAL CHURCH OF ST. JOHN THE DIVINE

Meditation in a Cathedral
112th Street and Amsterdam Avenue
865-3600
Daily 7 A.M.–6 P.M.
Subway: IRT 1 to 110th Street and Broadway
Bus: M4, M11, M104

This is far more than merely the largest church in the world (and one of the most impressive internally). It offers an amazing array of activities—music recitals, art exhibits, theatrical productions, dance performances, choral concerts, and lectures. There's always some event going on and it's usually open to everyone, free of charge. But—if nothing is happening when you visit—pause awhile at the Howard Thurman Listening Room (in one of the chapels behind the altar), where short meditation tapes based on Dr. Thurman's sermons are often played. Call 678-6945 for details. Alternatively, rest awhile on the cathedral lawns in a setting of Tudor-Gothic buildings and oak trees.

There's also that splendid walk through the heart of the Columbia campus nearby (116th Street between Amsterdam Avenue and Broadway).

18. RIVERSIDE CHURCH
Not just a church
500 Riverside Drive (near 123rd Street)
666-7600
Subway: IRT 1 to 116th Street and Broadway
Bus: M4, M5, M104

As at St. John the Divine, there's much more going on here than tours of the church and the carillon tower. Call 864-2929 for details on theatrical productions, dance performances, and music recitals; 749-8140 for information on the sixteen (plus) craft workshops; and 749-7000 for community affairs activities.

Also nearby is the Interchurch Center (475 Riverside Drive, 870-2200; Monday–Friday 9 A.M.–5 P.M. Free) with exhibitions of religious artifacts—icons, altar vessels, illuminated manuscripts, vestments, etc.

19. INTERNATIONAL HOUSE
500 Riverside Drive (near 123rd Street)
666-7600
Subway: IRT 1 to 125th Street and Broadway
Bus: M4, M5, M11, M104

This home of many foreign students in New York occasionally offers free public programs, and features an annual celebration of foods, dress, and music from around the globe.

Call for details.

20. A TOUCH OF GAUDI
Grant's Tomb
122nd Street and Riverside Drive
Subway: IRT 1 to 125th Street and Broadway
Bus: M4, M5, M104, Bx29

Don't worry, I'm not recommending a special visit to Grant's Tomb (once described as "the most overrated tourist attraction in the city") but if you happen to be in the area (you might wish to come and climb the carillon tower at Riverside Church for example), take a stroll around the tomb and admire the wonderful Gaudi-like benches. A South American artist, assisted by an army of local children, created these fantasy works in 1976 out of broken remnants of ceramic tiles. You'll need to make a double circuit to appreciate all the intricacies. The park across Riverside Drive just north of the church is a lovely shady place in the summer, or, if you're feeling ambitious, stroll south through Riverside Park (one of the finest walks in the city).

21. AFRO ARTS CULTURAL CENTER

2191 Adam C. Powell, Jr. Boulevard (between 129th and 130th streets)
831-3922/3
Daily 9 A.M.–8 P.M.
No general admission charge (for groups, however, the charge is adults
   $1.25, children 75¢)
Subway: IND A, D, or IRT 2, 3 to 125th Street
Bus: M2
A small but expanding collection of African carvings, bronzes, and religious artifacts in a part of town neglected by most city explorers. Combine a visit here with a trip to the nearby Studio Museum (2033 Fifth Avenue at 125th Street).

22. ST. NICHOLAS HISTORIC
DISTRICT (Striver's Row)

138th and 139th Streets (between Seventh and Eighth avenues)
Subway: IND AA, B, CC to 135th Street and St. Nicholas Avenue
Bus: M3, M10
Below the Gothic bulk of City College there's a remarkably cohesive segment of urban townhouse design built in 1891 and featuring the work of the city's leading architectural firms at that time —James Brown Lord, Bruce Price, and Clarence S. Luce, and the redoubtable McKim, Mead and White. Neo-Georgian and neo-Italian Renaissance are the primary styles. The development features a service alley down the center of the block (a rare feature in New York) closed off at both ends by ornamental gates.

23. CITY COLLEGE AND VICINITY

Convent Avenue (between 135th and 144th streets)
Subway: IRT 1 to 137th Street and Broadway
Bus: M3, M100, M101
Once a tourist attraction, City College is ignored nowadays by visitors and residents alike. But where else in the five boroughs can one find such a unified expression of "Collegiate Gothic" architec-

ture (black Manhattan schist stone and white terra-cotta) in a small but almost perfect campus? Both extremities of the original campus are delineated by ornate gateposts with wrought-iron arches, and as you explore you'll find a remarkably exotic array of grotesque gargoyles and other sinister trimmings on the richly detailed buildings.

And that's not all. From St. Nicholas Terrace there's a splendid view of the city (the St. Nicholas Historic District is immediately below), and at 142nd Street and Convent Avenue one suddenly discovers Alexander Hamilton's 1802 country home (Monday–Saturday 9 A.M.–5 P.M.) with its post–Colonial dignity somewhat compromised by its setting between a church and an apartment block.

Enjoy the refinement of the architecture on Convent Avenue itself and the adjacent side streets (142nd to 144th streets) and, as a final pause, visit the M. Marshall Blake Funeral Home at 150th Street and St. Nicholas Avenue, a magnificent (and little-known) essay in Victorian extravaganza.

24. AUNT LEN'S DOLL AND TOY MUSEUM

6 Hamilton Terrace (144th Street between Convent and St. Nicholas
  avenues)
926-4172/AU. 1-4143
Tuesday–Sunday by appointment
Adults $1, children 50¢
Subway: IND A, AA, B, CC, D to 145th Street
Bus: M3, M101

A little removed from the museum-metropolis of midtown but a totally absorbing display of over three thousand dolls, dollhouses, doll carriages, doll pianos, doll tea sets, and doll dresses plus a "touch and tell" room for children. Aunt Len is Lenon Hoyle. She's a doll too.

5
THE BRONX

1. OLD WEST FARMS
SOLDIER CEMETERY

2103 Bryant Avenue (at 180th Street)
Subway: IRT 2, 5 to Boston Road/West Farms Square
Bus: Bx20, Bx26, Bx28, Bx36, Bx40

Just below the zoo is the oldest veterans' burial ground in the Bronx, with graves dating from the War of 1812. It's a tiny enclave (only about forty veterans), but Bert Sack, president of the preservation group, is proud of its designation as a Landmark site. If you're visiting the zoo, look out for this unusual place.

2. HALL OF FAME FOR
GREAT AMERICANS

West 181st Street and University Avenue (Bronx Community College)
367-7300
Monday–Saturday 10 A.M.–5 P.M.
Free
Subway: IRT 4 to Burnside Avenue, IND D to 182nd Street
Bus: Bx12, Bx38, Bx40

Admittedly not in the best part of town, but well worth a visit all the same. This Stanford White creation contains, within its 630 feet of shady arcades, 95 busts of the nation's most notable authors, educators, engineers, inventors, military men, lawyers, judges, theologians, businessmen, humanitarians, scientists, physicians, statesmen, artists, musicians, actors, and explorers. Each bust is accompanied by a quotation—for example, there's Mark Twain's:

289

> Loyalty to petrified opinion never yet
> broke a chain nor freed a human soul.

and the caustic Thomas Paine's:

> Those who expect to reap the blessings
> of freedom must undergo the fatigues of
> supporting it.

And so on. An enlightening experience.

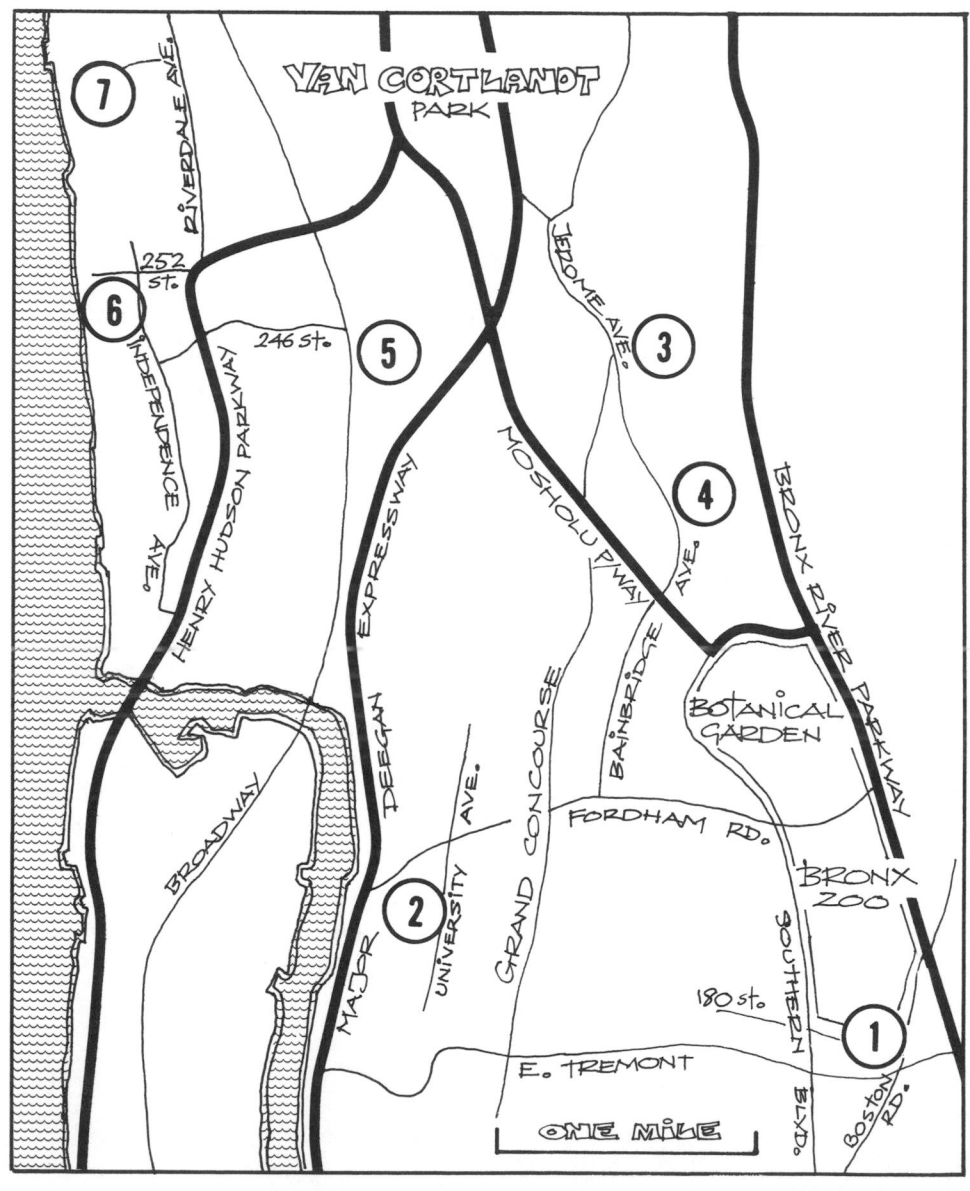

3. WOODLAWN CEMETERY

S.W. Entrance: Jerome Avenue at Bainbridge Avenue
Daily 9 A.M.–4:30 P.M.
Subway: IRT 4 to Jerome Avenue/Woodlawn
Bus: Bx4, Bx16

Green-Wood Cemetery (see page 298) has its splendid Gothic entrance but Woodlawn is, without doubt, the most beautiful cemetery in the metropolitan area, if not the country. It was founded in 1863 as a rural burial ground and has managed to preserve that flavor although surrounded on all sides by rapid development.

Pick up the map and guidebook at the Jerome Avenue entrance and wander through the wooded dells, by the lakes and past the incredible mausoleums, an encyclopedia of architectural styles memorializing such notables as Frank Woolworth, Fiorello La Guardia, Jay Gould, George M. Cohan, Herman Melville, Duke Ellington, "Bat" Masterson, Roland Macy, and Joseph Pulitzer.

Ironically, in this resting place for the departed, history comes alive.

4. VALENTINE-VARIAN HOUSE

(c. 1750) (Museum of Bronx History)
3266 Bainbridge Avenue (and 208th Street)
881-8900
Saturday 10 A.M.–4 P.M., Sunday 1–5 P.M.
Adults 25¢, children under 16 free
Subway: IND D to 205th Street

This sturdy example of a rough fieldstone dwelling was almost lost to the wreckers ball in 1964 but was finally moved and restored on city park land. Now it contains displays of Bronx history from Indian days to the present with special exhibits of Revolutionary War relics and early photographs.

5. VAN CORTLANDT MANSION (1748)

Broadway and 246th Street, Van Cortlandt Park
KI. 6-3323
Tuesday–Saturday 10 A.M.–5 P.M., Sunday 2–5 P.M. (closed February)
Adults 50¢, children under 12 free (free days Friday and Saturday)
Subway: IRT 1 to 242nd Street
Bus: Bx20 via Kingsbridge Road and Broadway

After a relatively short subway journey you can be frolicking in the fields and woods of Van Cortlandt Park, or reliving the early colonial days in this splendid example of a Georgian mansion. Nine rooms are normally open to the public. Many of the furnishings were used by the Van Cortlandt family, who occupied the house until 1889. My favorites: the Dutch bedroom with cupboard-style bed and the eighteenth-century dollhouse.

(Other nearby attractions, if you have a car, include the Wave Hill and Fonthill mansions.)

6. WAVE HILL

675 West 252nd Street (off Independence Avenue)
549-2055
Daily 9:30–4:30 P.M.
Monday–Saturday: Free; Sunday: adults $1, children under 14 free
Bus: Mid Manhattan/Riverside Express Bus
NOTE: Best to come by car and combine with a visit to the Van Cortlandt
   Mansion and Fonthill

This splendid 1843 Greek-Revival mansion with odd variations, once home for such notables as Theodore Roosevelt, Mark Twain, and Arturo Toscanini, was donated along with twenty acres of land to the Parks Department for use as an experimental horticultural center. There's an interesting range of exhibits, greenhouses, and various weekend activities often featuring musical recitals and folk dancing. Call for details.

Not far away in the estatelike grounds of the College of Mount St. Vincent is Edwin Forrest's odd Gothic mansion-castle, Fonthill, complete with tower, turrets, and battlements. Forrest was a famous Shakespearean actor in the mid-1800s and became even more notorious for his feud with William Macready, the noted British actor, which sparked off the Astor Place Riot of 1849 (see chapter 3). Hardly known for his modesty, he explained in a speech about his home:

> In building this house, I am impelled by no vain desire to occupy a grand mansion for the gratification of self-love . . .

6
BROOKLYN

1. WILLIAMSBURG

The heart of the district lies around Bedford Avenue and Keap Street
Subway: BMT J or M to Marcy Avenue and Broadway
Bus: B39, B53, B60, B61

Try to make two visits to this most unique of New York neighborhoods, home of the largest concentration of Chassidic Jews outside Israel. Come first on a weekday. If it's a fine day, walk across the Williamsburg Bridge from Delancey Street on Manhattan's Lower East Side instead of taking the subway. Explore the scores of Hebrew-signed shops, small and cramped, many selling exotic arrays of imported foodstuffs and the most truly kosher of all kosher products in the city. Pause and snack at the equally tiny restaurants with their chicken dishes, matzoh-ball soup, and gefilte fish. Marvel at the rich displays of silver ornaments and bowls behind barred windows.

Then on your second visit, come around dusk on a Friday evening or on a Saturday when all the stores are closed and the Satmar Jews (the most devout of all Jewish sects) celebrate their sabbath. The males dress in traditional black—black fur hats, long black coats gleaming as if polished, black trousers, black boots (and white socks). The streets are filled with hundreds of identically dressed Satmar males leading their sons to the synagogues. The females are less evident. A few walk together in groups, their wigs close-cropped and unstyled (according to Chassidic tradition, after marriage wives shave their heads permanently).

293

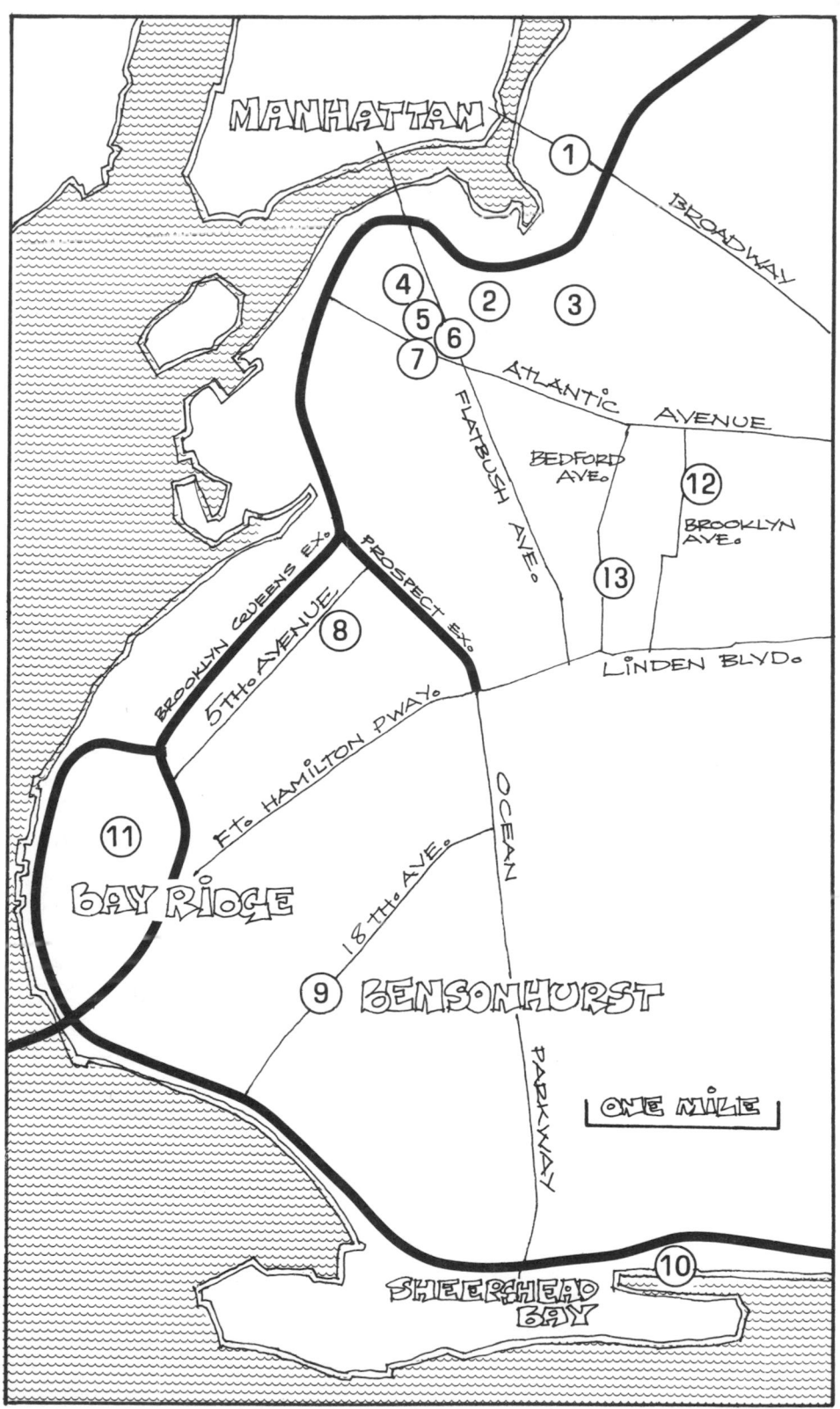

Even after a dozen visits you'll continue to be amazed at the cultural purity of this tiny oasis in the vast sprawl of Brooklyn.

2. FORT GREENE PARK

DeKalb Avenue at Fort Greene Place
Subway: IND GG to Fulton Street and Lafayette Avenue
Bus: B19, B38, B54

The area is what might officially be termed marginal, although such streets as South Portland Avenue and South Oxford Street, immediately south of the park, are magnificent material for brownstone buffs. If Park Slope and other Brooklyn neighborhoods are any indication, the renaissance will soon be here.

The park itself is a shady mound topped by a monument to the martyrs who died in the British hospital ships during the Revolutionary War. The views over the city from here or from the classical-revival conveniences are delightful. As one might expect, the park was designed by Olmsted and Vaux (on the site of old Fort Greene, a fortified hill in both the Revolutionary and 1812 wars).

3. THE PRATT INSTITUTE

DeKalb Avenue at Hall Street
Subway: IND GG to Lafayette and Washington avenues
Bus: B38, B54

Of course you've heard of Pratt, but have you been there? Not only is the campus known for its public activities and exhibitions (call 636-3600 for details) but also for the splendor of its Romanesque-Revival Library (an 1896 William Tubby creation) and Main Hall.

Take time to explore the adjoining neighborhood, particularly the mansion-lined Clinton Street and the Skinner House at Lafayette and Vanderbilt avenues, bedecked with an Italianate cupola and Greek-Revival trimmings on a building of Federal proportions. Exquisite!

4. AN EVEN MORE FABULOUS FIREHOUSE

365–67 Jay Street (near Fulton Street)
Subway: IND A, E, F to Jay Street/Boro Hall
Bus: B25, B26, B37, B38, B54

Although Brooklyn Heights has a fine firehouse (Empire Company No. 224, Hicks Street between State and Joralemon streets), the most prominent of all is, of cource, the Old Brooklyn Fire Department Headquarters on Jay Street—a towering masterpiece of red sandstone, dark brown brick, and copper-trimmed crenelations designed by Frank Freeman in 1892. Combine a visit here with a shopping trip along Fulton Street.

5. JUNIOR'S
386 Flatbush Avenue Extension (at DeKalb Avenue)
852-5257
Daily 6:30 A.M.–2 A.M.
Subway: Any train to Dekalb and Flatbush avenues
Bus: B15, B19, B25, B26, B45, B65

Anyone in New York who hasn't heard of Junior's just hasn't been here very long. Either that, or he doesn't like cheesecake.

6. THE WILLIAMSBURG SAVINGS BANK TOWER
1 Hanson Place
636-7334
Monday–Saturday 10 A.M.–3 P.M.
Free
Subway: Any train to DeKalb and Flatbush avenues
Bus: B25, B26, B52, B65 (and others)

You can't miss it, this 512-foot-high towering pinnacle of prosperity adjoining the Brooklyn Academy of Music. Visit the baronial banking hall with its ox-size fireplaces, huge cast-iron chandelier, its ceiling mosaic of the zodiac, and a second mosaic, thirty feet long, commemorating the original five Dutch settlements in Brooklyn. Then take the elevator to the twenty-sixth-floor observation platforms. A well-designed display here relates all the details of the 1776 Battle of Long Island to the panoramic vistas over the city.

At the base of the tower there's the wholesale Meat Market with some excellent bargains at the semiretail outlets.

7. ATLANTIC AVENUE
Between Boerum Place and Nevins Street
Subway: IND A, CC, F to Jay Street/Boro Hall
Bus: B15, B25, B26, B38, B41, B65

Farther east, beyond the restaurants, the bakeries, and the exotic

Jay Street Fire Headquarters

import stores on Atlantic Avenue, there's a burgeoning mini-district of antique and bric-a-brac stores between Willow Place and Boerum Place. Owners and locations keep changing, but it deserves a side trip if you happen to be in the neighborhood (see chapter 13).

8. GREEN-WOOD CEMETERY

Main Entrance: Fifth Avenue at 25th Street
768-7300
Daily 8 A.M.–5 P.M.
Subway: BMT RR, N to 23rd Street and Broadway
Bus: B33, B63

It's worth coming here just to see Richard Upjohn's Gothic Revival gatehouse, an incredible piece of architecture in an otherwise un-impressive part of Brooklyn. Inside the cemetery one enters a bu-colic environment of ever-winding roadways (22 miles on 478 acres!), lakes, manicured hills, and splendidly ornate mausoleums. Among the estimated 500,000 burials in the cemetery, notables include De Witt Clinton (father of the Erie Canal), Horace Greeley, the Reverend Henry Ward Beecher, both Nathaniel Currier and James Ives, "Boss" Tweed, Pierre Lorillard, Duncan Phyfe, and Eliza Gilbert, better known as Lola Montez. Truly "a haven of posthumous Americana."

Green-Wood Cemetery was the precursor of New York's parks. Because of its enormous appeal as a weekend picnic area in the 1850s, William Cullen Bryant and Washington Irving stressed the need for similar open areas throughout the burgeoning urbanity—hence Central Park and others.

Green-Wood is a little forgotten today. Come and enjoy its tran-quillity. Then, by way of contrast, especially if you come around a weekday lunch hour, slip down 25th Street to Third Avenue and experience a true dockland flavor of raunchy restaurants, bars, and boisterous street-corner gatherings of waterfront workers—a bit of real New York.

Green-Wood Cemetery Gatehouse

9. BENSONHURST

Eighteenth Avenue from 60th to 85th streets
Subway: BMT N to Eighteenth Avenue at 64th Street
Bus: B8

The flavor of Eighteenth Avenue is by no means as pronounced
as other, better-known Italian districts. But inside the salumerias,
the deli-groceries, the bakeries, and even the live poultry market
(Mapleton's at 6224 Seventeenth Avenue) you know it's authentic.
Modica's Latticini bulges with provolones, salamis, mozzarella,
and prosciutto rolls, salads, gallon cans of olive oil, and the best
pizza rustica in the neighborhood. Then there's the Flora Pastry
and Bake Shop (try their pane di semola), Milianelli's (whole-
wheat pasta and unusual ravioli), Charlie's Fish Market, Gloria's
(melt-in-the-mouth sfogliatelle), and a dozen other delights.
Spend time here. It grows on you.

10. A REAL DEEP-SEA
FISHING TRIP

Sheepshead Bay (Neptune Avenue)
Subway: IND D or BMT N, QB to Sheepshead Bay
Bus: B44, B49

Most party-fishing boats leave Sheepshead Bay between 6 and 7

A.M. off into the choppy Atlantic in search of bluefish, striped bass, fluke, flounder—even the big tuna. Costs range from $8–$20 per adult, and if nothing else you'll come back with a whopping appetite. Fortunately, there's the famous Lundy's Restaurant and Joe's Clam House just across from the boats. Take a day off work and gain a fresh perspective on life in the city. (If you arrive late and the fishing boats have left, don't despair. Stroll around the bay to the Manhattan Beach Park and spend a lazy day in this idyllic ocean-front setting.)

11. BAY RIDGE

Subway: BMT RR, N to Bay Ridge Avenue/Fourth Avenue
Bus: B37, also B27 Express
NOTE: You'll see more if you go by car.

Cut off from the rest of Brooklyn by the moatlike extension of Owls Head Park, Bay Ridge seems a place apart, a serene community of gingerbread mansions (once the homes of the tugboat barons) and quaint Revival-style row houses around Senator Street. The old Irish bars on Third, Fourth, and Fifth avenues have now received a Friday's-style face lift and appeal to a younger crowd of brownstone renovators—newcomers to the neighborhood. Stroll west on Bay Ridge Avenue to the pier with its fine

Bay Ridge Mansion

views of Manhattan, then wander south through the shoreline park—admiring the great mansions around 86th Street.

In addition to enjoying the general charms of the neighborhood visit two of the most worthy stores in southern Brooklyn. Lund's (8122 Fifth Avenue) reflects the Scandinavian heritage of the community with its whole-wheat rugbrød, Swedish rye limpa, sweet yeast coffee breads (Christmas and Easter), plus a delectable array of puffy Danish pastries.

Nearby at 7719 Fifth Avenue is Fredricksen and Johannesen with their own array of traditional Scandinavian meats and canned imports. Try the homemade sausages (pølse or korv), fish-pudding, corned lamb, and rullepølse (a spicy meat roll made from a Danish recipe).

12. THE BROOKLYN CHILDREN'S MUSEUM (Muse)

145 Brooklyn Avenue at St. Marks Avenue
735-4400
Tuesday–Sunday 1–5 P.M.
Free
Subway: IND A, E to Kingston Avenue and Fulton Street or
  IRT 2 to Kingston Avenue and Eastern Parkway
Bus: B44, B45

A marvelous "hands-on" learning complex for children, particularly organized groups from New York schools. (Enter through the ornate subway kiosk.) Everyone is welcome to enjoy the displays of more than forty thousand artifacts in cultural and natural history and technology, although it's normally best to call in advance to check out the special programs. Favorites with the kids (of course) are the stream that runs through the heart of the museum, the windmill, the greenhouse, and the steam engine. Latest innovations include a.children's resource library, a new series of workshops called "explore-its" (the kids enroll themselves), and a special "take-home" collection of museum pieces.

13. NEW MUSE COMMUNITY MUSEUM

1530 Bedford Avenue
774-2900
Tuesday–Friday 1–6 P.M., Saturday 10 A.M.–6 P.M., Sunday 1–6 P.M.
Free
Subway: IRT 2, 3, 4, 5 to Franklin Avenue

This dynamic center for black culture in Brooklyn reflects the black contribution to the city's development and features permanent and special exhibitions, children's programs, workshops, jazz concerts, planetarium shows, poetry readings, etc. There are so many things going on here it's best to call in advance for details.

NEIGHBORHOOD TOURS

Many of the lesser-known neighborhoods in Brooklyn—Bedford-Stuyvesant, Boerum Hill, Crown Heights, Gravesend, and Cobble Hill—are all experiencing bouts of enthusiastic brownstone renewal. Sure there are problem areas, but grass-roots tours provided by local individuals who know and love these areas give visitors renewed faith in their bootstrap renaissances. Call Louis Singer at 875-9084 (6–9 P.M.) or the Bed-Stuy Restoration Corp. at 636-1100 for more information. If the telephone numbers have changed, put that down to progress and call the New York Convention and Visitors Bureau (90 East 42nd Street) at 687-1300 for the new numbers.

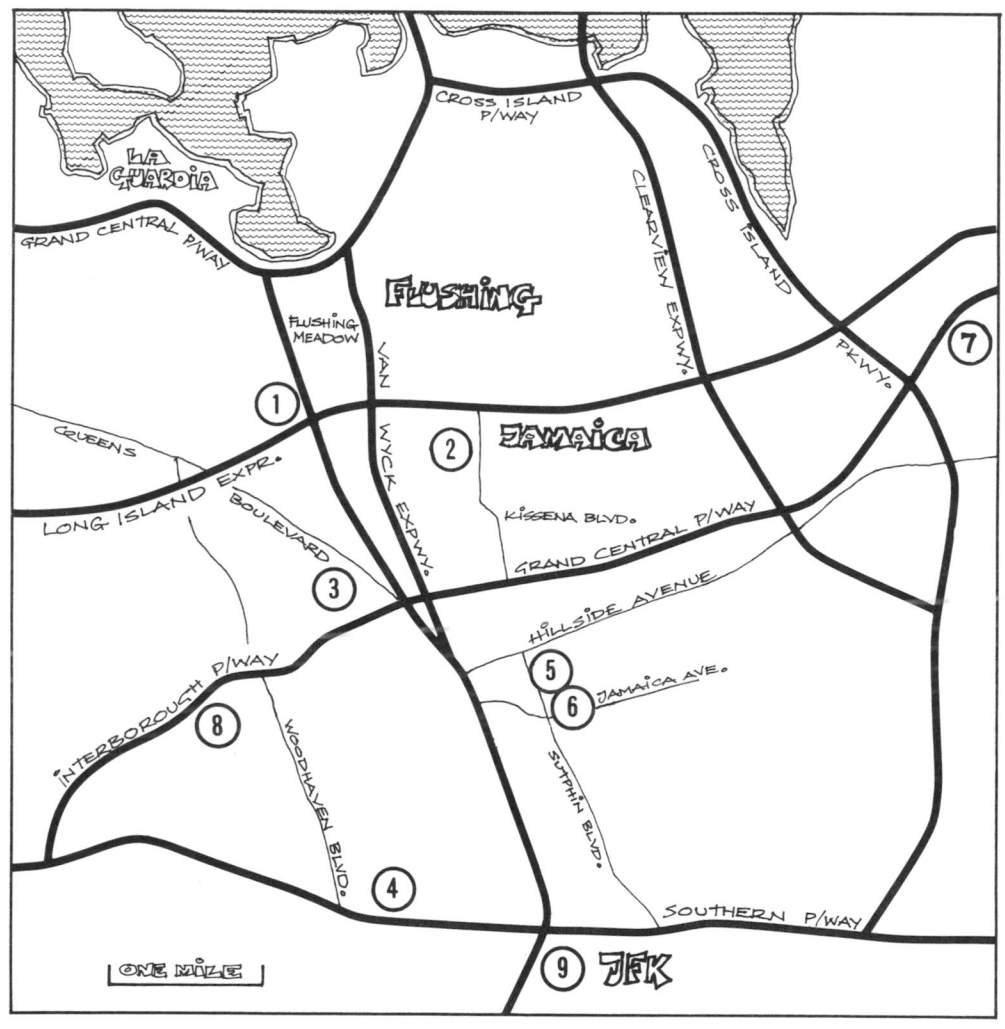

7
QUEENS

1. THE HALL OF SCIENCE

Flushing Meadow Park
699-9400
Wednesday–Friday 10 A.M.–4 P.M., Saturday 10 A.M.–5 P.M., Sunday
  11 A.M.–5 P.M.
Contribution
Subway: IRT 7 to 111th Street
Bus: B58 to 108th Street and Corona Avenue

You can't miss the rockets, towering above the trees, but there's plenty more here of interest to adults and children—excellent displays of communication technology, nuclear energy, space exploration, plus an amateur radio station, a planetarium, and a weather center. Also lectures, films, and special programs for youngsters.

Combine this with a visit to the nearby Queens Museum (in the New York City Building—Tuesday–Saturday 10 A.M.–5 P.M., Sunday 1–5 P.M. Free) and examine the vast scale model of the five boroughs (amazing details down to the design of individual bridges and vest-pocket parks).

2. QUEENS COLLEGE
ART COLLECTION

Queens College, Paul Klapper Library, Flushing
520-7243
Monday and Wednesday 9 A.M.–8 P.M., Tuesday and Thursday 9 A.M.–
  6 P.M., Friday 9 A.M.–5 P.M.
Free

305

Subway/Bus: IRT 7 to Main Street, Flushing—transfer to Q17, Q25, or
   Q25–34 to the college

As it can be a rather lengthy journey getting there, it may be best
to call ahead and check on the museum's special exhibitions of
primitive, Egyptian, and European art. Little-known outside
Queens.

3. FOREST HILLS GARDENS

Enter under LIRR bridge by Forest Hills Station (Seventy-first Avenue
   and Greenway Terrace)
Subway: IND E, F, GG, N to Forest Hills/Queens Boulevard
Bus: Q23, Q60

Past the odd towered and turreted Forest Hills Inn where visiting
tennis stars once stayed during tournaments at the nearby Forest
Hills Tennis Stadium is a unique housing development of curving
streets and large shade trees, a convincing replica of an English
village. Grosvenor Atterbury, the designer, was actually inspired
by the "Garden Cities" movement which during the twenties was
considered an ideal way to relocate low-income families from the
slums of English cities. The philanthropic Mrs. Russell Sage had a
similar idea here when she initiated the project, but by 1923 the
development had become fashionable, attracting many notable
residents.

Come stroll down Deepdene, along Beech Knoll, and Ivy Close.
All that's missing is a herd of cows on their way to milking, and a
village pub near the green.

4. AQUEDUCT RACE TRACK

Ozone Park, Jamaica
Subway: IND A to Aqueduct and North Conduit Avenue (also nonstop
   specials from 42nd Street and Eighth Avenue daily)
Bus: Q7, Q10, Q11 (also specials from the Port Authority)

You've heard the commercials, you know about the one-and-an-
eighth-mile dirt track and the one-mile-and-seven-furlong turf
course, you know everyone says it's great fun . . . so — go. (You
really can get all the way there by subway.)

Forest Hills Inn

5. KING MANOR (1730)

153rd Street and Jamaica Avenue, Jamaica
523-1653
Monday and Wednesday 1:30–4:30 P.M.
Adults 25¢, children under 12 free
Subway: BMT J to 160th Street (walk west to King Park) or
  IND E, F to Parsons Boulevard (walk south to King Park)
Bus: B53, B56, B22, Q44

Home of the "almost-great" Rufus King, the manor grew between 1730 and 1806 from a small one-story cottage to an appropriately dignified county seat for this senator, diplomat, and near-president. Furnishings range from colonial to nineteenth century, and special exhibits include a display of hats and a wonderful array of needlework samplers. An unexpected surprise in this part of Queens.

6. STORE FRONT MUSEUM

(Paul Robeson Theatre)

162–02 Liberty Avenue, Jamaica
523-5199
Tuesday–Friday 9:30 A.M.–4:30 P.M., Saturday 11:30 A.M.–3 P.M.
Free
Subway: IND E, F to Parsons Boulevard or BMT J to 160th Street

Both permanent and changing exhibits of black history and culture with artworks, photographs, and special programs, theater performances, workshops, and "celebrations." Call for details.

7. COLONIAL FARMHOUSE RESTORATION

73–50 Little Neck Parkway, Floral Park
468-4355 or 740-0747
Saturday 11 A.M.–1 P.M.
Free
Bus: Q12a, Q44a to Little Neck Parkway (walk to 73rd Road)
NOTE: Best to come by car.

At the time of writing, this project for renovating a 1758 farmhouse and re-creating a 52-acre farm environment of the colonial era was still in progress. Could be excellent. Call for details.

8. CEMETERY BELT

There's a most unusual four-mile drive on the Interborough Parkway from Jamaica Avenue in East New York to Queens Boulevard at Kew Gardens along the appropriately named "terminal moraine." It's an apparently endless landscape of cemeteries among wooded hills and vales. There are (at least) seventeen of them, plus a golf course and a park. An odd but pleasant change from the tract housing on the flatlands below the moraine.

9. KENNEDY AIRPORT —DIVERSIONS

The plane's late and you're stuck for hours on a plastic bench watching a slot-TV—right? Wrong. Admittedly, diversions are a little scarce but you can:

  —linger over a large meal (all-you-can-eat salad bar and all you can drink) at the International Buffet in the International Arrivals building (995-3611).

—visit the art displays on the second level of Eero Saarinen's TWA terminal, the upper level of the International Arrivals building, and between gates 14 and 22 in the East Wing.

—attend a service or meditate in the three chapels across the parking lot from the International Arrivals building. (The synagogue has a small museum of Jewish religious artifacts.)

—browse for hours in the airport bookshops (hardbacks too, and foreign publications) in each wing of the International Arrivals building.

8
CATEGORY
MINI-TOURS

PUB POETRY READINGS
(The Village and Elsewhere)
The following pubs normally offer regular poetry-reading sessions for the price of a drink. Call for details:

Cedar Tavern, 82 University Place (between 11th and 12th streets) 675-9555
Chumley's, 86 Bedford Street (at Barrow Street) 989-9038
Dr. Generosity's, 1403 Second Avenue (at 73rd Street) 861-2230
The Locale, 11 Waverly Place (at Mercer Street) 674-0860
West End Bar, 2911 Broadway (at 113th Street) 666-8750
White Horse Inn, 1713 Second Avenue (at 89th Street) TE. 1-9750

STREET CLOCKS
A dying species, but a few beauties remain:

The Hecla Iron Works masterpiece at 23rd Street and Broadway, cast in 1884
The Seth Thomas clock in front of the Morgan Guaranty Trust Company near the corner of Fifth Avenue and 42nd Street
The "Bloomie's" clock outside the famous Bloomingdale's department store at 59th Street and Lexington Avenue

310

IMPROVISATIONS

Three working "showcase" establishments for new talent:

The Comic Strip, 1568 Second Avenue (between 81st and 82nd streets) 861-9386
Catch a Rising Star, 1487 First Avenue (at 78th Street) 794-1906
Improvisation, 358 West 44th Street (at Ninth Avenue) 765-8268

Show times and attractions keep changing, so call for details.

SUBWAY SERENDIPITY

A combination of mediocre graffiti artists and poor maintenance has taken much of the fun out of subway exploration. However, here are a few worthy remnants:

The elevated station at the end of the IRT 1 line at 204th Street and Broadway. Billboards try to hide it, but you can tell it's a beauty.
The IRT subway entrance at Broadway and 72nd Street. A classic classic.
The IRT station at 168th Street and Broadway, once likened to "an old gymnasium."
The Lexington Avenue line's Wall Street station has some of the best remaining tilework in the city.
IRT South Ferry station has a few exquisite bas-reliefs of sailing boats (with baroque garlands).

CLASSICAL RECITALS (usually free)

The following institutions normally offer regular free recitals to the public. Call for details:

Church of the Incarnation, Madison Avenue and 35th Street MU. 9-6350
CUNY Graduate Center, 33 West 42nd Street (between Fifth and Sixth avenues) 790-4395
Donnell Library, 20 W. 53rd Street (between Fifth and Sixth avenues) 790-6463
Frick Collection, 1 E. 70th Street at Fifth Avenue, 288-0700
Goethe House, 1014 Fifth Avenue (between 82nd and 83rd streets) 744-8310

Greenwich House Music School, 46 Barrow Street and Seventh
Avenue, 242-4772

Juilliard School, Lincoln Center Plaza, 799-5000; also Lincoln
Center Library, 799-2200

Manhattan School of Music, 129th Street and Broadway, 749-
2602

Mannes College of Music, 157 East 74th Street (between Third
and Lexington avenues) 737-0700

Metropolitan Museum of Art, 81st Street and Fifth Avenue, 879-
5500

Museum of the City of New York, 103rd Street and Fifth Avenue
534-1672

New-York Historical Society, Central Park West and 77th Street
TR. 3-3400

Trinity Church, Broadway and Wall Street, 285-0800

CHESS PLEASE

The most popular gathering place for chess lovers is of course the
southeastern corner of Washington Square. However, for those
who prefer more sheltered surroundings there are the following:

CHESS HOUSE, 143 West 72nd Street 221-9564

Open, so they claim, all the time for 75¢ an hour (backgammon
and cards too). You can watch for free.

CHESS SHOP, 230 Thompson Street 475-9580

A store with seventeen tables at 50¢ an hour. Coffee and lessons
available too.

CHESS CITY, 2130 Broadway (at 75th Street) 595-0923

A slightly more exotic combination of chess, backgammon, and
Scrabble tables, bar, lounge, and even a disco.

THE M101—4¢ A MILE

How about a twelve-mile bus ride from City Hall to Fort George
(193rd Street) for 50¢? (Then you can join the Inwood/Washington
Heights walk—see chapter 10.)

Alternatively, take the MTA's two Culture Bus Loops on weekends and holidays ($1.25 per loop/day) and come home with two
free guidebooks to all the sights en route.

WHAT'S ON—FOR FREE?

To keep up with everything that's happening in the way of no-cost or low-cost activities such as:

poetry readings
music recitals/choral concerts
theater/films
lectures/seminars/workshops
folk/jazz/rock
fairs/festivals/exhibitions
walking tours/house tours
children's shows

you'll normally find these useful:

New York Times Weekend Section
Daily News Special Friday Section
New York magazine ("What's Free" series or similar)
Village Voice
Soho News
Our Town, Wisdom's Child, and a score of neighborhood papers
The New Yorker Magazine
Unique N.Y.

INDEX

315

Dick Cavett
Channel 13
356 W 58 St
ny ny